Crying For
Help

SUNDAY TIMES BESTSELLING AUTHOR

CASEY WATSON

Crying For Help

This book is a work of non-fiction based on the author's experiences. In order to protect privacy, names, identifying characteristics, dialogue and details have been changed or reconstructed.

HarperElement
An Imprint of HarperCollins*Publishers*
77–85 Fulham Palace Road,
Hammersmith, London W6 8JB

www.harpercollins.co.uk

and *HarperElement* are trademarks of
HarperCollins*Publishers* Ltd

First published by HarperElement 2012

1 3 5 7 9 10 8 6 4 2

A catalogue record of this book
is available from the British Library

ISBN 978-0-00-743658-3

Printed and bound in the United States of America by
RR Donnelley

Find out more about HarperCollins and the environment at
www.harpercollins.co.uk/green

To my wonderful and supportive family

Acknowledgements

I would like to thank all of the team at HarperCollins, the lovely Andrew Lownie, and my friend and mentor, Lynne. I'd also like to add a special thought to all those working within the care system.

Prologue

8.15am, Wednesday 15 October
Transcript of a call to emergency services, [location given]
Response Centre

999 OPERATOR – *'Police emergency. Can I help you?'*

YOUNG GIRL – *'It's my mum. I think she's dead.'*

OPERATOR – *'Can I have your name and address, lovey?'*

YOUNG GIRL – *'Yes, I'm Sophia, I live at [address given].'*

OPERATOR – *'Okay, sweetheart. That's great. Now, how old are you?'*

SOPHIA – *'I'm almost eleven.'*

OPERATOR – *'Thank you, Sophia. Now, listen – there are some police officers on their way to your house now, so you just stay on the phone talking to me until they get* to you, okay? Then you must let them come in. Okay, lovey? You understand that?'

SOPHIA – 'Yes, okay. But she's dead. I think she must be. [Pauses.] She's fallen down the stairs, I think, and there's blood. She's very cold.'

OPERATOR – 'Okay sweetheart. I understand. You just keep talking to me, okay? Stay on the phone. The officers will be there in just a minute or two, all right? Is there anybody else with you?'

SOPHIA – 'Yes, there is. My friend, Caitlyn. We had a sleepover. I don't know what to do. Oh, hang on, Caitlyn's gone to the door. I think it's the police. Yes, they're here.'

OPERATOR – 'They're there? All right sweetheart, I'll let you go and speak to them, you've done really well. Could you put one of them on the line for me so I can –'

[PHONE DISCONNECTS]

Chapter 1

Sometimes, I think it pays to trust your instincts. My own, like many women's, are sound in most respects, particularly that little voice that you hear from time to time which tells you something's not quite right; something isn't as it seems. You know, that hairs-on-the-back-of-the-neck prickle you sometimes get?

I had that, right away, when John Fulshaw got in touch. It was early January, and one of those really gloomy days, freezing cold, when, even though it was already two in the afternoon, it felt as if it had never really got light. I'd been standing by the window, looking out into the street, and thinking how dreary everybody looked as they plodded by. All dressed in black or grey or brown, hunched over, looking at the ground, collars up, shielding their necks and hands and faces from the bitter winter cold. I loved December, but I really hated January.

'What's up, Mum?' said my grown-up son, Kieron, who was with me, along with the family dog, Bob, and helping to take down the last of the Christmas decorations. I say 'said' but he actually had to raise his voice a bit, due to the music channel he and his sister insisted on having blaring out on the TV.

'Oh, don't set her off again,' chipped in Riley, my daughter. She was 22 to Kieron's 20, and had come over to help too. She paused to shake her head and to roll her eyes at the sight of my long face. 'It can't be Christmas every day, Mum,' she said, pulling a face at me. 'Despite what the song says, okay?'

I pulled a face back but they were both probably right. I needed reminding of that, often. I loved everything glittery and sparkly, always have, and hated the rest of the winter's dark days and dull colours. And this January already seemed particularly colourless. Not only Christmas had gone, but Justin had too, the 12-year-old boy who'd we'd fostered for the whole of the last year and whose leaving had left such a big hole in our lives. Sure, he still came to see us, and promised he'd keep doing so, but it wasn't the same. How could it be? For all the challenges he'd brought with him – and there had definitely been challenges – I really missed having him around. What I needed right now was a new challenge. Something to shake me out of my post-festive blues and get me all fired up once again.

And when the phone rang, it seemed John was going to supply one. John was our link worker at the specialist fostering agency we worked for. He'd also trained both me and my husband, Mike, for the job. It had been John who'd placed Justin with us, and once Justin had left us, just a couple of weeks before Christmas, it was John who had warned us that we'd both better recharge our batteries, because there would soon be another child who needed our help.

The recharging that had taken place, in true Watson style, had naturally involved plenty of parties and fairy lights, and, this year, since Riley and her partner, David, had blessed us in the autumn with our very first grandson, Levi, even more exuberance and cuddly toys than usual. Perhaps it was just the contrast, I mused as I went to pick up the receiver, that was making January seem so drab and dull.

It wasn't John on the phone, though; it was Mike, calling from work. John had phoned him there because he hadn't been able to get an answer from me.

'The kids and their racket, I expect,' I explained. 'They're both helping me get the decorations down and part of the deal seems to be MTV on full blast.' I pulled the living-room door closed to shut out the noise, so I could hear. 'So what's the news?'

'He's got a child he wants to talk to us about. But I couldn't talk, of course, because I'm working.' I smiled to myself. Mike was such a stickler for doing things by the book. He worked as a warehouse manager and he had his own office, but he'd never dream of taking time out for a personal call.

'How exciting! What did he say? Did he tell you anything else?' Suddenly my doldrums were gone the way of the Christmas tinsel. 'Did he tell you anything about him? Or her?'

'Her,' said Mike. 'It's a girl, by all accounts. But that's all I really know, because, like I said, love –'

'Don't worry,' I interrupted. 'You get back to work. *I'll* call him. A girl! How exciting!'

I could still hear Mike chuckling to himself as I put down the phone.

I was on the phone to John only minutes later, pausing only to have a sneaky cigarette in my conservatory (I was obviously banned from the rest of the house, particularly now we had our little grandson around). Suddenly the garden looked very different to how it had. I forgot about the cold and instead mused on how pretty the apple tree looked, covered in white frosting. I finished the ciggie – I really must give up soon, I told myself – and went back inside to fish out John's number.

He sounded very pleased to have heard from me. 'Yes, it's a girl,' he confirmed, 'and a real girlie girl too, so I thought she'd be right up your street.'

'She sounds good already,' I said. 'So. What's the situation? What's her background and what sort of problems does she have?'

I was hoping for something quite detailed about her, as Justin, our last child, had come with very little known background, and we'd learned the hard way about how being forewarned is forearmed. With him we'd been anything but. However, John was quick to fill me in and reassure me. 'That's the thing, actually,' he said. 'You're not going to have to follow the programme with this one. It's only short term.'

That seemed odd. Our kind of fostering was all about behaviour modification, to help re-integrate kids back into the mainstream, so we'd been trained to use a specific, points-based programme with the kids we cared for.

'Oh,' I said. 'How come?'

'Because she's already been placed long term with a mainstream foster carer.'

'Oh, I see. But?'

'But she – the carer, that is – has had some sort of mental breakdown, and needs to take extended sick leave for a few weeks.'

'Oh, dear,' I said. 'Was it related?'

'No, no,' he said quickly. 'Not that I'm aware of. She wants the child – her name's Sophia, by the way – to return to her when she's better.'

'So she's fine, then –'

'Apparently, though I'm told she does have medical problems of her own. But I can't tell you what they are because I don't know myself. I did meet Sophia but I was told not to bring up anything medical – not in front of her, anyway, which meant I couldn't get any proper facts. But I'll find out more tomorrow and get back to you, okay? Perhaps I could come round and meet with you and Mike on Friday.'

It was around then that I had that niggling sixth sense kick in. Just the feeling that there might be something John was holding back. I tried to dismiss it, because there was really nothing I could put my finger on. But it was there.

And for very good reasons.

'Another kid already?' Kieron said as I went back into the living room to tell them, by now with Levi, who'd woken up, in my arms. Riley cooed and took him from me, talking baby talk at him. 'Isn't it a bit quick?' Kieron added. 'You know, after Justin?'

It's easy to forget, when your children are grown up, that the things you do still have an impact on them. I'd been pretty low since Justin had gone, I knew, and I was touched to see the looks of concern on their faces. They glanced at one another now. 'Kieron's got a point,' Riley said. 'Are you sure you're ready?'

'Definitely,' I said, meaning it. 'I'm kicking my heels here, aren't I?' Which was true. Before Mike and I had switched to fostering, I'd been running a unit for troubled children in a big comprehensive school. It wasn't normal for me to have nothing to do but rattle round my house, even with my new grandmotherly duties. Then I paused. Perhaps I wasn't seeing things clearly. 'But how about you two? If you're not up for it, I could always ask to put it off.'

'Don't be daft, Mum,' said Kieron, obviously reassured by my determined manner. 'Be good to have another kid in. And if it's a girl, that's even better. I won't have to fight for my games console and footie games this time.'

'And we'll be able to do lots of girl stuff together,' agreed Riley. 'Baby stuff, clothes shopping, make-up and hair ... how old is she?'

'Twelve,' I said. 'And funny you should say that. John Fulshaw remarked that she was a very girlie girl.'

'So she's going to *love* Justin's bedroom, then,' Kieron said, laughing.

* * *

'Isn't it going a bit over the top to decorate the whole room again?' Mike wanted to know, once he was home from work and we were headed down to the chippy. I'd been planning on cooking, but what with getting the house sorted out, plus all the excitement of knowing we were getting a new foster child, I'd been too excited. Plus I fancied fish and chips.

'Oh, it won't be that much work,' I reassured him. 'And Riley'll help me, I'm sure.'

'Would have been no work at all if you hadn't gone so overboard doing it up in the first place,' he chided. That was Mike all over. He was so much more sensible and down to earth than me. A proper thinker. We'd been married fifteen years and I'd lost count of the times when he'd sat me down and said, 'Now let's just think this through ...' And he was right. I had gone a bit overboard for Justin, taking my football theme to perhaps rather excessive levels, with green carpet, football borders and wallpaper, a football clock – I'd even painted footballs on the bookcase and dresser.

'I'm sure she will,' Mike agreed, 'but look, love, are you definitely sure you're ready?'

Him too now! Had I really been acting like a nut job just lately? Because he was looking at me in the same way as the kids had. Yes, I'd been down, but how could I not have been? Losing Justin had really saddened me, but we had been warned to expect that. It was a grieving process I had to go through, no more, no less. Not surprising when you have such an intense relationship with a child. But I was over it and keen to move on now. Justin would always be a

7

part of our lives, but day to day I needed that new challenge.

'I *am* ready!' I said to Mike. 'And I am going to start re-decorating right away. And just you make sure you book that time off on Friday, okay? Honestly, love, I am *more* than bloody ready.'

Which was just as well, because it looked like we needed to be.

'It's a sad story,' John told us on the Friday morning. He'd arrived on the dot of eleven, as he'd promised, and come armed with a folder full of papers. I thought back to when he'd visited to tell us about our first placement, and how madly I'd rushed around the house, tidying and polishing. So much water had passed under the bridge since that time. John was very much like a friend now. So no big cleaning-fest; just three big mugs of coffee, as we gathered around the kitchen table to discuss the facts.

'Sophia only came into care about a year and a half ago,' he went on. 'Prior to that she lived with her mother – no siblings – who had been bringing her up alone. One-night stand, far as I know. Certainly no father in the picture. And then a tragedy: the mother – name of Grace Johnson – had mental health problems, by all accounts, and had a near-fatal fall down the stairs when Sophia was 11, which was thought to have been a suicide attempt.'

'Suicide?' Mike asked. 'That sounds grim.'

John nodded. 'There was a difficult family situation, apparently. Compounded by Sophia's illness. But I'll tell you more about that in a mo.' He consulted his notes, obviously scanning them for the important bits. 'Ah, here we are,' he said. 'The mother went into a coma – didn't die – from which she has never recovered. She's been classed as being in a persistent vegetative state, from which they don't expect her to recover. Very sad.'

We both nodded.

'So then it seems,' he went on, 'that Sophia went to stay with an uncle and his family – they formally fostered her – but after a year, when the uncle's wife fell pregnant, apparently, they decided they could no longer keep her. Even sadder. So at that point a different fostering team were approached, and that's when she was placed with her current carer, Jean. But, as you know, Jean's not well now, so that's where we're at.'

He sat back. 'God,' I said, 'the things some kids have to go through. And of course we want to help Sophia, don't we, love?' I turned to Mike.

He nodded. 'Absolutely. But tell me, John. You mentioned something about an illness. What's wrong with her?'

John sat forward again. 'That's what we need to discuss. Have the two of you ever heard of a condition called Addison's disease?'

We shook our heads. 'No,' I said. 'Never.'

'I doubted you would have. Neither had I, until now. It's rare, apparently – a disorder which destroys the adrenal glands. And it's even more rare for it to be diagnosed in someone so young. But it's controlled – she has to take tablets every day, which replace the hormones she'd be producing naturally – cortisol and, let me see, yes

– something called aldosterone, so, in that sense, it won't present you with too much of a problem. Apparently, it only becomes one if she gets stressed or feels under pressure …'

'Which she might well do at the moment, mightn't she?' asked Mike.

John nodded. 'Fair point. But I'm not really the one to tell you *how* it might become a problem. Apparently, social services are going to arrange for you both to have a quick tutorial with her doctor and her specialist nurse.'

'Okay,' I said. 'That sounds sensible. Better to know what we're doing than not. But how is she generally? Sounds like she's been to hell and back, from what you say.'

'I don't know, to be truthful,' John answered. 'There really isn't a great deal more on her file.'

Where have I heard that line before, I thought ruefully. It had become almost a catch phrase when we'd taken on Justin. John caught my expression and looked apologetic. 'I'm sorry,' he said. 'It's just that she hasn't been in care that long, and when they are fostered with other family members, they never seem to be as strict with the record keeping. I'll see what else I can find, obviously, but, in the meantime, how are you placed for taking her next Wednesday?'

'That's quick,' said Mike. 'How will we manage to fit in an initial visit? I'm sure neither she nor we would want to commit until we've met each other.'

'I know,' John said, the hope in his face clear as day. 'But I was hoping we could do that on Monday. Jean goes into hospital on Wednesday, you see, for tests, so it would get complicated if …'

'Fine,' I said. 'Monday is fine. The poor thing. But one thing, John.'

He nodded. 'Yes?'

'Why us? Why me and Mike? It sounds to me that this is a pretty mainstream and also very short-term placement. Why have you picked us and not a general foster carer? Is it the illness?'

He shook his head. 'Well, okay, partly,' he agreed. 'But mainly because her behaviour apparently *can* be a little challenging. Nothing major – and you'll know from experience that I don't use the word lightly. She's just a little undisciplined, it seems. And the feeling is – and this is strictly between you and me, okay? – that there's been a general lack of discipline in her life since she's been with Jean, and what with the complication of the Addison's – well, you can see how easily a child with that sort of issue can become manipulative if allowed to.'

'I get it,' I said. 'She needs some boundaries, then?'

'I think that's about the size of it. So it's right up your street. No points, as I say, as this really is just temporary, but just do what the two of you do so well. And don't let your heads swell, because I shouldn't tell you this, but it was my boss who suggested we place her with you. He said, "If anyone can turn her around, the Watson family can. After all, look how well they did with Justin."'

'That's nice,' said Mike, though I could tell by his voice that he knew he was being sweet-talked.

'And just as well I cracked on and got the room ready, then,' I added. 'Why don't you take John up to see it, love, while I put the kettle on again.'

11

My head was whirring while they went up to admire my creative efforts. The poor child. How tragic. To lose her mum – to lose all she had in the world – and to have to cope with what sounded like such a debilitating condition on her own. I wondered if she ever got to see her mother in hospital at all, and when John and Mike came back downstairs I asked.

'Yes, she does,' John said. 'Every six weeks or so, for an hour. Not that she gets anything out of it. She apparently gets really upset after each visit, which is why she doesn't go there more often.'

'Poor kid,' I said. 'It must be awful.'

'The world we live in, I'm afraid, Casey,' he said. 'Hey, but a great job on the bedroom. Fit for a princess! Oh, and be prepared, because it'll seem like she really *is* a little princess. She has quite an entourage, this one, in terms of a team. So you'll need plenty of cups at the ready ...'

When John had gone, Mike and I retreated to the living room, where we sat and talked about what was to come. A pointless exercise really, though one which we'd go on to repeat many times. You could never second-guess the future, particularly in our line of work.

'See, though,' I said. 'It was worth me getting all that decorating done, wasn't it? I'm like a walking girl guide motto. Be prepared!'

I said it in jest, but little did I know. Those prickles of mine didn't happen for nothing. Because *nothing* could have prepared us for Sophia.

Chapter 2

Monday morning arrived, and with it a fresh flurry of snow. Which made me groan because I'd just finished painstakingly polishing my wooden floors and now they were going to be trodden all over by soggy footwear.

'Do you think I should ask everyone to take their shoes off?' I asked Mike.

He shook his head. 'I wouldn't, love. It'll only take a quick mop once they're gone.'

'A quick mop!' I railed at him. 'As if! I've spent all bloody morning polishing these floors – and by hand! You should try it some time. It's –'

'Hey!' he snapped. 'Calm down! Stop flapping – the floor's fine. As is the rest of the house!' His expression softened then, if just a little. 'Look,' he said, 'I'll help you do the mopping, okay? And I'm trying to be helpful. So don't take your nerves out on me.'

He stomped off to the conservatory, and I felt a bit bad. I just wanted to make a good impression – I always did. And

Casey Watson

a spotless house seemed a good way to do that. It was probably my mother's fault, this obsession, I decided. We were Catholics, and when we were kids she was just the same as I was now – on account of the parish priest and the nuns forever calling round and, more often than not, doing so unexpectedly. She'd always be in a complete tizzy, so, just to be sure, she'd scrub the house from top to bottom every day.

But there was no time to dwell on the fate that might befall my wooden flooring, because just as I was finishing giving it a last careful scrutiny I could see a car – no, three cars – pulling up outside.

'Mike!' I hissed. 'Get back here! They've arrived. God, how many *are* there?'

He joined me at the living-room window and peeped out. 'Bloody hell, that's some posse,' he agreed.

The first car, which we recognised, held John Fulshaw, of course. The second contained a young girl – presumably Sophia – and two females, and in the third was another woman, plus a man.

We repositioned ourselves behind the front door in time to open it and welcome them, allowing a blast of cold air to swirl around our legs. It really was a bitterly cold day.

The young girl's smile, however, was warm. 'You must be Sophia,' I said, grinning at her and holding out my hand. She promptly shook it, seeming genuinely friendly. I ushered her inside, along with the others, where Mike took over with the traffic management, and herded them all in the direction of the dining room. Always good to have a table to sit around at such times, and the one in the kitchen was too small.

Not that we had enough chairs in the dining room, for that matter, and I winced inwardly as I realised he was off to get more from the conservatory; ones that I hadn't thought to wash down.

I mentally scolded myself. It didn't matter if the chairs weren't completely pristine. This was about Sophia's welfare, not what people put their bums on!

I glanced across at her to smile again, but now she was in whispered conversation, speaking close to the ear of one of the women she'd come in the car with. A woman who'd looked nervous from the off. I was just wondering whether this might be her social worker, when the woman promptly burst into tears, grabbed Sophia and pulled her in for a hug.

Glancing first at me – I clearly looked as dumbfounded as I felt – one of the other women took a step and pulled the two apart. 'Come on,' she said smartly, though not unkindly, at the two of them. 'Jean, you promised me you wouldn't *do* this. Come on, let Sophia go and then perhaps we can start the meeting. We haven't even got as far as introductions!'

Ah, so this was Sophia's carer, I thought. The one we'd heard was ill. So that would explain her rather strained and strange demeanour. But even so, as we all sat down, I reached under the table for Mike's hand and squeezed it. Something definitely didn't feel quite right here.

While introductions were made, I studied Sophia more carefully. In fact, it was hard to keep my eyes off her. She was only 12 years of age but she was a startlingly well-developed girl. With her height – she was around five foot eight, to my five foot nothing – she could easily pass for 16 or over. She was also seriously tanned – so much so that she looked like she'd just come back from the Med. Which she obviously hadn't, so did it come from a bottle? It certainly fitted – she dressed to kill, clearly knowing she had a figure to die for, emphasising her large boobs with a tight low-cut top, over skinny jeans and a pair of high-heeled boots. She was also sitting back, looking composed, with a strange smile on her face, as if allowing the proceedings to wash over her. All in all it was an arresting first impression.

Linda Samson, the supervising social worker, kicked off, explaining the facts that John had already outlined: that Jean was unable to look after Sophia temporarily and that as a consequence she needed a short-term placement.

Sophia leaned forward then, and to both my and Mike's astonishment said, 'Linda, could you please make a record of the fact that it's Jean who has asked for this, it's Jean that can't cope? Because I'm sure,' and her eyes flicked towards Jean as she spoke, 'that real mothers don't just dump their kids at the first sign of illness.'

I was gobsmacked. And Jean had started crying again. Linda's face reddened. 'Sophia, sweetheart,' she entreated. 'We have explained all this to you. You *know* what's going on. *Please* don't make matters any worse.'

Jean's tears, as Linda spoke, had become increasingly voluble. Was she really in any fit state to *be* here? Clearly not – because she then asked my unspoken question. 'Why did I come?' she sobbed. 'I knew I shouldn't have! Oh, this is all just too much! Sophia, please, darling, don't do this!'

I was absolutely stunned, and could see Mike was, too. He was looking at John with a plea in his expression. Was John going to say something, or should he?

'Okay, everyone,' John said, only moments before Mike did. 'Let's all try to calm down a little, shall we? Sophia?' He waited till he had her full attention. 'How about you and I have a quick tour of the house. See your room and so on. That will be okay, won't it, Casey?'

I nodded. 'And Bob's in Kieron's bedroom, John. Perhaps Sophia would like to meet him as well.'

Bob was Kieron's dog, a scruffy and adorable little mongrel whom he and his girlfriend Lauren had got from a rescue centre the previous year. I watched as the two of them left the dining room together, and almost felt the air stir as everyone exhaled. It was a bizarre situation and I knew Mike could sense it too. It was as if everyone in there was going out of their way not to upset this 12-year-old child in a woman's body.

'Erm, I'm a little confused,' I admitted, once I knew they'd be out of earshot. 'I thought all this had already been arranged.' I leaned forward. 'Are you okay, Jean?'

Jean nodded sadly, though she said nothing. It was Sam Davies, Sophia's social worker, who spoke up. 'It has,' she confirmed. 'It's just that it's all a bit raw for Jean and Sophia. It's Jean's first ever foster placement, you see, and she's obviously upset that she has to let go of Sophia so soon. What makes it worse, of course, is that Sophia sees it as so much of a rejection, however much we all reassure her that isn't the case. We can all see where she's coming from, I'm sure.' Everyone nodded. 'She really is terribly alone in the world. The only family she has left is the uncle, as I think you know, and he's made it very clear he doesn't want her. Packed her off the minute his wife got pregnant, by all accounts. Very difficult for a child who's already been through so much …'

'Which is why we feel it's so important that Sophia has a solid team around her,' added Linda. Yes, but more like an adoring retinue, I silently thought. 'Jack?' Linda went on. 'Would you like to explain your role?'

Jack Boyd was a small, jovial-looking Irishman. His job, he explained, had been to be a 'friend' to Sophia, taking her out once a week, to an outing like bowling or the cinema. He'd carry on, he said, to ensure continuity, if we wanted. Sophia had his mobile number, he added, and often liked to call him, especially if she was upset. Mike, who'd stayed silent, taking everything in, now chipped in. About something that, in the midst of all the upset, I had completely forgotten about myself.

'Sophia's Addison's disease,' he said to Jean. 'Can you tell me about that? We have to visit the doctors to find out a little more about the management, but can you shed any light on the challenges it throws up for you?'

Jean looked slightly nonplussed. 'Oh, I'm sure the medical team will tell you everything you need to know,' she said. 'You just have to watch out for the warning signs of her getting stressed, really, because that's dangerous. Like getting a bit snappy and irritable. That's when I know, because she's normally *such* a sweetie.'

The rest of the posse smiled an indulgent group smile when Jean said this, and once again I got the sensation of this group of people treading on eggshells, even when the girl wasn't in the room!

But then she was – she and John re-entered the dining room at that moment, and she immediately went over to behind Jack's chair, where she stopped a moment, to ruffle his hair. It seemed an unlikely gesture, and a little out of place. He lurched forward slightly, having not anticipated it, as those of us had who were sitting opposite, saying, 'Ah, give over, you little rascal!' He glanced across to us. 'She's always picking on me, this one. I have to have my wits about me, so I do.'

'It's just because I love your accent, Jack,' she told him, sitting down again. She turned to me now. 'Don't you just love the Irish, Casey?' she wanted to know. She was laughing out loud now and everyone else looked uncomfortable.

I smiled at her. 'Well, you'll meet some more Irish people in our house, Sophia. My two brothers married sisters from Ireland – from Belfast. We often visit them. And they come here with their kids all the time.'

Sophia stopped laughing now. Abruptly. 'Oh, I don't think that'll be the same, will it? Not if they're women.'

'Sophia,' John interjected, before I could close my now open mouth. 'Have you anything you'd like to ask Mike and Casey, before we finish up?' The sense of tension in the room was almost palpable.

'I don't think so,' she said mildly. 'The room is lovely. Really lovely. And your dog is adorable … Oh, I know! How old are you both? I don't like old people. Mike, you look quite young, though. Are you older, Casey?'

I was stunned at the girl's cheek, but not half as much as the fact that a couple of others in the room had actually *giggled*. This was some 'professional' team. It really was.

'You know, Sophia?' said Mike pleasantly. 'Just for future reference, it's not really polite to ask an adult their age. But, since you ask, Casey's younger than I am.'

'Well then,' said Linda, clearly keen to get away now. Sophia herself didn't open her mouth. 'If there's nothing else, I think we can wrap this up now. I'm sure, Casey and Mike, you'll have more questions to ask, so be assured that one of us will always be on hand to answer them. All our numbers will be on the paperwork that we'll be bringing on Wednesday morning, and I'll also leave you the address of Dr Wyatt, Sophia's doctor. Your appointment with him is at 1 p.m. on Wednesday, by the way, so plenty of time to get to –'

'That's a point,' said Mike. 'Where is this doctor based anyway?'

Linda handed him the sheet with the address on. 'He's here. It's –'

'The Lake District!' Mike gasped. 'Cumbria? But that's a couple of hundred miles away!'

'You only have to attend once a month or so,' Linda said quickly. 'Unless there are complications …'

'I should hope so!' Mike snapped. 'It's a six-hour round trip! It would have been nice if someone had told us this before!'

Sophia, who had been about to leave the room, now turned around. 'Aw, diddums,' she said, and it was clear she was getting her own back. 'Doesn't Daddy like driving?'

Sam pushed Sophia's coat into her arms. 'Stop being silly,' she snapped. It was the first time I'd heard anyone admonish her.

Mike was furious, I could see, so I grabbed his hand and squeezed it, hoping I could help him calm down. What hope had we if she could wind him up so comprehensively, and so quickly? Not a lot, I decided. Not a lot at *all*.

We saw them out – all bar John – with fixed smiles on our faces. What were we about to take on? *See beyond*, I kept telling myself. *See beyond the bad behaviour to the hurting child beneath*. So I looked, but, by God, it was hard.

'Quite a team she has there, eh?' John said, to break the silence that was threatening to swallow us all up, minutes later. We'd moved into the kitchen now, and Mike had set about washing up the cups, the crockery rattling furiously as he did so. The hall floor was suddenly the last thing on my mind.

'She didn't come across at *all* like that the last time I met her,' John added limply. 'Like a different girl completely …' He tailed off.

'Bloody hell, John!' I said. 'That was completely bizarre. It was like they were all absolutely terrified of upsetting her; pandering to everything, pussyfooting around her … Does she turn into a werewolf when crossed? Is that it?'

John pulled out a kitchen chair and sat on it, looking weary. 'I've never witnessed anything like that before,' he admitted. 'All my dealings with that team have been on the phone up to now, and up to now they've all seemed really switched on. I'm sorry,' he said. 'You're right. It does all feel a bit of a challenge, doesn't it? To be honest, I only agreed to taking the case because it was going to be so short term. And it *won't* be for long, I'm sure, because, as you can see, Jean really wants to keep her, long term.'

'Is she really strong enough?' Mike said. 'I can't see it myself. But I hope she does.' He frowned. 'Because, much as I hate to say this, I smell trouble. I think there's much more to this girl than meets the eye.'

John was, of course, relentlessly apologetic. He apologised for not being able to find out more about Sophia's background or her illness. He apologised for not knowing the doctor was so far away. He apologised for not knowing about the apparently worrying prospect of what might happen if she got a little 'stressed'. And he promised that he would do everything he could to find out more – because forewarned was forearmed.

We reassured him that we weren't going to take it personally – because it wasn't *his* fault, was it? It was just going to be a challenging sort of placement, we all agreed, and challenges, we also agreed, were what we were all about. Even so, as Mike and I waved John off from the doorstep, I couldn't help feeling that there were challenges and there were challenges, and that this one might not be to our liking.

'You know, love?' I said to Mike, reaching out for a hug. 'I was really looking forward to having a new child to foster, and now, you know what? I'm not sure I am any more.'

He pulled me in. 'I know, love. It all looks a little daunting, doesn't it? But I suppose that's exactly what we get paid for. We'll just have to do our best, eh? See how it goes. And remember just how much she's had to cope with in her life. She's probably feeling angry at the whole world.'

Mike was right, of course. We both knew we had to see past the behaviour and remember that she was a child who had not yet hit her teens, and was without a mum – without any family to speak of. Couple all that with what sounded like a very complicated and, possibly, life-threatening condition, and it was no wonder she was angry and demanding. I sighed as it hit me just how difficult this might be. And not just because Sophia would be a difficult child to manage. It was because I had a sixth sense – no, I *knew* – that all the efforts we made at establishing boundaries, which we badly needed to, had the potential for being undermined at every turn by the team of professionals who seemed intent to let her have her way all the time and, in doing so, turn her into a monster. Couldn't they see they weren't helping her development? They were just adding to her sense of entitlement, her bad manners and her unrealistic expectations; not a great recipe for a happy adult life.

I could only hope one thing, that we *could* make a difference. Even if it seemed, on the face of it, like a tall order.

'The coast is clear!' I told Riley, over the phone, twenty minutes later. 'Can you come round with Levi and cheer me up?'

Bless her, my daughter is an absolute sweetheart, and I knew seeing her and my lovely grandson would make the prospect so much less bleak. I set about making lunch for the three of us – Riley, Mike and me – before Mike had to rush off back to work.

'So was she awful?' Riley asked, as soon as she arrived. 'You sounded pretty down on the phone.'

I'd certainly felt it. As I'd said to Mike before she'd arrived, I now felt pretty silly, having gone so bloody overboard on the bedroom. And I had – well, me and Riley had – to a ridiculous degree. There were pink fluttery butterflies hanging in the window, two layers of contrasting pink curtains, with silver sequins dotted over them, matching bed linen and fluffy pink cushions. The bed had also been transformed by a glittery pink canopy, which hung from the ceiling and flowed over the pillows. The walls sported an array of butterflies and fairies, and the offending football-adorned bookcase was now gleaming white, and sat among mushrooms (Riley's idea – garden ornaments), upon which sat more fairies … It really was a room fit for a princess. Trouble was, what we seemed to have was less a princess than a little madam.

But as Mike had pointed out, aiding that transition was our job. But he'd looked at me gloomily, as if reading my thoughts. 'Screw the room, Casey,' he'd said. 'That's the least of our worries.'

It was good to have Riley here to break the tension. 'Tell you what,' I said now, 'I'll go and dig some toys out for Levi. Mike, why don't you tell Riley all about it, love?'

I went off to the blanket box under the stairs, knowing Mike would be able to stick to the facts and not get overemotional, like I would. I didn't want to seem overemotional about it, as I knew the kids would just fret even more about whether we'd done the right thing.

Funny, I thought, pulling out the box and lifting the lid, how you have expectations in life, without any evidence to back them up at all. I'd collected a lot of these toys when we'd first discussed fostering, mistakenly thinking we'd have lots of little children around. Naïve, really – it was the older kids who needed our kind of specialist help. The ones a way down the line; the really damaged ones. Still, I thought, pulling out a singing pig for Levi, maybe the toy fairy knew I'd soon have my first grandchild. It was a nice thought after a troubling kind of morning.

When I returned to the kitchen, Mike and Riley, thank goodness, were both laughing.

'Sounds like you've got a proper little madam on your hands!' Riley said, echoing my own thoughts.

'Dad's filled you in, then?' I asked her.

'Yes, he has,' she confirmed. 'Though don't worry, Mum. You'll soon have her learning our ways. No airs and graces in this house!'

I nodded. 'But I am worried about Kieron,' I confessed. My son has a mild form of Asperger's syndrome, which makes him vulnerable in lots of little ways. He doesn't see bad in anyone, much less any kind of guile, and I suspected, with him being young, not to mention tall and good look-ing, that he might be a target for Sophia's attentions. 'I think he's going to find her a bit overwhelming,' I said. 'She seems a bit over the top in the touchy-feely department – you saw the way she was with that Jack, didn't you, Mike? She's definitely a bit flirty around men.'

'A bit?! And he was mortified,' Mike agreed. 'So we'll just have to prepare Kieron. You know, make it clear that he'll need to keep his distance.'

'And put some rules in place, for definite. Even if she's not going on the programme. She needs some guidelines more suitable for a girl of her age.'

Which was what we did, over the course of the next twenty-four hours, as well as filling Kieron in on how unlike most 12-year-old girls she was, and how running around in boxers might be a very bad idea. I also contacted my old school – the one I'd worked in before the career change into fostering – and secured Sophia a place there to start the following Monday. Finally, I spent a little while on the internet, trying to find out what I could about Addison's disease. It seemed to be as described – something life-long and incurable – but which, with tablets, seemed straightforward to manage. The only alarming thing I read was that people with the disorder could have 'crises', when the levels of hormones fell so low they could die, if not treated immediately by injection. That sounded worrying, and I made a mental note to ask the doctor a bit more. Then I called John Fulshaw, to fill him in too, and was taken aback by his response.

'Oh, Casey, I can't tell you, I'm so grateful to you and Mike. After yesterday morning I really thought you'd be calling me to say you'd changed your minds.'

'Not at all, John,' I told him. 'We're giving this a go. It'll be different, for sure, but we'll find a way through it.'

All that done, and with Mike at work and Kieron at college – he was there doing a course in music and media, which he was loving – I trotted off to the conservatory for a sneaky cigarette. I must try to stop, I chided myself, as I did every time, but I couldn't seem to. I smoked very little, but that emergency packet of twenty that I kept above the fridge-freezer was an absolute lifeline in times of great stress. And I *was* stressed, I thought, as I opened the patio doors and lit one.

But if I'd known just how much *more* stressful my life was soon going to become, I think I would have booked myself in for an asbestos lung replacement, ready.

Chapter 3

I was feeling pretty confident when I woke up on the Wednesday morning. I didn't know why, exactly, but I was certainly glad of it. I glanced at the alarm clock – it was just before seven – and decided I would quickly nip downstairs, grab the morning paper and a coffee, and come back up to bed for half an hour. Mike had already gone to work; he had to go in for about an hour. Then he'd be back by nine, ready to welcome Sophia and her entourage, before our long trip to see the Addison's doctor.

You deserve this, I told myself, as I slipped back under the cosy, still-warm duvet. So enjoy it. Got one heck of a lot of challenges ahead …

I was downstairs, showered and dressed, by eight thirty, with my hair, which is black and curly, tied in a ponytail. Some days there was nothing else I could do with it. This was one of them. Typical, I thought, as I put the kettle back on. But no matter. I looked calm and casual, I knew, in leggings and a warm baggy jumper, but, sadly, my rush of confidence had gone the way of the shower gel – down the plughole – as thoughts of the day ahead began claiming my attention. A long drive, a lecture on Addison's, another long drive, then the reality of welcoming Sophia into our home and lives.

I glanced at my watch. Just time to sneak a cigarette and coffee in the conservatory before Mike returned home and the cavalry arrived. I shivered in the cold as I stood there and smoked it, and wished I'd put the heating on an hour earlier. I also wondered who'd turn up with her this time. Surely not all that lot who came on Monday? I put out the cigarette and wandered back into the living room to see.

Yup. It *was* all that lot, it seemed. By the time I got to the window I could see that three cars had already pulled up in the road outside. But, looking closer, I could see that this time there were fewer people in them. Or rather, getting out of them: John Fulshaw from one car, Linda Sampson from the second and Sam Davies from the third. Sophia herself was already standing by my open gate, seemingly directing operations.

She was dressed to the nines – fur coat, matching hat, her face caked in make-up – and holding the gate open for her retinue to pass through. I stood, open-mouthed, as I watched the tableau before me. I simply couldn't get my head around the quantity of luggage that seemed to be spewing from the various car boots. I counted them out: four huge suitcases, at least six cardboard boxes and what seemed to be a stack of canvas paintings. I was gobsmacked.

Where the hell was all this stuff going to go? And more to the point, why had she brought all this with her, when it was going to be such a short placement?

Equally unbelievably, and I could hear it all clearly from the window, was that this 12-year-old seemed to be barking orders at the adults – and, more incredibly, they seemed to be listening.

'Careful with that artwork!' I heard her bark at John, as he passed her. 'Any tears in those and you're going to have to pay for it!' She then clapped her hands together – this was beginning to feel like some bizarre slapstick movie – and said, 'Chop chop! I don't have all day!'

Sophia turned then and saw me gaping out of the window. She smiled and waved at me, and then, if my eyes weren't deceiving me, actually clicked her fingers to beckon me to the front door. Upon which I, on some mad autopilot, and in keeping with her other minions, almost fell over my own coffee table in my rush to get to the hall.

'Hi, love,' I said, emerging from the door just as she'd sauntered down the front path. 'Good grief, you have a lot of luggage, don't you? Can I help? Do you need a hand with anything?'

'Hi,' she responded, marching straight past me. 'No thanks. You can just tell them to take everything up to my room. I don't do carrying,' she then finished, sweetly.

Them? Now I recovered at least some of my senses. 'I don't think so,' I said, speaking also to the adults who were now assembling, partly obscured by the procession of belongings. 'We'll just leave it all in the hall for the moment, I think. We can take it –' and by which, I made a mental note, I *meant* we '– all up to your room later on.'

Nothing terrible happened. No explosion. No strop. She just shrugged and wandered off into the living room, leaving me, mouth slightly agape again, standing in her wake, while she muttered something to herself about 'the incompetency of idiots'. It honestly beggared belief.

But it was also so absurd as to be hilarious with it, especially as I watched John wrestling with two pink suitcases, which he half hauled, half threw into my hallway. I had to bite my lip to keep from laughing, and his withering expression only made it worse. He gave me an old-fashioned look. 'Don't,' he said under his breath. 'Okay? Just don't.'

We all congregated, eventually, in the living room, where I invited everyone to take a seat while I made some hot drinks. The hilarious expression on John's face had really lightened my mood, and I was chuckling to myself as I pulled mugs from the cupboard.

'What's so funny?' asked a voice. Sophia had joined me in the kitchen.

'Oh, nothing,' I said, glad she'd felt able to come and join me, at least. 'It was just seeing John grappling with those cases of yours. You okay, love?' I glanced across at her. 'Feeling all right?'

Her expression changed to one of what I could only describe as condescension. '*Derr*,' she said in an exasperated voice. 'You don't have to look at me like that, you know. I'm not *dying*!'

'I know,' I said nicely, through my slightly gritted teeth. 'I didn't think so for a moment. I just wanted to make sure you're okay. After all the upheaval of *moving*, that was all.'

Her face back-tracked slightly, even if her voice didn't. 'Hmmph,' she muttered. 'Yes, well, I'm fine.'

And with that she turned and sauntered off back to the living room, leaving me once again staring after her, agape. Right, I thought, making my mind up at that moment. No more Mrs Nice Guy from me. I needed to let this child know who called the shots around here and put an end to all this pussyfooting around. It would do her no favours – *had* been doing her no favours. It made her unpleasant to be around, and that wasn't going to help her. It wouldn't help *me* to help her either. I finished making the drinks and took the tray into the living room, where the three adults were sitting, Sophia back among them, trying to make small talk among themselves.

'Right,' I said cheerfully to one and all. 'Here you go. Help yourselves to biscuits, by the way.'

Sophia's glance towards Sam was as pointed as she could make it. 'Sophia doesn't like to be around biscuits,' Sam explained nervously. 'It's her Addison's. She has to be really disciplined about sugar, because the steroids she takes give her a really huge appetite, and if she indulges ...' She looked back towards Sophia as if for help. Then I noticed her and Linda exchange glances. 'Well, it's obviously not terribly good for her to get fat.'

I picked up the plate of biscuits and offered it only to the adults, equally pointedly. She clearly needed to learn discipline, period. 'I'm sorry,' I said. 'I clearly have a lot to learn, don't I?'

'Yes, you *do*,' Sophia answered, folding her arms across her chest.

'Now, Sophia –' began Sam, sounding nervous about even speaking. Jesus, what was the matter with these people?

'Come on, sweetie,' she added, leaping up and putting her arm around her, as if she wasn't standing there smiling but in huge floods of tears. 'D'you want to show me your room? I could help you make a start, carry some things up. Leave the others to sort out the boring paperwork, eh?'

I could have happily slapped Sophia's social worker then. Not only was she undermining me – bad enough in itself – but she was also disregarding the girl's rude behaviour. Which wasn't very professional of her at all.

As soon as they'd left the room, I rounded on Linda, the supervising social worker, who, right now, seemed to be supervising nothing. 'You know,' I said, 'pandering to her every whim isn't going to help her. She needs boundaries, a bit of discipline ...'

'I agree,' John chipped in. He could see how cross I was and seemed keen to support me. It wasn't too late, I thought, for us to change our minds, and he knew it. But that wasn't his motivation, I decided. He was genuinely trying to second a valid point. 'She does seem to wrap everyone around her little finger,' he continued.

Linda, unsurprisingly, jumped straight to her defence. 'I know it seems that way,' she said. 'But try to look beyond her behaviour, *please*. Underneath the front, she's feeling

Casey Watson

lost and abandoned and alone. She'll settle down, I promise. Give it a couple of days. Things will be fine. Honestly
they will.'

But her tone belied her words. She knew no such thing.
This wouldn't be a team I'd be getting much support from,
I decided. Once again, as had been the case with our last
child, bar John, we'd probably be on our own. Was that
how it worked with our kind of specialist 'extreme' fostering? That Mike and I were considered so able they could
throw anything at us, secure in the blind faith that we'd
cope?

But before I had a chance to say something regrettable,
Mike himself walked in, having come back from work.
'Morning all!' he said cheerily. 'Everything okay here?'
The three of us seemed of like mind. End of conversation.
We all got our heads down and ran through all the
paperwork.

It was only once John and Linda were finishing up and I
cleared the mugs that I could have a word with Mike on our
own.

'What's up, love?' he asked, once we were both in the
kitchen. 'You could cut the atmosphere in there with a
knife!'

'Oh, just more of the same. Our little madam's been busy
being one again. And it seems no one in her "team" has got
the confidence to take her on. I just had a bit of a moment,
that's all. Nothing to worry about. She'll find things rather
different now, starting today. And none too soon, because
that lot seem to be creating a monster.'

But once back in the living room I had cause to eat my words. Sophia and Sam had come down from upstairs now, and Sophia was visibly and genuinely distressed as she hugged both the women and said her goodbyes. I felt a pang of guilt. This was a desperate 12-year-old girl, trying to make sense of an appalling situation. Perhaps Linda had been right, and I'd been wrong. I must learn, I decided, that my usual acuity *re* character wasn't quite as infallible as I thought. I also knew nothing about the emotional toll of being the victim of an incurable disease. Sophia had perhaps been right in that, too. I did have a lot to learn this afternoon. Speaking of which … 'Look at the time,' I said. 'We really need to get off.'

'Right,' said Sam, disentangling herself from Sophia. 'And we'd better leave you all to it. I'll phone you in a day or so, Sophia, okay? And come to see how you're doing in a week or so.'

I moved closer to Sophia as everyone trooped back out of the door, automatically putting an arm around her waist. She needed affection, I thought. Physical contact. Even though her manner so often seemed to suggest otherwise, the child inside needed love more than anything.

We waved them off, Sophia rubbing at her tear-stained cheeks with her other hand. Then she turned to me. 'Where's your son? Didn't you say you had a teenage son?'

Her voice was completely different now. As light and sunny, suddenly, as the day was dark and cold.

'Kieron?' I said, shocked. 'Yes. He's at college today. You'll meet him tonight. When we get back from your doctor's –'

35

'Okay!' she said brightly. 'Coats on then, is it? As you say, it's a long way. Time to go!'

It was a very, very long three hours, that journey to hospital, as all three occupants of the car – Mike, myself and Sophia – retreated into their own minds and thoughts. I tried several times to start conversations with Sophia initially, all of which were mildly, but decisively, rebuffed by her lack of interest in giving me more than one-word responses. I then tuned the radio station to one I thought she might like, but this, too, was pointedly rejected. She simply pulled an MP3 player from her pocket and plugged herself into that. 'I think that's you told,' whispered Mike.

She's 12, I kept telling myself, locked alone with my anxieties. (I couldn't talk to Mike, of course, because she wasn't six inches from us.) She's 12. Think back, Casey. That's what 12-year-olds are like, even 12-year-olds with the most benign of families and backgrounds. She's on the cusp of adolescence, too; no, that was wrong. Physically at least, she was well into it. So perhaps I was reading too much into things. She'd also been overindulged and was clearly using her disorder to manipulate the adults around her. She just needed guidance, support and that healthy dose of discipline. That, I decided, would help her immeasurably. And as a virtual orphan in the world, boy, did she need help.

But I couldn't help but wonder at these extreme swings in behaviour: one minute full of herself, the next happy-clappy, and then, out of the blue, appearing really upset. What mood would be on offer when we arrived at the hospital, I wondered? I was beginning to realise that we just couldn't second-guess her.

'Happy', as it turned out, just as soon as we got there. The sullen mask was stashed away along with the earphones for her iPod, to be replaced by what I could only describe as the sweetest, friendliest expression imaginable.

'Follow me,' she commanded, though in the nicest of manners. 'I know this place like the back of my hand! Casey,' she turned to me, 'you are *so* going to love my doctor. He's called Dr Wyatt, and he's absolutely *gorgeous*.' She was so excited, she was practically squealing.

'Right behind you, love,' said Mike, as we both hurried along in her wake.

Less inclined to stampede down the corridor than Sophia was, we kept her in sight but still failed to keep up, and by the time we reached the correct clinic's reception she was already charming the receptionist.

'Ah, you must be Mr and Mrs Watson,' the young woman said. 'I'm Wendy, by the way. Me and Sophie go back a long way, don't we, honey? Do take a seat. Dr Wyatt will be with you very shortly.'

Mike and I sat down on the leather sofa we'd been assigned to, leaving our young charge gaily chatting to the receptionist. But we didn't have to wait for very long. After only about thirty seconds a man emerged from behind a door, and promptly bellowed 'Sophie!' as if greeting a dear friend who'd been thought lost at sea and had unexpectedly fetched up. I noted that he, like Wendy, hadn't called her Sophia. They were obviously all very close. *Very* close.

Sophia's response was equally enthusiastic. 'Oh, it's so nice to see you!' she cried, leaping upon him, and so forcefully that I thought she might topple him over, or, even worse, jump up into his arms and swing her legs round him. Thankfully, neither happened, but most astonishing to my mind was that the doctor didn't even seem to flinch. 'Nice to see you too!' he said, when she finally put him down. 'I'm Steve Wyatt,' he then said to us, coming to shake our hands. 'Paediatric endo-crinologist. Very nice to meet you both as well.'

Mike and I began to rise, but he flapped a hand to indi-cate we should stay where we were. 'No, no. You can sit a while longer,' he explained. 'Sophia likes to have her consul-tation in private – just myself and her nurse, if that's okay?'

He could probably tell from our expressions that this seemed a little irregular – after all, we were *in loco parentis*. 'I know it seems a little strange,' he added, rather less confi-dently, 'but it's what Sophia wants and we have to accept her wishes. But it should only take around fifteen minutes and then of course you can come in so we can go through the management and so on. Okay?'

'Well, if that's the way it has to be …' Mike answered. 'Is that okay with you, Sophia?'

'Well, I do like to see my doctor in private,' she nodded, and then they turned around and went back into the room.

'How bizarre,' I said to Mike, once we were alone. 'We should have insisted on being allowed in with her, shouldn't we? Don't you think? It feels all wrong not to be in there. How odd.'

Mike shrugged. 'What's new? Everything seems bizarre about this child. Run of the mill, she isn't. Why should this be any different?'

'But why the "private" thing? What's he privy to that we're not allowed to know about? I mean, I understand the whole business of patient confidentiality. But she's a child. And she's in care. And it's our job to care *for* her. So if there are things we should know and which are important and no one's telling us ...'

Mike squeezed my knee. 'Don't fret, love. We'll be in there soon enough. And we can ask. Perhaps we'll get a chance to have a word with the doctor on our own at some point. In the meantime, I need a coffee. The heat in this place is making me sleepy ... You want one?'

'Do bears live in the woods?' I asked him, grinning.

While Mike wandered off in search of a vending machine, I idly flicked through the magazine I'd brought with me. But only a couple of minutes later the doctor's door flew open and a stressed-looking nurse came rushing out, clutching a purse. I was then shocked to see her rushing back, only half a minute afterwards, now holding a bottle of water and a bag of peanuts. Blimey, I thought, poor love. Talk about NHS cutbacks – were their tea breaks now measured in seconds, or what? Mike ambled up with our coffees soon after, and I was just about to share my little witticism with him when he said, 'You see that?', nodding towards Dr Wyatt's consulting room. 'That was apparently for Sophia. Had a bit of a turn, by all accounts. Brain fog, the woman called it. Needed an immediate protein boost.'

'Oh, my God,' I said, panicked. 'Should we go in?'

Mike shook his head. 'Apparently not. I did ask her at the machine. But she said she'd fetch us in once they'd sorted things out.'

I took the coffee from him. 'I don't know about you,' I said, 'but this Addison's thing scares me. It's clearly a serious illness and we know nothing about it. *Nothing*. How on earth are we going to cope when it's just her and us?' I meant it, as well. Just how *would* we cope? I had no confidence that half an hour with Dr Wyatt was going to help much. This was obviously something that could come on and be life threatening at any moment, and for the third time in as many days I repeated the same mantra – that I mustn't fret, that it was short term, that we wouldn't have her long … but how dreadful, I thought guiltily, to be wishing a kid away when she'd only been with us five minutes!

Mike, who could read my mind – well, most of the time, anyway – put a reassuring arm around my shoulder. 'Stop worrying, love, eh? Think about it logically. They wouldn't have trusted us to care for her if they didn't think we could cope, would they? Let's just see what the doctor says and take it from there. And remember what they say about women and teabags …'

I laughed. He was right, as I'd proved to myself often. You really *didn't* know how strong you were till they put you in hot water. And becoming a foster carer, above all, had proved to me that I was one hell of a lot stronger and more capable than I could ever have thought.

I sipped my coffee, awaited our summons and tried to think positively about things. But I didn't know then, though I very soon would, just *how* hot this water was going to turn out to be …

Chapter 4

Addison's, clearly, was a very frightening disease. Despite Dr Wyatt's cheerful, matter-of-fact manner, this wasn't something Mike and I could listen to lightly.

Our all-you-need-to-know lesson wasn't long, but it was complex, so I was grateful that the doctor passed us various leaflets and brochures as he spoke, which we could take away to digest more fully later, along with a big box of medication, which included the steroid injection paraphernalia I'd read about and which scared me. I hated everything about injections.

But the reality of the disease hit home straight away. Sophia's Addison's disease meant her adrenal glands no longer functioned, which had implications for all sorts of bodily processes. The two vital hormones she needed – cortisol and aldosterone – had to be replaced by taking daily medication – several times a day – and though it seemed this was usually sufficient to manage it, all sorts of things could affect how much she needed, including eating patterns, how well she was and how much stress she was under. If she didn't get those hormones, via the tablets she was taking, she would die – it was as stark a fact as that. She had, therefore, to be mindful of taking her tablets at all times; an onerous responsibility for anyone, let alone a child – and when you factored in the appalling circumstances of this particular child's life … well, it was a pretty sobering thing to even think about.

On a practical level, it was all about discipline. She had to eat regularly, and follow a diet that, though not that restrictive generally, prohibited the sort of random snacking on junk that other children of her age so often tended towards. Her medication did, as Jean had said, mean she could easily put on weight, something that would make her condition even harder to manage, as well as having negative psychological effects.

The worst-case scenario, the doctor pointed out, would be the onset of an 'Addisonian crisis', as it was called. If she had one of them, as a result of either a high temperature or other stress, it really was a life-and-death situation. Hence the injection kit he'd given us. I could only hope we'd never have to use it.

It was a hell of a lot to take in at one sitting, but we needed to try to get our heads around it all because, as Sophia's carers, for however short a time, we had to have the means and knowledge to be able to put it into action.

Sophia wasn't with us now. When we'd been invited into the doctor's office, where he sat behind an enormous desk, Sophia perched on a stool to one side, he'd suggested that she might like to go off with the nurse for some fresh air.

After all, as he pointed out, grinning at both her and us, she was already something of an expert on Addison's disease and didn't need to sit through all the boring stuff.

We'd taken the opportunity to bring up the slightly odd business of her being so adamant about seeing him alone. Wasn't it all a bit cloak and dagger?

'I know it seems that way, Mrs Watson,' he'd agreed. 'But unfortunately my hands are tied. There are certain parts of Sophia's file that she doesn't want disclosed, and I'm afraid that I have to respect that. All I can say is that they in no way affect her condition, nor do they hamper your ability to care for her.'

Which, frustratingly, left us none the wiser.

'The main thing,' Dr Wyatt explained now, his medical briefing complete, 'is, of course, that you become attuned to the symptoms of a steroid insufficiency. Headache and/ or dizziness, nausea and/or vomiting, wobbly knees, fuzzy thinking – the thing is, *at all costs*, to avoid a full-on emergency, so it's always better to be safe than sorry. Increasing her steroids temporarily won't cause her any harm, though long term they very much can. But it's all in the literature,' he finished up, cheerfully. 'And you can call us any time you have concerns. Oh, but one more thing.' He nodded towards the door now. 'There's also low blood sugar to look out for. It's another common problem with Addisonians, but easily dealt with. As happened just now, give her a small bag of peanuts or something. Some of my patients swear by things like scrambled eggs, too. It's the protein boost that helps. You'll find she craves salt as well. Just the one thing ...' He paused again.

'What's that?' Mike asked him.

'The one thing, of course, as you've no doubt been told, is that Sophia's been known to fake crises and low blood sugar. In fact, that's probably what she did just then. For effect.'

I tried to take this in. 'But why?' I asked.

'She's a 12-year-old girl,' the doctor said. 'One who must take pills all the time and eat sensibly. Which must be galling. Especially when her peers can chow on what they like. But if she says she feels sick or dizzy … well, she's learned, of course, hasn't she? That it's a sure route to getting attention.'

'But how are we supposed to know if she's faking or not?'

Dr Wyatt shook his head. 'Please don't stress overly,' he said. 'It's just a question of making sure she follows her routine. If you make sure from the outset that she takes her pills in front of you – when she's with you, that is – give her a healthy packed lunch and a well-balanced evening meal, there's no reason at all why she should have problems. Oh, and get her school on board, of course. If you're really very lucky, they might have someone on the staff who's familiar with the condition. But if not – and it's doubtful – then it's really just a case of them exercising vigilance as well.' His tone was reassuring, but I wasn't reassured. I had no idea the condition could be manipulated like this and how much of a close eye we would have to keep on her. 'And this could *really* be life-threatening – this crisis thing?' I asked him.

He nodded. 'They happen only very rarely,' he said, 'but potentially yes, one could be. The trick is to stave it off before it even looks like happening. Prevention is always so much better than cure.'

I thought grimly about the average adolescent's mind. Being told you might do some damage to yourself in the long term never stopped armies of kids taking up smoking, trying drugs and getting drunk as skunks, did it? But for attention? Mr Wyatt seemed to read my mind. 'The problem with Sophia,' he said quietly, 'is that she resents her condition and wants to prove she controls *it*, rather than the other way around.'

'Or maybe she's just manipulative,' Mike suggested. 'And likes to control those around her.'

Dr Wyatt nodded. He looked slightly taken aback by Mike's comment, but I got the feeling he did understand. 'It's certainly true that some young people with chronic illnesses can be manipulative,' he agreed. He then looked at his watch. Quite a lot of time had passed now. There were obviously more patients waiting. 'But unless she tells us how she feels, I'm afraid we just don't know,' he finished. 'But please do get in touch,' he said, rising, 'if you have further questions or need help. That's what we're here for ...'

We were all quiet, lost in our own thoughts, during the journey back home. I was busy going through everything again in my head: the complicated nature of this new routine. I was expecting each child to be different, of course; with my first foster child, Justin, who counted major food issues among the many manifestations of how badly he'd been damaged, I'd had to create a wall chart and update it on a regular basis, detailing every aspect of all our upcoming meals. Not only did I have to write up exactly what we were having, but also when we were having it, almost to the minute. If I didn't do this, he got terribly anxious and difficult, especially in the early days and weeks he was with us. It did improve, but it would create tension, even months down the line, if we ever deviated from it. Deciding on an impromptu take-away instead was, we soon realised, not an option.

This new routine, though, was a whole other ball game. This was medical and complex and stressful. I had to observe Sophia's daily tablet taking, keep a track of her supplies, ring up for regular repeat prescriptions and collect them, and keep two emergency kits – one at home, and one for school trips and so on – to hand and ready for action at all times. Not such a huge amount really, but that wasn't the point – it was just the enormity of the responsibility. I had honestly not realised until that very moment quite how serious a chronic disease like this could be.

I sighed heavily. Blow the long-term health implications for me – I was stressed and I really craved a cigarette.

I turned to Mike. 'Could we stop at the next services?' I asked him. 'I need to pick up a few bits.'

'And a cig?' he said, grinning. 'Course we can, love.'

We stopped at the next services – about an hour away from home – and all got out of the car. After such a long time in the car it was good to be able to stretch our legs, but Sophia, once she'd done so, climbed straight back in. 'I don't need to go in, do I?' she wanted to know. 'I'm tired. I think it's the heat. Plus the stress of the journey.'

'You go on, love,' Mike said to me. 'I'll stay here with Sophia. Get your bits. See you back here in a bit.'

I bought the bread and milk I needed and ducked round to the corner of the building to the smoking area. I really must research this disease properly, I decided. I didn't feel comfortable not knowing everything I could know about it. If I was going to be able to look after Sophia properly, then I needed to know when the wool was being pulled over my eyes.

I stubbed out my cigarette and walked back to the car, and the rest of the trip home passed without incident. Sophia, true to her word, seemed sleepy indeed. She didn't stir for the rest of the journey.

Happily, for all concerned, the rest of the day went pretty well. When we got home Kieron had already arrived back from college, and their first meeting seemed a success all round. Sophia took to Kieron instantly, it seemed to me, and our evening meal felt as relaxed as it would have done usually, Sophia laughing and chatting and being generally very sweet.

But there was still *something* – a vague sense of unease I couldn't shake. I'd definitely been rattled by the doctor's revelations about Sophia having been known to fake symptoms, but not *that shaken*. After all, I'd spent almost all of the previous year with a much more obviously distressed and challenging child under my roof. I'd also had years of experience working with difficult children; it was almost in my blood to tease out what made these kids tick. But this one, I thought, was somehow different; more unfathomable. And so chameleon-like, it was frankly spooky.

Still, I thought, waking slowly and strangely serenely on Thursday morning, another day, another chance to get to know Sophia better, another opportunity to make a difference to the world. But my serenity didn't last long. 'Damn!' I thought, seeing the alarm clock beside the bed. Nine o'clock and I'd only just woken up!

I'd have to get my act together, I thought grimly, as I threw off the duvet and registered that, once again, Mike seemed to have forgotten to switch the heating on. But no bad thing, perhaps, to be driven from my bed. This time next week we'd be back in the thick of a new school term. I had to snap myself out of this post-Christmas languor, and *fast*.

I dragged my dressing gown around me and hurtled downstairs, fully expecting to be greeted by the sight of my young charge, looking fed up and abandoned, in the kitchen. Or worse, waiting to take her tablets – it had to be in my sight, of course, and she knew that – and going rapidly downhill even as I slept.

But I needn't have stressed. A quick glance around confirmed she wasn't downstairs, and another back upstairs – for I was now, of course, going to have to be hyper-vigilant – confirmed that she was still sleeping soundly.

Time, then, to relax for a short while in the conservatory, with my own company, the paper, a sneaky cigarette or two and my sheaf of Addison's disease information pamphlets. Pausing only to flick the heating switch and grab a mug of coffee, I opened the back door and went out into the conservatory.

But I'd not been in there two minutes when Bob trotted in, tail going nine to the dozen, closely followed by footsteps, which I assumed must be Kieron's. Bob slept on his bed every night, so it made sense. But then he spoke and it wasn't a he. It was Sophia.

'Wow, it's so cold in here!' she observed, not inaccurately. I was pretty cold myself. After all, it was January. And this was a conservatory.

'It'll warm up soon,' I said, turning round to greet her properly. 'I just put the heating back on, so –'

I stopped and gaped then, on seeing her, pretty much lost for words. She'd come down in what's generally described as 'baby doll' pyjamas. But there was nothing doll-like about them, and certainly nothing babyish, either. They were not only very short and frilly, and fashioned from scarlet nylon, they were also very, very transparent.

'Good Lord!' I said. 'No wonder you're cold, dressed like that! Haven't you got anything more suitable to put on?'

'What d'you mean?' she asked, innocently, looking down at the wisps of material. 'It's a nightie. All my nighties are like this.'

'Then we'll need to get you some new ones. Do you at least have a dressing gown?'

She shook her head. 'I don't wear them. Anyway, what's wrong with this? Jean lets me wear these.'

I put my stash of leaflets down and stood up to return to the kitchen. It was making me feel cold just looking at her. 'Sweetie,' I said, 'quite apart from the fact that you'll catch your death, there are no men at Jean's house, are there? But here …' I thought instantly of the rapport she'd struck up with Kieron, and how he might react, faced with such a sight. He wouldn't know where to look. He'd be mortified. 'Well, it's just not appropriate, love, okay? Though, I have to say –' I couldn't help voice what I was thinking. After all, the child was *12*. 'I'm surprised she let you wear those sort of nightclothes, in any case.'

Sophia stuck her lip out. 'Well she *did*.'

Best, perhaps, I thought, to let this go for now. She was bound to be sensitive about Jean, after all. 'Well, we'll see what we can find when we go shopping.'

'We're going shopping?'

'Yes,' I said, heading back into the kitchen. 'This morning. With my daughter Riley. And my grandson, little Levi. You'll love him,' I assured her. 'He's gorgeous.'

'A baby?' She brightened instantly. 'Oh, I love babies! How old is he?'

Baby talk, I thought. Never failed to come in useful.

If the idea of Levi had put such a smile on Sophia's face, actually meeting him in the flesh would, I knew, have her squealing with delight.

I was biased, obviously, but my little grandson was just lovely. Born the previous October, he was now just beginning to recognise faces, and delighted everyone with his broad toothless smile. It had been a shock, Riley starting a family so young, not least to her, I think – but she and her partner David had been together for a couple of years now, and they were a really solid couple. They were also turning out to be wonderfully relaxed, natural parents; Riley was obviously really cut out to be a mum.

And me a nanna, even though when they'd first told us, it had taken Mike and me a few days to adjust to the idea of becoming grandparents at the youthful age of 40 and 41 respectively. In our heads we were still just young newly-weds ourselves!

Little Levi couldn't have come at a better time, either, as it was just before we had to say farewell to Justin, our last foster child, which had been a wrench and a half, to say the least.

I smiled as rustled up some scrambled eggs for us both, and Sophia took her tablets. She had two different pills to take in the mornings, then further doses of one of them twice more during the day. I smiled at her as I watched her carefully re-close the bottles. It would be nice to have another youngster in the family mix again. Whatever the travails ahead, I was sure I could handle them. Underneath all the outward behavioural oddities, this was just another child who needed some stability and love, after all.

'And Mike's going to pop out and get some picture hooks on his way home from work,' I told her, as she tucked into her eggs. 'So he can put up all your paintings in your room for you.'

She pulled a bit of a face. 'I don't know why Jean bought all those canvases for me, to be honest,' she said. 'I just pointed to one I liked when we were out shopping one day, and next thing she, like, started this whole collection for me.'

I had wondered about them myself, as had Mike. It did seem an odd thing for a 12-year-old to have her own art collection. And even though they were prints, and not originals, this *was* an art collection, there was no doubt about that. They were all by the same artist, and clearly of some quality. I'd initially wondered if they'd come from her mother's home. But apparently not. Sophia had seen the first one when she and Jean had been on a trip to London, and Jean had bought it for her right away. 'And she got the rest of them by mail order,' Sophia explained. 'I think the woman who painted them used to send them herself.'

'Well, it was nice of Jean to do that for you, wasn't it?' I said.

'I s'pose,' she agreed. 'But Jean was pretty easy like that. I could get anything I wanted from her, basically.'

Again, I was brought up short by her words. What an inappropriate thing to say to another adult! I could imagine kids in a playground making comments like this, but here? To me? Another foster carer? I smiled anyway. 'Is that right?' I said. 'Hmm. Well, I think you'll find I'm not quite such an easy touch. I value my money too much, I'm afraid!'

This didn't seem to faze her. Quite the contrary, in fact. 'Ah, yeah,' she said, polishing off her last mouthful of toast. 'But I happen to know how much allowance foster carers get for kids, and it's only fair it gets spent on us, isn't it?'

Astonishing. Just astonishing. 'Hmm,' I said again, 'well, I don't know what you've heard – and I'm surprised people have even talked to you about this, to be honest – but believe me, that allowance is not there as pocket money, to be spent on anything and everything a child wants. It's to *care* for you, Sophia. To pay for your keep, plus things like outings and holidays, and clothes – speaking of which, we'd better get our skates on. Riley'll be here with Levi any minute.'

Sophia stood up and took her plate over to the sink, looking completely unconcerned. I nodded towards the hall. 'Go on, scoot upstairs and get yourself dressed and ready, okay? Oh, and don't forget to make your bed!' I called after her.

My God, I thought, as I poured hot water onto the few bits of crockery. That girl really knew how to push buttons. Sounded like she had Jean wrapped right around her little finger – and didn't seem to care who knew it, either. It was going to be a learning curve for Sophia, living with us, I thought wryly.

But, as I'd find out, it would be an even bigger one for me.

Chapter 5

Levi was beginning to recognise faces now, and it was wonderful to see the big grin he gave me when I swooped towards the pram and lifted him up. Grandchildren, I decided, should be available on the NHS.

'How's my little man, then?' I asked him. 'As gorgeous as ever? You want a coffee, love?' I asked Riley. 'Sophia's still upstairs getting ready, so we've got time.'

Riley nodded, and went to flick the switch on the kettle. She then nodded towards the hallway. 'How's it going?' she whispered. 'What's she like?'

I raised my eyebrows a touch. 'You'll see!' I whispered.

As if on cue, Sophia clattered down the stairs, and came into the kitchen smiling, but looking (well, as far as I could tell on our few days' acquaintance) uncharacteristically shy around Riley. Which was interesting. Riley had a big, big personality, but she definitely wasn't the intimidating type. Not unless she needed to be, anyway. In fact, where my and Mike's fostering was concerned, she was a godsend. She really cared about what we were doing, and wanted to help wherever she could. In fact, she was already talking about doing fostering herself, once Levi was a little bit older. She smiled broadly.

'Hi! You must be Sophie, then,' she said brightly. 'Nice to meet you!'

'Soph*ia*,' she corrected. 'My name is Soph*ia*. *Not* Sophie, okay? Just so you know.' There was a sudden flash of anger in her eyes.

Riley nodded slightly, but didn't otherwise react. Even though I knew she'd seen it too, bless her. 'Oh, I'm *so* sorry,' she said nicely. 'I must have heard wrong. Anyway, this little man here is my Levi. D'you want to give him a cuddle?'

The flash subsided just as quickly as it had appeared. And just as she'd intimated to me earlier, Sophia seemed very keen, holding her arms out as I handed him over, and now cooing, 'Look at you! You're so sweet! Oh, and look at your beautiful black curls!' She turned to Riley. 'He obviously gets his hair from you and your mum!'

Which was true. We all of us had thick, raven locks. 'You wait till you hear him scream,' Riley laughed. 'He gets that from Mum too!'

'Hey, you!' I chided. 'Anyway, let's do this coffee. Time's getting on and we need to head out.'

'Casey,' said Sophia. 'Is it okay to put down the baby? I still need to finish getting ready.'

'Oh,' I said. 'I thought you were ready already.'

'Er, not quite,' she said, already leaving the kitchen. 'I still have to do my hair.'

Casey Watson

'She looked pretty ready to me,' Riley said, once Sophia had run back upstairs.

'Me too,' I agreed, puzzled. 'Oh, well.'

'So, what's the lowdown, then?' Riley asked. 'How's things going? She seems sweet enough.'

'Yes, she is. Well, at least intermittently. But there's a whole lot going on underneath the surface, obviously. Been a pretty grim time for her, these last couple of years.' I told Riley about the incident with the nightwear and what had happened at the hospital. 'I'm not quite sure I have a handle on her yet, to be honest. She seems to swing from mood to mood without any real warning. But, as I say, when you think about her background … well, there are bound to be challenges ahead, aren't there? Still, she seems to have taken to you, anyway.'

Riley nodded. 'Well, to Levi, at any rate. Actually …' She lowered her voice. 'I did notice she kept looking at me when she thought I couldn't see. And rather strangely, too. You know? Kind of assessing?'

'I know what you mean,' I said. 'I've felt that too. It's like she has a mask in place most of the time. And it's only when she lets it slip that you get a glimpse of what's going on beneath. I'm sure she's built a very big strong wall to protect herself …' I handed her her coffee. 'But I'll get there.'

'Well,' said Riley, 'if anyone can, you can, Mum, I'm sure!'

'I appreciate your confidence,' I said drily.

And speaking of masks, it was a full fifteen minutes before Sophia returned, and when she did we were both open mouthed in shock. She had changed, in that time, out of all recognition. Gone were the perfectly appropriate jogging bottoms and hoodie she'd been wearing, and gone also was the perfectly neat and brushed hair. Instead, she'd curled the latter to within an inch of its life, and changed into skinny jeans and a tight black vest top. But it was her face which was the most arresting thing about her. She had plastered it in make-up; really trowelled it on. Dark foundation, dark lipstick, a swathe of eye shadow, thick mascara – she looked more like an 18-year-old, headed for a night on the town, than a 12-year-old girl going shopping.

It was Riley who found her voice first. 'Goodness, you look very glamorous!' she observed diplomatically. 'But it's freezing outside. You'll catch your death! You want to go upstairs and put something thicker over that?'

'I've got a jacket,' Sophia responded. 'I'll be fine.'

'Sweetheart, isn't that rather a lot of make-up to be wearing?' I added gently. 'You know, they won't allow you to wear it like that at your new school next week, don't you?'

'That's fine,' she said airily. 'I just like to make an effort.' She turned to Riley then and smiled sweetly. 'Don't you wear make-up, Riley?'

If it was intended as a barb, it was a sharp one. But Riley didn't flinch. 'Not much, during the day,' she said mildly. 'I do when I go out, but when it's light, in the daytime, I prefer to keep it looking natural. I could show you some tricks of the trade, if you like.'

Bless her, I thought. She was doing the same as I was. Remembering that this wasn't a peer, just a young girl, in the midst of an appalling situation. But one with strong opinions, too. 'That's okay,' she said. 'But I like it like *this*, thanks.'

Upon which I think we both decided the best course of action was to draw a line under any more discussion of Sophia's eyeliner. 'Come on,' I said, pretty much at the same instant Riley did. 'Let's head to town and do our girlie shopping.'

Twenty minutes later we'd made it into town and hit the shops, and to a passer-by we probably looked like a perfectly normal family gathering, except I couldn't shake off the feeling that had been stalking me since Sophia's arrival – that I had to be on guard, be alert, keep an eye trained on her all the time. Not physically – she was too old for me to worry about her running off and getting into scrapes – but just this vague nervousness, like she was this unknown quantity you had to keep checking on. It was her smile, I think. The fact that it never reached her eyes. As if it was stuck on, and could be whipped off in an instant.

But I had a mission on and I intended to complete it. 'How about these?' I suggested, once we were in a shop selling nightwear, and I was holding up the umpteenth pair of pyjamas.

Sophia shrugged indifferently. 'Whatever.'

I bit my lip. She wasn't being so different, I reminded myself, from plenty of other girls of her age. In the end I selected a few sets of PJs myself, together with a fleecy dressing gown that came with matching slippers.

'Cheer up,' said Riley, helpfully, as we exited the shop. 'I had that dressing gown and slippers from Mum at Christmas, and they're really cosy –'

'Oh, she likes dressing girls up as old ladies, then, does she?'

I don't think Sophia intended it for my ears, but I certainly heard it. Riley rounded on her. 'Sophia! You could at least try to be grateful!'

'And since you didn't want to help me choose them, what do you expect?' I added levelly. 'And as Riley just said, a little gratitude really wouldn't go amiss.'

I was busy thinking how this was what she most needed, her rude behaviour reined in a bit, just like I'd always made a point of doing with my own kids, when I realised she was about to burst into tears. It was incredible. One minute so cheeky, the next looking so wretched. Was this why everyone pussyfooted around her? Because you simply couldn't discipline her for fear of her cracking up? I sighed inwardly. That wasn't useful at all. If so, how could anyone help her?

I stopped scowling and instead scooped her into my arms.

'I'm so sorry, Casey,' she sobbed. 'I didn't mean to be rude. Thanks for my pyjamas.'

'It's okay, love,' I soothed.

'I'm just missing Jean so much. It's hard …'

'I know,' I said. 'I know. Now then, you probably need to stock up on toiletries, don't you? Shall we do some proper girlie shopping now, eh?'

I glanced at Riley as I said this, noting her sceptical expression. But I made a sign to let her know that I didn't want her to say anything, even though I knew exactly what she meant. Early days, I thought. Only early days yet.

And the next hour passed agreeably enough. Though we were soon to see yet another sea change.

'How about we have lunch in that new organic café?' I suggested. I'd clocked it before Christmas and they'd seemed particularly baby-friendly.

'I'd promised to go and meet David,' Riley began. David ran his own business – he was a professional plasterer – and at the moment was working close by. 'But I guess I could tell him to come and meet us here instead, couldn't I?'

Sophia's ears pricked up. 'David?' she said. 'Isn't that your boyfriend? What's he like?'

Very much to Sophia's liking, seemed to be the answer, because lunch soon became excruciating. If she'd seemed a bit over-enthused with her endocrinologist, now Sophia was utterly rapt. She hung on David's every word, kept flicking her mane of curls all over and giggled excitedly at pretty much everything he said. If it hadn't been so uncomfortable, it would have actually been comical, for she sat, chin on fist, gazing at him adoringly.

Riley, however, wasn't too amused. 'Elbows,' she chided. 'This is a restaurant, Sophia.' Which not only earned her a withering look, but also a giggle at David and a roll of her eyes. 'Ooh, er! Is she always so fussy?' Sophia purred.

Now I was getting really uncomfortable. 'Tell you what,' I suggested to Riley, ignoring Sophia's comment. 'Why don't you walk David back, and we'll head to the market with Levi?' I had a few bits to buy, and she could easily catch us up. And it might stop her bursting a blood vessel.

But as soon as we were alone with the baby, Sophia turned to me, oblivious. 'Oh, Casey, he's well fit,' she said, stopping me in my tracks. 'How old did you say he was?'

'I didn't,' I pointed out. 'But way too old for you, young lady. And also taken,' I added pointedly.

She giggled again, then, but was happy to push Levi to the market. She chatted animatedly to me as she did so, as well, even though one of her comments was that pushing a baby was great because it always made you such a 'man magnet'.

I made light of it, but by now I was having serious concerns. She was attracting male attention not because she was a young girl pushing a pram. She was attracting it by the way she was wiggling as she did so. This girl had been sexualised – and to a increasingly worrying degree. Which rang alarm bells. What had happened to her that we hadn't been told about?

We'd been told to expect it at some point, of course, but when the letter arrived that Friday from social services it was to inform us that Sophia's next visit to her mum would be taking place just a week on Sunday.

My musings about why Sophia behaved around men the way she did were now nudged out of pole position by my worrying about that. I didn't know why, quite – I'd dealt with plenty of bad things in my time – but I was filled with this sense of foreboding. The tone of the letter didn't help, either, making it clear that the whole thing would be emotionally exhausting for her, and that we'd have to be extra vigilant about her taking her medication, as her stress levels would be particularly high. We might even, the letter warned, have to make her take more hydrocortisone, as the stress might deplete her reserves. Finally, it advised that the visit might be upsetting for us to witness; in short, the letter seemed to say, *brace yourselves*.

The timing, I thought, was very poor as well. We'd already been told that these visits were infrequent, so why arrange one in the midst of so much upset in her life? She'd have barely been with us a fortnight! I gathered up the rest of the post and went into the kitchen. I could hear Sophia coming down, accompanied by Bob. She'd definitely made a friend in our little mutt, at least. Which was pleasing; pets were so good at soothing troubled souls. And so uncomplicated with it. Just what she needed.

'All right, love?' I asked her as they both came into the kitchen. I was pleased to see she was wearing her new pyjamas and dressing gown.

'Yeah, fine,' she said, smiling. 'And it's a lovely day, isn't it?'

'Nice to see some sun,' I agreed. 'Even if it's perishing out there. Let me just let Bob out then I'll make you some breakfast.'

'I'll do it,' she said. 'Out through the conservatory, is it? I can stay and keep an eye on him too.'

'Don't forget your tablets.'

'I won't!' she responded brightly.

'Then I'll make us both a nice fry-up, shall I? I've got bacon, I've got mushrooms, I've got eggs …'

'That would be lovely,' she said, grabbing her meds from the fridge. 'But no mushrooms for me, thanks. Mushrooms are yuk!'

Well, well, I thought cheerfully, as she followed Bob into the conservatory. Was I at last seeing a glimpse of the girl behind the mask? The girl she might once have been?

And could be again, I hoped, if she got the right kind of help and support. Poor, poor kid. None of us could make things right for her – not where her mum was concerned, anyway. But at least we could all go some way towards making her life more manageable; give her some tools with which to better deal with her demons. But thinking of her mum reminded me I now had to puncture her seemingly happy bubble. But not yet. I would choose my moment. Do it later.

The 'later' turned out to be lunchtime, because the morning had continued in much the same cheerful vein, and I figured she was in a good frame of mind. She'd played in the garden with Bob for ages, even though it was perishing, and once I'd done all my housework and told her I'd make something she particularly liked for lunch she seemed genuinely chuffed at my suggestion.

Which wasn't out of the blue; I wasn't a mind reader. With our first foster child, Justin, having such issues around food, and because our kind of fostering was geared to particularly damaged children, minimising any anxieties that didn't need to be there was a really big help. And with issues around food being quite common in kids who'd been in the care system (unsurprisingly, given how insecure they tended to be, not to mention having to compete with older and bigger kids in children's homes and so on) Mike and I had devised a questionnaire. It was something kids who came to us could fill in before they moved in, and gave them a chance to list all the things that mattered to them. Foods were the major part, but we also included things like favourite colours, favourite TV shows, any hobbies that mattered to them and so on. It all helped to make the transition process just that little bit less stressful, and, in Sophia's case, I knew she liked cheese and beans on toast.

'Ooh, lovely!' she said, seeing it, as she joined me at the table. 'You've done it just how I like it, Casey. Thanks so much.'

'You're welcome,' I said. 'I'm looking forward to trying it, as it happens. I've never had beans and cheese on toast together before.'

'Oh, you'll love it,' she assured me. 'It's gorg. Really *gorg*.'

Perhaps this was my moment. 'By the way,' I said lightly. 'I had a letter from social services earlier. They've arranged for you to visit your mum Sunday week.'

A full minute passed before she responded in any way. She just carried on eating, mechanically putting forkfuls in her mouth. Then she finally lifted her head. 'And?'

'And nothing,' I said, keeping my tone breezy. 'I just thought I ought to let you know. Are you okay, love?'

'Yes, I'm fine,' she said, putting down her knife and fork. 'Actually,' she said, 'I'm not really hungry. Is it okay if I go upstairs and finish my unpacking? I still have some things to sort out.'

'Yes, yes, love,' I said quickly. 'Of course that's okay. We did have that big breakfast this morning, after all. Probably not a good idea to … well …'

But I stopped speaking because by now she'd already left the room. I sat there not knowing what to think. Had that gone well or hadn't it? At least she hadn't kicked off or become visibly upset. And going quiet and wanting some time alone – well, that seemed normal. After all, how *did* you deal with having your mum effectively dead, yet still there, alive in a hospital bed? The closest analogy I could think of was having a loved one with Alzheimer's – still there but not there. Not to communicate with, anyway. But that tended to be problem for adults with their elderly parents. This was a *child*. It was unusual and grim territory.

I got up and cleared the table. I'd leave her with her thoughts for a bit. She knew where I was if she wanted to talk about it. But she'd only known me a few days so I doubted she would. Instead I went to ring John Fulshaw so he was kept up to date. She stayed up there – I could hear the odd clatter of drawers opening and closing – for pretty much the rest of the afternoon. I must remember, I thought, as I pottered around downstairs, to warn Mike and Kieron that she might be a little preoccupied.

And just *how* preoccupied we were soon to find out. I'd roasted a piece of gammon for our tea, and also done as I'd intended: warned both Mike and Kieron of the news I'd imparted that lunchtime, and how they'd probably find her a little sad and subdued. But when she rattled down the stairs, obviously having heard Kieron's voice, she seemed quite the opposite: bright as a button.

'Hi Kieron,' she said, as though they were mates from way back. 'Good day at college? I've got school next week. *Groan*. But maybe you can help me with my homework!'

Mike gave me a look as if to say 'Quiet?', while Kieron shook his head emphatically. 'Trust me, you don't want me helping you,' he said. 'You'll get it all wrong. I was rubbish at school.'

'Only joking!' she came back with. 'I'm actually quite brainy. Get it from my mum's side!' Then she laughed like a drain.

The silence was uncomfortable and further eyebrows were covertly raised, and I moved the conversation on to less delicate topics as I carved the meat and plated up the meal. I was twitched. There was just no predicting this child.

And I don't think any of us could have predicted what would happen next, either.

Chapter 6

The tea dished up now, we all trooped into the dining room and sat down, and still on the tack of making light conversation Mike immediately resumed where I'd left off in the kitchen. 'This gammon's nice, love,' he said. 'Have you glazed it with honey?'

'Yeah,' I said. 'I put it on before I –'

'Well, the bitch *was* warned.'

We turned as one to Sophia, because it was she who had spoken, and I don't think any of us were sure we'd heard her right. Had she *really* said that? She couldn't have, could she? After all, she was smiling and eating her tea.

'I, er, yes ...' I carried on, refusing to believe my ears. 'I glazed it before I put it in the oven. Boiled it first and then –'

'I do love my mummy, she's so sweet,' she sighed this time. I wasn't imagining it, then. She was talking to herself.

'That's nice,' I said gently. 'I'm sure she loves you too.' Mike and Kieron had their heads down, clearly keen to leave me to it. And Sophia seemed oblivious to me too.

'Bitch looks lovely,' she said next. 'Lying there all cosy. All cosy tucked up in bed.'

There is was again. 'Bitch'. I leaned towards her.

'Sophia, love,' I said. 'Whatever do you mean?'

Once again, it was as if she couldn't hear what I was saying. 'Bitch should have died. She made her own fucking choice though.' Her voice was mesmerising. Quiet and even and calm. Almost sing-song, like she was soothing a restless child.

Mike put his cutlery down. 'Sophia!' he said sharply. It was enough to seem to startle her. She looked across at Mike with a puzzled expression.

'I don't know what you're going on about,' he said to her firmly. 'But we don't speak like that in this house, you understand? That's enough, okay? Now finish your tea.'

He resumed eating, but Sophia was still looking at him in shock. 'Don't speak like what?' she asked him. 'I don't know what you mean.'

Kieron, by now, was almost choking on his dinner. 'Come *on*,' he said. 'God! You know exactly what you said!'

'It's all right, Kieron,' I butted in. 'Let's just leave this for now, eh? I put a lot of effort into tea and it'll soon be flat cold.' I gave him a look, to say 'leave it', and thankfully he did. We finished the meal, which we'd now lost all appetite for, in silence. Only Sophia seemed intent on clearing her plate.

And once she'd left the table and gone up to her room, we gathered in the kitchen to discuss it over the washing up.

'Mum, she *really* freaks me out,' Kieron said. 'I'm actually scared of her.'

Mike and I exchanged glances. We understood what he meant. 'So what do we do now?' Mike wanted to know. 'There's something wrong with that girl, and they never told us that, did they?'

'I'm going to email John,' I decided. 'Get it all down. Everything that's happened. And I'll copy it to her social worker, too. And log it. In fact, I think I'll do that now.' I kept a detailed daily record of events for the children we fostered. It was part of our training to make sure we recorded everything. It formed an important record that could be filed for future use. Shame some of the other branches of social services we dealt with were less conscientious about doing such things, I thought wryly.

'Good plan,' Mike agreed.

'And let's hope they move her,' Kieron said. 'Because she's weird. I fully expected her head to start spinning! She sounded like something out of *The Exorcist*!'

'Come on,' I said. 'Kieron, it wasn't *that* bad. The time to worry is when she starts spouting Latin and spewing green slime!' It was inappropriate and unprofessional, but the words just came out of me and both Mike and I laughed. But it was a release of tension more than anything, because this really wasn't funny. We were all of us, I think, a little spooked. I pulled myself together. 'Love, she's just a *child*. A child with a lot of emotional problems. And emotional problems can manifest themselves in all sorts of ways.'

'I know that,' he said. 'But she scares me, even so. Dad, can you put a lock on my door?'

'Don't worry, son,' Mike reassured him. 'We'll get everything sorted. As Mum said, she's just a kid. Nothing to be scared of. Okay?'

'Exactly,' I agreed. 'Let's not get over-dramatic, eh?'

But even so, I was troubled. I was almost 100 per cent certain that Sophia had no idea she was saying those words out loud. And if that was the case … well, surely someone at social services knew more than they were telling us. I knew the info on her illness mentioned this 'brain fog' symptom, but even so it just didn't stack up. I went to bed that night, deep in thought, determined to get to the bottom of it. And it seemed I wasn't the only one unable to put it out of their minds. After an hour of fitful tossing and turning, Mike nudged me.

'You awake, love?' he said.

I grimaced. 'What do you think?'

I rolled over to find him staring at the ceiling. 'You know, love,' he said. 'I think that kid has really got to Kieron. I know we all made light of it, but did you see him when we were watching TV earlier?' He turned to face me. 'He was chewing all the skin off his fingers.'

I had noticed, even though I hadn't said anything. And Mike was right. It was a sign. Kieron hated change and found stress and upheavals hard to deal with. The way he was, if someone so much as moved any of his carefully catalogued DVDs, he could get anxious and upset. We all knew that, of course, because it had been like that all his life, so as a family we just worked around it. Kieron had never been the sort of boy for whom you'd arrange a surprise party. He needed routine and order and *no* surprises. He'd managed so well to adjust to and become close to Justin, but Sophia was a very different prospect. And him chewing his fingers was a sure indication that he was even more stressed by her being with us than he was letting on.

I wasn't worried about the chewing itself – our doctor had told us it was quite common in people with Asperger's – but I was definitely worried about the welfare of my son. Our decision to foster could only work long term if it didn't adversely affect our own kids, after all.

'I know,' I said to Mike. 'I did notice it. Let's hope it's something that will settle once she's been to see her mum. Maybe it's the thought of it; maybe it flips some mental switch … We'll have to keep our fingers crossed, won't we? But I'm definitely going to go into Sherlock Holmes mode in the morning. And if I find out they're holding stuff back …'

'You mean Monday,' Mike said. 'We've got the whole of the bloody weekend to get through yet …'

To our great relief, however, Saturday started well and carried on without any incidents. In fact, better than well, even, as Riley came over, and made a sustained effort to get to know Sophia better, regaling her with tales of her new school – both Riley and Kieron had been pupils there – and a lowdown on the best and worst teachers. Kieron had already called Riley to fill her in on the dinner-table mutterings, so she obviously knew which topics to avoid.

After a light lunch the three of us headed off to town and, as it was snowing again, we left Levi in the care of Mike and Kieron. Kieron usually played football on a Saturday afternoon, and Mike took him, but with the match having been cancelled because of the weather they were just as happy watching it on TV instead. Plus, Mike pointed out, he had to get his grandson into football nice and early. But perhaps I should have realised the calm and order wouldn't last. Sophia had been with us just four days now – even if it felt so much longer – and every one of them had involved some sort of drama.

When we returned, laden down with Sophia's school uniform and stationery, it was to find my evening had been hijacked by the boys' continuing football plans. After dinner – I'd made a hearty stew and dumplings, which were devoured in no time – Kieron explained that it was pretty much a life-and-death situation that they be allowed to see the Liverpool match highlights, having not been able to see two games at once earlier.

'But supposing I've got something I want to watch?' I argued. 'Last time I checked, it was me who's been on the go all afternoon, not to mention whipping up your cordon bleu dinner ...'

Mike laughed. 'I did point that out to him, love, honest. Only fair. And this dinner is incredible, by the way. Best stew in the universe.' He winked at Kieron.

'Oh, go on then,' I said. 'I can see I'm outnumbered. I have stacks of ironing to wade through, in any case. Well, unless – Sophia, is there anything you'd like to see on telly? That would take it to stalemate.' I grinned at Mike.

She shook her head. She'd just finished wiping her plate clean with a last slice of bread. If I could do one thing right for her, I thought, it would be to feed her. 'No, I'm fine,' she said brightly. 'Got to sort out all my new school stuff.

And I've got a DVD I want to watch anyway. Not that I don't like football,' she added, looking coyly at Kieron. 'All those men running around in shorts and stuff.'

I tutted as I stood up and started to clear the table. 'You're much too young to be thinking about men in shorts, madam! Now, come and give me a hand with the dishes before you disappear.'

'We'll do them, Mum,' Kieron offered. 'Only fair, after all …'

But I said no. Getting to know a child, I'd always found, invariably seemed to happen most naturally in those little pockets of opportunity when you were doing something else. I headed off with Sophia into the kitchen.

'Do you look like your mum?' I asked her, once we'd got the washing up under way. She'd been talking about some of the things they used to like on TV when she was younger, so this seemed a good time to delve deeper.

'I suppose so,' she said, shrugging. 'A bit. We've both got blonde hair and blue eyes, but I'm taller. Actually, people often used to think we were sisters.'

I passed her a plate to dry up. 'Bet your mum loved that,' I said. 'I always do when people mistake me and Riley for sisters.'

'Though I'm prettier than she is. And I don't think we do.' She continued to wipe the plate for a few moments. 'But she still had more boyfriends.'

This brought me up short. What an odd thing for a 12-year-old to say. 'But you're only young, love,' I said. 'Bit early for boyfriends, isn't it? Plenty of time for them as you grow up.'

She turned to face me, looking deadly serious. 'But I *am* grown up. I have boobs and everything, don't I?' I certainly couldn't argue with that. She was incredibly well developed for her age. Physically, at any rate. I smiled at her.

'Thing is, love, it's not just about your body developing,' I said gently. 'Just because you develop physically, doesn't mean your mind and emotions keep pace. Sometimes it's hard when you look older than you are –' She seemed to like hearing that, I noticed. '– because people expect you to be more mature than you can be … or even *should* be. As I say, plenty of time for boys in a couple of years or so.'

But though I smiled as she skipped off to her room, seemingly satisfied, the little niggle of unease in my mind began to itch. She was so much a child in a woman's body. And with her circumstances, her condition, her tragic orphan status, well, she was vulnerable to all sorts. And her provocative manner around men was disturbing. How did she get to be that way at such a young age?

I've always hated ironing. In contrast to all the other domestic chores – and I knew I was borderline obsessive about my housework – ironing was the one that I tended to let pile up. So my ironing pile was generally teetering by the time I got to it, and tonight was no exception. Still, once I got under way, it at least gave me some 'me-time'. I'd do it out in the conservatory, lost in my own little world, listening to my favourite golden oldies radio station, with the consolation of at least having the odd sneaky fag break without anyone in my family nagging me. Which they did, almost constantly, about when I was giving up. Mike had, a

74

couple of years back, and was now one of those evangelical ex-smokers, and, to be fair, I had too, for a while. But it always seemed like something stressful came along to derail me, and I'd be back to square one, puffing away. I'd have to set a new date, get stocked up with those wretched inhalators. But not yet. Not right now, with so much on my plate.

I'd just finished my cigarette, and was back to about the sixth of Mike's shirts when Kieron popped his head around the door. I'd been at it for an hour now, and had lost track of time. 'Hello. You okay, love?' I asked him.

'Not exactly,' he said. 'I think you need to come and get Sophia. Dad's going to go mad in a minute.'

I put the iron down. 'Why? What are you on about? Where is she?'

'She's in the living room, dressed like a hooker, Mum, honest. And she's all over Dad. It's so *embarrassing*!'

I came round from behind the ironing board and followed him back into the house. I could hear Mike even before we got in there. 'Look, I told you,' he was saying. 'And I won't tell you again. Get back over there. I want to sit on my own. And while you're at it –' By now we'd both entered the room. 'You can get those ridiculous things off and put on some of those pyjamas Casey got you!'

I was gawping by now, because I couldn't believe my eyes. Sophia was getting up now, on seeing me, but had been perched on the arm of the sofa, close to Mike, with her hair once again curled and her face plastered in make-up: deep-red lipstick, blue eye shadow, mascara. But it was what she was wearing that most grabbed my attention. She had on a short, see-through red-and-black flimsy nightie, trimmed with red satin, beneath a matching satin dressing gown, which was unfastened. Kieron had been right. She did indeed look like a hooker.

'What on earth do you think you're playing at, young lady?' I asked her.

'Oh, God!' she flounced. 'You lot are all so strait-laced! I was only teasing …' She looked across at Kieron. 'Oh, just look at your face! I'm only teasing,' she said again, sweetly.

'Move it, Sophia,' Mike said. 'Like Casey said. *Now!* And you can stay up there till you're fit to be seen, too.'

'Jesus!' she said, before stomping from the room. 'What is *wrong* with you all?'

Mike was the most wound up I'd seen him in a long time. Pacing the room, pushing his hand though his hair. This had obviously really affected him, and I didn't know what to say. 'You're going to have to sort this out, Case,' he said quietly.

'She's mad, Mum,' Kieron said, plopping down on the sofa. He was looking pretty agitated too. 'Honestly, she's mad. Who'd *do* that?'

'Do what, exactly?' I asked. 'What was she doing?'

'Coming on to Dad,' Kieron said. 'Like really going for it.'

'She was even trying to tickle my bloody neck!' Mike added. 'We really do need to sort this,' he went on. 'And fast. This is potentially dangerous territory. We've got to protect ourselves here.'

He was right, of course. We'd covered this sort of thing in training. Damaged children could display lots of inappropriate behaviours, inappropriate sexual behaviour being one of them. And it was a potential minefield for carers in a fostering situation, because damaged children could also make damaging allegations. Mike was right. We had to nip this in the bud. But just as the serious nature of what was happening was kicking in, we were startled by an unexpected explosion of laughter from Kieron.

'I'm sorry, Mum,' he said, trying and failing to stop the giggles; in fact he looked like he'd wet himself if he carried on much longer. 'It was just so funny! You should have seen Dad – he was beetroot! I actually thought he was going to burst into tears!'

'It's not funny, Kieron!' Mike barked, but then his mask slipped away, and he too started laughing hysterically. Which started me off. I just couldn't help but join in. But even as I laughed I couldn't quite believe what was happening. This wasn't *funny*. So how was it we were all in this state? Was this girl going to drive us all insane?

We all composed ourselves eventually and, thankfully, Sophia didn't reappear. When I went upstairs to check on her, and make sure she took her meds, she was as meek and childlike as could be.

Nevertheless, we'd have to sit down and spell out the ground rules in the morning and, once she was at school, I'd also go into her bedroom and confiscate all her unsuitable nightwear. She could have it all back when she went back to Jean, and not before.

Which made me think about Jean's breakdown. Were jigsaw pieces falling into place here?

In any event, Monday couldn't come soon enough.

Chapter 7

I woke up on Sunday thinking something quite unusual. I woke up and wished it was Monday. Had it been Monday, I could have gone downstairs and rang John Fulshaw's office, and maybe got some guidance – not to mention information – with which to arm myself before tackling Sophia. As it was, I would just have to get up and get on with it, even though what I really wanted to do was pull the duvet over my head and hibernate for the rest of the winter.

I got up, though, because the day wouldn't sort itself out, taking care not to wake Mike, who needed his lie-in. He seldom got to sleep in, even at weekends; there was always someone needing him to pop down and sort something out at the warehouse. Best let sleeping dogs lie for a bit, bless him.

But when I came out on to the landing it was to hear the sound of the shower already going and, above that, the cheerful sound of Sophia singing. I shook my head as I went down the stairs to make my coffee; it was like she had the ability to pull a switch and forget everything that had gone before that moment. I tried to imagine myself in her shoes – after all she'd been through, and now dumped in an unfamiliar home, with unfamiliar people, and knowing she was likely to be getting yet another rollicking … yet nothing seemed to faze her at all.

Defence mechanism, maybe? But perhaps she *should* be fazed. She wouldn't cope in the world unless she learned certain behaviours were unacceptable; and sexual behaviours in particular. Coming on to grown men was a dangerous business. She could get herself into all sorts of worrying situations. If ever a child needed a guiding hand, she did, and it felt like no one had so far stepped up to the plate.

So be it, I thought, taking my coffee and cigarettes into the conservatory for a think.

By the time I came back in, a few minutes later, Sophia was in the kitchen, dressed, and looking in the cereal cupboard. 'Morning, Casey!' she said brightly, her smile guileless.

'Morning,' I said back. 'And I'm glad you're down bright and early, because you and I need to have a little talk, love, don't we?'

Now she grimaced, and then rolled her eyes. 'Look,' she said, as she gathered up the cereal box and a bowl and spoon. 'If it's about last night, I'm sorry, okay? I was only trying to have a bit of fun. Just bored, that's all.'

I joined her at the kitchen table. 'Love, it's not okay. It will never be okay for you to carry on like that around grown men. And I think you already know that, as well, don't you?'

'Okay,' she said. 'And like I say, I'm sorry. And I promise I won't do it again if it upsets you.'

That brought me up short. Not so much the words as the subtle but definite emphasis she'd placed on the word 'you'.

'Sophia,' I said, 'you didn't upset *me*. You upset *them*. You made yourself look a bit silly, and you also made them embarrassed to be in the same room with you. You don't want that, surely? For them to feel uncomfortable around you?'

She flushed pink now, under her tan, which immediately made her seem closer to her real age. She shook her head. 'No,' she said in a smaller voice now. 'I don't. Can you tell them both I'm really, really sorry?'

I told her I would, and that that would be the end of the matter, and decided to myself that this was what the girl needed – for the child in her to be teased out and rein-stated. The sexual precocity and manipulative behaviour went hand in hand, I thought. What we needed to reclaim was the remainder of her childhood, by putting some secure boundaries in place.

And so far, so good. Because the rest of the day went so well that by the time it was Monday morning I felt confi-dent once again that we could make headway.

I was going to drive her myself that morning, but had agreed that from the Tuesday she could walk across the field, alongside all the streams of other children who passed our house on the way – it was on one of the main routes to the high school. I was quietly pleased she'd been keen on doing this, too. I'd envisaged a few days – if not longer – when she wouldn't have the confidence to strike out on her own in that way. I was also pleased that she seemed to be taking responsibility for her medication. She'd taken her morning pills at breakfast and carefully packed the day's supply into their special bag and put it in her backpack. I would be taking in the school's emergency injection kit myself.

'There you go, love,' I said, handing her the packed lunch I'd made for her. 'And there's some peanuts in a separate bag in there, in case you get tired or have PE.'

'Thanks,' she said. 'But you're not going to take me right in, are you? I don't want the other girls to think I'm a baby.'

'No, of course not,' I reassured her. Poor love. Must be pretty hard for her, changing schools again. 'I'll just take you to the office so you can meet Miss Summers and then I absolutely promise I'll leave you to it.'

I didn't need to outstay my welcome anyway. I'd already had a long chat on the phone with Rachel Summers, Sophia's class teacher, and we'd run through all they needed to be aware of in relation to the Addison's. They'd never come across it either, but I knew I could trust the school to look out for her anyway. Not only had they risen to the challenge of my last foster child, Justin, they also knew me – well, many of them, anyway – as before fostering I'd worked there for several years. I'd run 'the unit', the informal name for my pastoral care classroom, where I'd take on the school's most challenging and demanding children, trying to get to the root of their behavioural difficulties and turn them around so they could make the most of their time in school. I'd had all sorts over the years, from the bullied to the bullies; all the kids that, for whatever reason – and it was normally related to difficult home lives – were struggling to find their place in the world. It was that job that had ultimately led me to fostering, as I realised that, though I loved it, I could do so much more on a one-on-one basis, taking care of one child at a time. I dropped Sophia off at school without incident, fifteen minutes later, and decided that since I now had the luxury of a day off I'd pop round to Riley's and see what she was up to. After the intensity of the last few days it would be good to do something normal – even if it was just to tag along when she went shopping.

It was also good to get my hands on little Levi.

'This is early for you, Mum,' Riley observed as she reached for the kettle and I reached for Levi.

'I've just dropped Sophia at school so I thought I'd take the opportunity to see how my little baby's doing.'

'Not as little as I'd like to be,' she joked. 'Not with all the baby blubber. But still your baby, if it makes you happy.' She was such a wag, my daughter.

We didn't go into town in the end, Riley having decided it was too cold, so, as was normal, I somehow ended up spending half the morning helping with the washing and the ironing and with having a proper clean of the bedrooms and bathroom. Not that I minded really; I enjoyed making things sparkle and shine, and had the bonus of some quality time with her and Levi. That said, it was still lunchtime before I came back downstairs.

Riley was making tuna sandwiches and coffee. 'Mum,' she said, as I came back into the kitchen. 'Does your new phone have an alarm setting or a diary function or something?' I grinned at this. I'd had my 'new phone' for a couple of months now, but I was still not entirely sure what all the buttons did. Hence the ribbing. 'Because I keep hearing this beep – every five minutes or so – and it's just occurred to me that that's what might be making it. Could it be? I can't think what else it might be.'

I reached for my bag. 'Yes, it might be. It does do that. Very irritating. I've never been able to work out how to switch it off. I should ask Kieron ...' I fished my phone out and immediately saw what the problem was. It wasn't an alarm. It was telling me I'd missed a call. 'Oh, lord,' I said. 'It's the school. And – oh God – they called over an hour ago. I hope it's not something bad.'

Riley tutted as she cut the sandwiches. 'Oh dear,' she said. 'If she's getting into trouble already, you are really going to have your work cut out, Mum!'

We both frowned simultaneously, remembering Justin. It felt like hardly a week went by when the school weren't ringing me about some misdemeanour. And some of them pretty serious. But I shook my head. 'I wasn't thinking that. I was thinking more the illness.'

'Oh, of *course*.'

I pushed the return call button.

The phone was answered promptly, and when I explained who I was, I was put straight through to Alan Barker, Sophia's head of year.

'I'm so sorry,' I said to him. 'I didn't have my phone with me. What's happened?'

'Nothing to worry about too much,' he replied. 'So please don't worry. It's just that I think Sophia might have overdone it a bit during break this morning. She's been complaining of feeling dizzy, and she doesn't look very well, to be honest.'

I was confused by this as I'd definitely seen her take her tablets. 'Oh, dear,' I said. 'Do you want me to come and get her?'

'If you wouldn't mind,' he said. 'Just to be on the safe side. It could just be first-day nerves of course, but I'm told she has been running around a fair bit ...'

'No, that's absolutely fine,' I said. 'I'll be there in ten minutes.'

I told Riley what Mr Barker had said, between grabbing my coat and taking mouthfuls of sandwich. 'All a bit odd,' I concluded. 'She took her meds okay. She had her packed lunch and her snacks. God, I hope it's not going to be this borderline all the time. It's not what the doctor led us to believe, for sure.'

Riley looked sceptical. 'Maybe it's not that. Maybe it's just to get some sympathy, some attention. It wouldn't be out of character, based on what we've seen so far.'

'I know,' I said. 'But we can't just assume that, can we? Not with something so potentially serious. Anyway, I'd better run. Thanks for the sandwich, love.'

'What you had of it!'

Riley saw me out, and as I left she called me back. I turned around.

'Just you keep your guard up, Mum, okay?'

I laughed it off, but was she already seeing things I wasn't?

When I got to school Mr Barker and Sophia were already waiting for me in reception. I could see Sophia was giggling at something he was saying.

I didn't know Mr Barker well, as he'd started at the school not long before I left to begin fostering, but I liked him and knew he'd keep an eye on Sophia. He was very upper crust, and was nicknamed 'the dog', because of his name, but I doubted that was the witticism he was sharing. But he'd obviously taken her mind off her malaise, and to me she looked the picture of health.

'Ah, Mrs Watson,' he said now. 'Thank you so much for coming. As you can see, Sophia's feeling a bit better now, aren't you? But we obviously didn't want to take any chances.'

'Of course not,' I said. 'Come on, love.' I turned to Sophia. 'Let's get you home so you can have a nap.'

'I told them not to bother you,' she said to me as we walked back across the school car park. 'You shouldn't have had to come out and get me. I didn't want to come home. I told them I'd be fine in an hour, if they just let me rest.'

I patted her shoulder. She was so much taller than me that I couldn't put a friendly arm around it. 'Don't worry, love,' I said. 'They were just being careful. They probably don't have enough staff available to keep a proper eye on you. If you're well you're in class and if you're ill you go home.'

She shrugged then, a teenage 'whatever' expression on her face, and I wondered if perhaps Riley had been right, that she'd feigned the dizziness to get attention – but not that much attention. They'd probably been used to managing her Addison's in her old school. So perhaps she hadn't figured on being sent home. Or maybe the opposite was true: she actually *liked* being sent home, and her telling me otherwise was just to keep me sweet. Oh, it was all so confusing, trying to read her.

And once at home, her manner changed again.

'C'mon, missy,' I said, forestalling her from flopping down on the sofa with the remote for the afternoon. 'We need to get some water and a salty snack inside you, and then you have to go to bed for a bit.'

I was pleased by how readily the 'rules' came to mind. Mind you, I had studied the huge amount of info very thoroughly. She'd obviously been running around a lot, and needed to rehydrate. She also needed salt. I wasn't sure exactly why that was – so much science! – but the advice was clear. And then she needed sleep. But she shook her head. 'No need,' she said. 'I'm fine.'

'Clearly not,' I persisted, 'or the school wouldn't have sent for me. Come on,' I said. 'Into the kitchen, so we can get you sorted before some shut-eye …'

She pointed the remote at the TV and it hummed into life. 'I told you,' she said slowly. 'I am *fine*.'

Okay, I thought. Okay. Deep breath. 'Sophia, you might *feel* fine, but I need to *know* you are. So would you please turn the TV off and come with me.'

Before I could even finish, she'd flung the remote onto the coffee table with a loud clatter, leapt up and turned the television off by hand.

'Satisfied?' she asked me, her tone caustic as she pushed past me.

I exhaled slowly and followed her into the kitchen. 'Yes, thank you. Though perhaps next time we'll have the teachers deal with this in school. That way, you'll actually be able to *stay* there.'

I left the room feeling duped. And also cross. How did you handle something like this – something with so much scope for manipulation? You obviously couldn't call her bluff – she might end up seriously ill. But at the same time, this amount of power over people was doing her no good. I lit a cigarette, out in the conservatory. One thing was clear. I wouldn't be able to give my habit up any time soon. But, feeling calmer, I decided to give her the benefit of the doubt. This could all be related to the stress of the visit to see her mother at the weekend. I must make allowances for that. And, as if on cue, Sophia appeared then, in the conservatory doorway. 'I'm sorry, Casey,' she said haltingly. 'You know, about just now. I just get a bit ratty when I have a wobble with my meds.'

I patted the seat beside me. She sat down. 'But I don't understand,' I said. 'I thought your consultant said your medication levels were stable.'

She shook her head. 'Not if I get stressed. Or if I do a lot of extra exercise.'

'But surely you know not to do that? I know I read somewhere that if you're doing more than normal exercise, then you need to take some extra steroid before you do it, don't you?'

She nodded. 'But I didn't *know* I was going to be doing that, did I?' She frowned. 'But you can't *not*, can you? Not when everyone's got a game on, and you're the new girl … I don't want to look like I'm some stuck-up cow who won't join in, do I?'

I couldn't argue with that, and I felt sorry for her. It must be tough.

I clasped her hand and squeezed it. 'I know,' I said. 'I know. Now how about that sleep, eh?'

I was pleased about our chat, and, actually, it didn't really matter. If she had made herself ill accidently, or did it on purpose, it didn't make any odds. What mattered was that we kept on communicating. I'd have a word with the school in the morning, just to keep them in the loop, and make a point of reading up some more on her taking extra medication. This, I decided, was all completely sortable. I just needed to know exactly *how* to sort it.

I was in a much better frame of mind as I set about making our dinner – steak and chips with all the trimmings, plus my own home-made peppercorn sauce. And by the time Mike and Kieron got home, Sophia and I agreed that we were both absolutely starving, and that if they didn't come to the table pronto we'd eat theirs as well.

It set the tone for a nice relaxed family dinner. We weren't the Waltons, but sometimes it made me so happy just to sit round the table as a family, chatting about nothing. But it seemed the 'nothing' part was going to be short-lived.

'How'd your first day go?' Mike asked Sophia as he began tucking in.

'Okay,' she said. 'I made a new friend called Lucy. She seems nice.'

'One of many, no doubt,' Kieron chipped in with. I was pleased. He seemed to be making a real effort to get along with her.

'Oh, no,' Sophia said, before delivering the news that the rest of the girls already hated her.

'But why?' I asked.

'Because all the boys fancy me, of course,' she answered. I opened my mouth to comment and then I closed it again. She was twelve. Twelve-year-olds were inclined to make pronouncements like that. Particularly pretty ones like Sophia.

'Oh, you'll make more,' Kieron persisted, shrugging it off. 'Don't you worry.'

'Oh, I'm not worried,' she said. 'I don't want to have friends really, anyway.'

'Why ever not?' Mike asked.

'Because you can't trust them.' Her face darkened. 'My last best friend, Chloe, tried to turn me into a lesbian. And –'

'Sophia, love,' I interrupted. 'Shall we talk about this later? Not a topic of conversation for teatime really, is it?'

'But she did!' Sophia persisted, now fired up, eyes flashing. 'And my caring mother didn't give a damn! *Oh, Sophia, stop complaining, she's just being friendly, stop moaning* … Yeah, right, Mum. Like she ever gave a damn!'

'Sophia,' I said, shocked. 'Please, just *leave* it. We can discuss all this later. Now calm down and let's all just finish our tea, eh?'

She put her head down and continued eating, as the conversation juddered back to life.

'Lovely steak, love,' said Mike.

'Flattery will get you everywhere,' I answered.

'Uurgh! Pass the sick bucket,' Kieron whined. '*Please.*'

Sophia smiled too, and the tense moment seemed to have passed. And as I'd promised her, we would definitely talk about it later. It was clearly something she badly needed to get off her chest.

That and a whole heap more, besides.

Chapter 8

It's a special place, my conservatory, especially in the evenings. It's nice any time – my haven, my place of solitude overlooking the garden – but at night time it really came into its own. With the soft lighting, you couldn't see the jumble of garden furniture stacked in the corner; all you really noticed were the two sofas, both covered with fleecy throws, and accessorised with piles of colourful cushions. It was cosy, too, the heating having been on all day, the perfect place to sit and relax.

The washing up done and the boys off watching football, I carried through my coffee and Sophia's glass of milk and placed them on the little pine table that sat between the sofas. Then I sat down myself and patted the space beside me.

'There,' I said. 'Peace at last. Come on, sit down and rest your legs, love.'

She duly sat next to me and leaned back. 'It is true,' she said. She had obviously been dying to tell me about it. 'She did make me a lesbian, Casey. I know she did.'

'It's not up to her,' I said. 'It's up to you. Do *you* think you're a lesbian? What I mean is, do you like girls the way you like boys?'

This wouldn't have been a conversation you'd have with many 12-year-olds, I thought. But she was very well developed, and aware of it, too. And I'd come across that many children now whose stories would make some people's hair curl. Out of the mouths of babes and all that, sadly.

She glanced across at me. 'Casey, I *do* know what a lesbian is. And no, of course I don't. It was just that one time I, well, you know, *did* it with Chloe.'

I had to think carefully before speaking. 'And it really doesn't mean anything. You know, lots of girls experiment with kids of their own sex when they're your age. It doesn't mean they've committed to being gay. It's just – well, like I say – experimenting.'

'But Chloe said it made me one, because I let her.' She pulled her legs up underneath her, so she was half-turned towards me. 'And when I asked my mum – I was worried, I really was – she was, like, "Oh, stop going on." She didn't even want to know.'

I wondered then at Sophia's overt flirting around men. Was she trying to prove a point? And to herself? 'I think maybe your mum was trying to explain it, like I am, that it doesn't mean anything, so you shouldn't worry about it. After all, you have years ahead to work out who and what you are. I think you should just put it out of your mind.'

Instinctively then, seeing her anxious face – which now seemed very childlike – I reached an arm around her shoulder and drew her in towards me. She responded by throwing her own arms around me and hugging me so tight she nearly squeezed all the breath out of me.

'Oh, Casey,' she said, letting me breathe again finally. 'Thanks. Thanks so much for listening. My mum never listened to me, *ever*.'

I could have said 'I'm sure she did', but I didn't know that to be true, and I didn't want to trot out platitudes. It wasn't as if there was a relationship that could be rebuilt here. That was the tragedy. And it was also important that she work through all the issues she had around her mother. I had no idea what sort of a mother she had been, after all. So instead I just speculated. 'Perhaps it just seemed that way, because she was trying to make light of it. Like I said –'

'I don't mean just about that. I mean *everything*. Like when her boyfriends would touch me up. She *never* listened. She *wouldn't* listen. Des. He was the first. Used to come up – just like that – and squeeze my boobs. And when I told Mum she just laughed. I *hated* him.'

I felt an all too familiar sense of dismay. 'Did you tell anyone else?'

'Not at first. Later, yes, lots. With the next one, I did. But not at first. Not with Des.'

The next one? Oh, God … 'But that's serious, Sophia. Are you sure? I mean, are you sure he was doing it deliberately?' I felt a fool for even asking. But this was a potentially serious matter. And I had Mike's words of caution now fixed in my mind.

'Of course I'm sure. How can you do something like that by accident?'

'And your mum didn't do anything?'

'I told you. She just said I was being silly. So I just decided in the end that I would make his life hell instead.' Her expression hardened. 'I thought if she wasn't going to get rid of him, I would. I just moaned about him all the time, saying how mean he was to me, and I'd refuse to eat when he was there till in the end he stopped eating with us. And they'd argue about me all the time, and he'd get mad, and in the end she threw him out. Good riddance!'

'But afterwards,' I said. 'Did you tell her the truth afterwards?'

Her features changed radically, even as I watched. 'Oh no, I didn't need to. It was lovely again without Des. Just me and Mum, together. Girls together. We used to stay up late, watching chick flicks and eating popcorn … Or reading girly mags together, no men to bother us. It was *so* lovely …'

She seemed almost lost in her own little world now, and I wondered if all these revelations had been triggered by the prospect of seeing her mother again. I couldn't begin to imagine how hard that must be for a child. Your only parent effectively dead, and yet you had to keep going back … seeing her lying there … just awful. The poor, poor kid. She'd started to cry now, I noticed.

And then her voice changed again, her lip curling. 'Didn't fucking last, though, did it?' I could feel her body stiffening now beside me. 'Oh, no, I wasn't enough for her, was I? Never enough. She was man mad, my lovely mother.' She looked sharply at me now. 'D'you know, she'd only been seeing Steve a week when she moved him in!'

'So he came to live with you after Des, then?'

She nodded. 'After a week, that was all!'

'This was the "next one" you were talking about then?'

Her sudden laugh made me jump. 'Oh, yes,' she said, still looking at me but now through me. 'And the last. You know what that bastard did?'

I didn't need to answer. She seemed on autopilot now, the tears streaming down her face unchecked. I took hold of her hand as she spoke. 'He tried to rape me. He waited till my dear mother had gone out to a parents' evening – a parents' evening, can you believe it? I was just sitting in my room, doing my homework, listening to music, when in he came. And he was like, "All right, babe? What you up to?" Then he came over to look at my homework, and …'

She had to stop then, because she was really crying now. Huge gulping sobs. She was finding it difficult to catch her breath. And from behind her I caught sight of Kieron, just about to open the door from the kitchen, so I pulled her close to me again and waved at him not to. 'It's okay, sweetheart,' I soothed. 'Take as much time as you need. You need to get all this outside of you, don't you?'

She pulled back slightly and sniffed. 'It's okay … It's okay.' She sniffed again, ran the back of her wrist across her face. 'He pushed me on the bed then,' she continued, gathering a little more composure. 'And yanked my pyjama bottoms down. And I was going mental at him. Kicking him and thumping him and screaming. He tried to hold his hand over my mouth but I was biting it, really hard.' She looked disgusted, remembering. 'And then he undid his jeans and then pulled them down and got his dick out and then he tried to have sex with me. I was scared to death, but I never stopped fighting him – and I'm strong …' Thank

95

the lord for that, I thought. 'And I think he got scared then, about all the racket I was making, because he stopped then and he slapped me round the face. Called me a prick teaser, then, he did. Said he'd kill me if I ever opened my mouth.'

'Oh, dear God, love, that makes me so angry! Please tell me you told your mum *this* time.'

She sniffed again, and wiped her eyes. 'Oh yes,' she laughed then, almost hysterically. 'Oh, yes, as soon as she got home and he'd stomped off to the pub. I told her everything. All of it.'

'Good, love. That's good. And what did she say this time?'

'She said ...' Her lower lip began quivering. 'She said ... She was like, you lying little *cow*! She said I'd destroyed one relationship and now I was trying to do it again!' Agitated now, Sophia kicked her legs out from beneath her and, moving to the edge of the little sofa, twisted towards me. 'You know what she said, Casey?' I shook my head. 'She said I really thought I was something, didn't I? She said, and what made me think *her* men would prefer *me*? She called me a jealous bitch. Yeah, that's exactly what she called me.' Her anger had overtaken her pain now. 'Yeah, and lots of other lovely mummy things like that.'

'Oh, sweetheart,' I said. 'I can't believe it!'

'Nor could I – she was just so *horrible* to me – but it's true. And *that's* when I realised just what a shitty mum she really was. I warned her. I did. I told her straight. Either him or me, I said. Because I wouldn't be sticking around if she *chose* him.' She let out a heavy sigh. 'But she did. She did anyway.'

I was stunned. Despite all the years I'd been dealing with dysfunctional families, I still found it shocking when a mother wouldn't put her own child – her very flesh and blood – first in that kind of situation. Yes, there were mothers like Justin's, who, addled by drug addiction, had their kids do all sorts in order to get their next fix. But to simply call your child a liar and, worse, a jealous bitch – that was quite something. And how old must Sophia have been – eleven? Ten, even? It beggared belief. And thinking of Justin made me think of something else. I knew I had to explain to her that the nature of what she'd told me meant I would have to both record it and also share it with the rest of her care team.

I took a deep breath. 'I'm so glad you've managed to get all this out,' I said, cuddling her. 'I'm sure you'll feel much better for having talked about it, hmm?' She smiled wanly. Finishing her story seemed to have knocked the stuffing out of her. 'And you know,' I went on, 'what has to happen now is that I've got to put it in my log book. Because this is serious and these men should have to pay for what they've done, shouldn't they?'

But, to my astonishment, she suddenly burst out laughing. 'What's the fucking point of that?' she asked incredulously, pulling back and gaping at me. 'I mean, go ahead and tell who you want, but what difference is that going to make to anything? And how would anyone find them anyway? I barely knew the names of any of the blokes she had round. I only knew those last two because I used to have to listen to her shouting it when they were *doing* it,' she spat. 'Go on, if you want to, Casey. Tell anyone you

97

want to. But you'll be wasting your time, I promise. Don't forget, she's my only witness and she's a fucking cabbage!'

I stared back at her, momentarily speechless, my brain whirring. The fact that she used the word 'witness' seemed telling. 'Have you already told anyone about this, Sophia? I mean, anyone other than your mother?'

She shrugged. 'What's the point? Who's ever going to do anything about it? Who *can* do anything about it?' She stood up then. 'Honestly, Casey, stop looking at me like that. It's done. It's finished. And I need to go to bed now.'

She walked to the kitchen door then and turned back towards me as she opened it. 'Don't look so worried,' she said again. 'I'm okay now. I'm a big girl now. Really I am. Night.'

I stayed in the conservatory for another half an hour, just to try and get my head around the things she'd told me. If her allegations were true – and they certainly seemed to fit, instinct told me – then no wonder she had so many issues. There had obviously been massive unfinished business between her and her mother, and, since tragedy had struck, it would never now *be* finished; a scarily big load of psychological distress to sit on the shoulders of such a young girl. And then there was the issue of the attempted rape by her mother's boyfriend, and Sophia's assertion that her mother had refused to believe it. I'd seen and read about plenty of cases where mothers, fearing the loss of a boyfriend or spouse, would shut their eyes to what was being done to their kids, almost before their eyes, and that was shocking enough in itself. But to actually accuse your barely pubescent daughter of not only lying, but trying to compete with you for them – that was something else again. I would need to ask John to do some more digging, I decided. It might not be seemly to speak ill of the dead (or in a vegetative state, for that matter) but if Sophia had any hope of making a good life for herself she needed someone to step up to the plate and get the truth out there about her mother.

It was with this very much in mind that I went up to bed. Mike was still awake, reading, so once I'd undressed and snuggled up to warm my toes I told him, in hushed tones, everything Sophia had told me. He's a gentle soul mostly, but he was angry. A lot angrier than I'd seen him in a while, in fact.

'Fucking animals!' he hissed.

'Shhh, Mike. And mind your language!'

'I'm sorry, love,' he said, 'but it makes my blood boil. And I'm telling you, something had better get done about this. No wonder these kids come to people like us with such messed-up heads! How come none of this is on her bloody file?'

'Shh!' I said again. 'Sophia's going to hear you!'

'Well, good, frankly. Perhaps she *should* hear me! She should certainly know someone's on her side. Fucking animals!'

I had never heard Mike quite so riled up before. Never heard him swear like that, either – not if there was a chance one of the children might hear him. He'd always been a stickler for things like that. 'I know, love. I feel the same,' I said, stroking his arm, trying to calm him down. 'But she's got us on her side now, hasn't she? You and me, love. *We'll stick by her*. And that's a promise.'

But as I lay in bed, waiting for sleep to creep up and overtake me, all I could think of was one of my mum's favourite sayings. *Never make a promise you can't keep.*

Chapter 9

After the revelations and drama of the weekend, the following week was turning out to be something of an anticlimax, and that was absolutely fine by me.

I'd been on to John Fulshaw first thing on the Monday morning but, as Mike and I had both expected, there was nothing on Sophia's file about an abuse allegation. 'You know,' John said, 'I have to tell you, Casey, I have heard mutterings about her having a tendency to make stuff up, to be honest.'

'But if there's nothing on file ...'

'That may be because she has made an allegation, but it wasn't recorded because it wasn't deemed to be true.'

'I don't know, John,' I said. 'My instinct is the opposite. It *does* ring true. I know I barely know her but I've been around children her age for half my life. I think I have a pretty good instinct for when a child is telling the truth.'

'And I know to trust that instinct of yours, Mrs Watson! Look, leave it with me. I will do some sleuthing and get back to you asap.'

John had also agreed both with my feeling that such a thing would help explain some of Sophia's inappropriate and worrying behaviours and also that, if it *was* true, then it should be investigated.

Sophia herself, now she'd opened up a bit about the travails of her life, seemed to be happy to forget about them. And at last she seemed to be settling in. We had no upsets, no arguments, no displays of pique or temper all week, and I allowed myself to hope that we could make some solid progress; I felt we'd become closer now she'd decided to confide in me, and if ever a child deserved a break, Sophia did. She was almost entirely alone in the world, after all.

By Friday, I was especially pleased to hear from Mr Barker that, while he was still a bit concerned about Sophia's health, he was generally very pleased about how she was settling in. She was clearly a bright girl, with the potential to do well academically, and if she could achieve well in school it could make a real difference in her life.

I put the phone down and went back to the cleaning I'd been doing, feeling seriously positive for the first time since she'd come to us.

I returned to the living room to find Kieron, who had a half-day off from college, standing in front of our big living-room mantelpiece mirror, duster in one hand, spray cleaner in the other, flexing his biceps and pulling faces. Housework generally, he hated, but mirrors he liked to do. I rolled my eyes. He was honestly that vain.

'Kieron, you big poser!' I said. 'I thought you were supposed to be helping me, not practising your Mr Universe pose!'

'Mother,' he said, sweeping his hands down his torso. 'It takes a great deal of willpower not to keep looking at this. You may mock, but most females find me irresistible ... Anyway, who was that on the phone?'

I returned to my own dusting and he to his. 'Oh, just school.'

He rolled his eyes. 'Oh, God. What's she done now?'

'Oh, it was nothing like that. They were just giving me an update. She's actually getting on rather well, they said.'

Kieron stopped polishing then and turned to me. 'Mum,' he asked, 'is it true what Dad told me, that she's been abused?'

'That's what she said, love. Though there's nothing in her file. So I'm waiting for John Fulshaw to come back to me once he's done a bit of investigating. I mean, kids do sometimes make stuff up –'

'Why the hell would anyone make something like that up?'

'Oh, for lots of reasons. To get attention ... to get someone they don't like into trouble. But your dad and I are inclined to believe her. It would explain a lot of what's happened with her, after all. But don't you worry – we'll get to the bottom of it, I'm sure ...'

'Oh, I wasn't worried,' he said. 'It's just that I was thinking. I mean, if she does make stuff up, she could tell lies about all of us, couldn't she?'

What Kieron said brought me up a bit short. It had never occurred to me to think about that, and I could have kicked myself – how stupid of me. If she *had* been lying about her mother's boyfriends, then she was a pretty accomplished actress, and Kieron was right to point out that she could cast him and Mike in similar roles. I shook out my duster, with a snap.

'Good point,' I said to Kieron. 'We do have to be careful. Perhaps I'll dig out the safe care paperwork so we can have a read through it again, eh? Just to check we have everything covered.'

The safe care agreement was one of the guides foster carers had, commonsense guidelines about how things were done to protect the family against false allegations. 'Though I do believe her, as it happens,' I said, 'sad though that is. But don't worry about it, eh? And remember, unless we hear differently we *have* to believe her. Way too many kids in care, after all, are much worse off than they might have been if just one adult had taken what they said seriously.'

'Like Justin,' Kieron said.

'Just like Justin,' I agreed.

'Still,' he mused, getting back to polishing his reflection. 'Even so, you never know.'

I didn't share what Kieron had pointed out to me with Mike. I didn't want to stress him, given the unfortunate episode the previous weekend, and, besides, I felt it important that we stood together regarding Sophia. She'd confided in me, and both Mike and I believed what she'd said. If Mike was now having doubts about that – which I wondered about, since he'd clearly spoken to Kieron – we could so easily go down the road of just trying to deal with the symptoms, rather than really getting to grips with the root cause. I knew we were only her foster carers, and very short-term ones at that, but this girl was so messed up, and if abuse *was* part of the cause, then we had a duty to clarify it and address it.

And when Sophia got home from school I felt we *were* making progress. She had some gripes about the girls – who all still *hated* her, apparently, because *all* the boys fancied her – but listening to her woe-is-me moans was actually quite refreshing because it was just like listening to any child of her age.

But the relaxed ambience wasn't to last. The dinner cleared away, we were all in the living room catching up on the soaps, when Sophia, quite out of the blue, began laughing.

'Oh, I can't wait to see my lovely mummy this weekend!' she said gaily, as if her mummy was fit and well and going to take her for a picnic, not lying in a coma in a hospice bed. *Oh God*, I thought. Not that again.

I gave Mike and Kieron warning glances before responding. I felt she was after a reaction, but the best thing would be to play it down.

'Yes, it'll be nice, love, won't it?' I responded mildly. 'And we'll set off nice and early, so we can ...'

I trailed off as she'd now stood up and walked across the room, a strange, puzzled expression on her face. She then turned, as she reached the door. Now she looked at me. 'By the way,' she said. 'I haven't taken my last tablet today. I'm not sleeping well, and it just makes it worse.'

Mike was on his feet before I was. 'Come on, love. You know you have to take it. Your doctor said you mustn't start interfering with your medication, without first –'

'Erm,' Sophia interrupted him, grinning. 'I think you'll find that it's my body, my disease and my problem,' she responded. 'And I'm not taking it, and that's that, okay? If the world looks like ending, *then* I'll call the doctor. End of.'

She walked out of the living room and started up the stairs. 'Sophia!' I called after her. 'Get back down here. Stop being silly.'

'Just forget it!' she shouted down. We then heard the slam of her bedroom door.

'What the hell was all *that* about?' Mike said.

Kieron, too, looked stunned. 'God, she's mad, she is. Is this all about the visit to her mum?'

'I don't know,' I said. 'But I imagine so.'

Mike frowned. 'Well, she obviously can't *not* take it.'

'I know,' I said. 'I know. But let's just leave her for a bit, eh? Then I'll go up and talk to her. See if I can persuade her.'

I spent half an hour watching but not seeing the telly – I think we all did. The whole thing with her mother had really been playing on my mind. After the allegations she'd made about the boyfriends, and the ultimatum she'd given her mother, it was hardly complicated psychology to figure out how badly her mother's attempted suicide must play on her mind. It was unfinished business of the worst kind. It couldn't *ever* be finished, could it? So here she was, having to keep returning to those horrible memories; she'd wished her mother ill, and then her wish had come true. And every few weeks or so she had to stare that reality in the face. Though I felt awful thinking it, it would be better if her mother *had* died, because no one seemed to hold out any hope of a recovery. The chances this far down the line were frankly negligible.

Once I felt I'd waited long enough, I made my way upstairs to her room. I couldn't find her pills, so I assumed she'd taken them with her, perhaps taken one, even. I knocked softly on the door. 'Sophia?' I called gently.

'Go away.'

'Can I come in, love? I just want to talk.'

'No. Go away. I just wanna be left alone.'

'I'm sorry, love,' I said, 'but I need to come in. I'm responsible for you and I need to know you're okay.'

As she didn't respond to that, I turned the handle and pushed the door open. She was lying on the bed, fully clothed. The lights were off but I could tell she'd been crying, and my heart went out to her. She wiped her eyes and sat up, her expression stony.

'How dare you come in when I said no!' she barked angrily. 'Get out! I mean it, Casey! Get out! Leave me alone!'

She stood up then, and straight away I could see she was unsteady. She had to put her hand out against the wall to get her balance. 'I'm not taking it, okay? I'm not taking it, so just fuck off!' She was really yelling at me now, as she staggered towards me. Realising she meant to push me out bodily – from her own body language – I began slowly backing towards the landing. 'Go away!' she shrieked. 'Go away, go *away*!' Her eyes weren't focusing, and I could see she was losing all control. And in that state she was scary; I knew I was no physical match for her. 'All right, love,' I tried to soothe, 'that's fine. Go back to bed now. I can see you're upset, so I'll go back downstairs again, okay? You lie back down, now. Look, I'm going. See?'

This seemed to satisfy her and she turned and lurched back onto the bed. Mike had come upstairs now, hearing the shouts. 'What the hell?'

'Shh!' I whispered, frantically gesturing him to go down again. I followed close behind and went straight for the phone. 'I'm calling an ambulance,' I said, as I dialled 999. 'She's in a right state. God, this disease is a bloody nightmare!'

Ten minutes later – ten minutes during which the three of us sat, not knowing quite what to do, bar drink coffee and fret – the ambulance arrived, disgorging a brace of paramedics, who were reassuringly smiley and in control. I felt immediately calmer just showing them through the door.

One went straight upstairs while the other asked for details.

'So what have you done so far?' he asked me.

'Nothing,' I said. I felt such an idiot. 'I should have made her take her pill, shouldn't I? Forced it down her somehow.'

'Love, you think she would have let you, state she was in?' Mike countered.

'I suppose not,' I agreed. Though it didn't make me feel any better.

But the paramedic did. 'It's not life and death,' he said, obviously seeing my concern. 'Don't panic. She'll be *fine*. Probably just low blood sugar.'

'There,' said Mike. I could see the relief on his face. 'Listen,' he said, turning to the paramedic. 'Can we get you a coffee or something?'

'Coffee? Who said coffee?' came a voice from the doorway. 'Stiff drink, more like.' He was grinning. 'Proper little madam you've got there, haven't you? Told me I could 'eff off out of her bedroom. Charming! Is she always this delightful?'

It broke the tension a little, having the paramedics laughing in my kitchen. They dealt with all sorts, and seemed to take everything in their stride. I explained that we were fostering Sophia, and that we were still feeling our way.

'Absolutely understand,' he said. 'And you might find her a bit less demanding from now on. She gave me plenty of attitude, so as well as her tablet I gave her some back. About frightening everyone and wasting our time. Listen, you really don't need to worry too much about something like this. There's a simple rule of thumb here. And it's stress, physical stress. If she has any sort of fever – gets the flu, say – or has a bout of diarrhoea and vomiting, that's when you have to call the doc about upping her meds. The other thing, obviously, is emotional stress. The body doesn't differentiate between a temperature and a mental trauma – it'll go into shock just the same. So again, if in doubt, call the doc or give her more steroid. You have an injection pack?' I nodded. 'Well, you mustn't be afraid to use it. Jab it in, do it fast, get it done.'

I felt the colour drain from my face, but the paramedic grinned. 'It's rare for that to happen,' he said. 'So you'll probably not have to. As I say, don't worry. Forewarned is just forearmed.'

I smiled at this. How many times now had Mike and I said it? 'I'm just so sorry we had to call you out,' I said. 'This is all new to us, and I just wasn't sure what else to do.'

The paramedic shook his head. 'No, no. You did absolutely the right thing, Mrs Watson. Any time. That's what we're here for. Anyway, we'll get off – oh, and our notes will go off to her GP. And you get a good night's sleep. Don't lie awake worrying. She's fine now.'

But none of us were fine. I saw the paramedics out, and when I came back into the kitchen to make us all another coffee the expressions on Mike and Kieron's faces hit me like a slap. They were sitting in silence, both looking so upset and bewildered, and it hit me – did they deserve all this, really? It was my job. My responsibility, and yes, they'd both been such rocks. And Mike had gone through the training with me – I couldn't have decided to foster without my husband's full support. But, hand on heart, was I asking too much of my family? This wasn't just a case of bringing my work home – work *was* home. It was the business of bring children to live with, and be supported by, our family, that our kind of fostering – any kind of fostering – was all about. But was my desire to make a difference actually making the worst *kind* of difference? Committing my own family to much more than they'd bargained for? To all this?

It had been so hard at first, with Justin. We'd all been new to it, and had had to make adjustments. But this felt different. Where with Justin I had a clear plan and all my experience to draw on, here I felt completely out of my depth. And it wasn't just the illness, it was the whole situation. She was so complex, so unpredictable, so difficult to manage. I really didn't know where to start.

Mike must have seen the look of despair on my face. 'Stop beating yourself up, love. It's not your fault. We all know we can't pick and choose the kids they send us.'

I know, I said, mechanically making more coffees. 'But I hate that you and Kieron have to be witnessing it all. It was different in school. I know I would sit down and tell you about some of the kids. But at least it didn't affect you. Not in this way.'

'It's your *job*, Mum,' said Kieron. I could have hugged him. 'We all knew it would be the problem kids we'd be having, didn't we? So it was never going to be a bed of roses. But if you didn't do what you do, where else would kids like Sophia go? If it wasn't for people like you, Mum, they'd be dumped in secure units, wouldn't they?'

I nodded, but sadly. Already my son, who up till a couple of years ago had been so innocent, knew the language of social services, and all about the kids on the scrap-heap. And he was right. The kids we were trained to take in *were* on the scrap-heap. They were the kids with such intractable problems and attendant 'challenging' behaviours (how was that for an understatement?) that no one else, literally, would have them.

'It'll get better,' said Mike. 'I'm sure it will. And remember, we're only going to have her for a short while anyway. Once Jean recovers she can have her back and we can get back to normal. Well,' he grinned, 'as normal as it ever is in this house, anyway. And when she does, I think we should plan a nice little holiday. All of us. Invite Riley and David and little Levi as well.'

'Perfect,' said Kieron. 'Brilliant idea, Dad. Somewhere nice and hot. Right, then – when's she going?'

We all laughed then, and I felt much better. My family were perhaps not as badly affected as I'd feared, and, if they were, they were prepared to slog it out. So who was I to question it? *Let's just get this wretched weekend over with*, I thought, as I climbed into bed, and fell into a fitful sleep. Little did I know that, after the weekend, I would be questioning absolutely everything.

Chapter 10

I was awake at six on the Sunday morning, the prospect of the day ahead being grim enough to ensure that, as soon as I was conscious, my brain wouldn't let me sleep again. I knew it didn't affect me personally, but there was something deeply unsettling about the prospect of taking a 12-year-old girl to visit her comatose mother, and it made me anxious in ways I couldn't quite pin down. I didn't know if we'd be going in with Sophia, but I suspected we might be. It would be distressing for her, surely, and she'd need our support.

But what would it be like to go in there, seeing Sophia's mother like that? I had this vision – learned from years of watching hospital dramas on TV – of her lying there, motionless, wired up to stuff, the rhythmic sound of a ventilator hissing the only noise in the deathly hush. What did you do in a situation like that? Did Sophia talk to her? Did she have any sense of the hopelessness of the situation? And what about the future? What was it doing to her, psychologically? I found it creepy and disturbing. I couldn't help it.

But it wasn't for me to think about the future. I needed to concentrate on the here and now. I crept soundlessly from the bed and went downstairs, a delighted Bob, who could hear a pin drop, trotting along excitedly at my heels. I felt like death warmed up and he felt a million dollars. A dog's life, I thought. I'd quite like one of those.

Saturday, surprisingly, had been a good day. Sophia had come down bright and early, immediately apologised – somewhat sheepishly – for her 'strop' the night before, and then, having done her homework, happily accompanied me to Riley's. Once there she'd played with Levi for much of the afternoon, letting Riley and me have a good chin-wag. We couldn't talk about my number one stress of the moment, of course, but then that was probably a good thing. I didn't want to burden her.

We'd then all gone to a ribs restaurant in the evening – a planned treat for Sophia as the chain was one of her favourites. And everyone had had a nice, uncomplicated time. Perhaps this was something I should get used to, this see-saw existence. It would just be nice not to be thumped down so hard, and so often; to stay at that good end a bit more often.

After I'd made myself a coffee and let Bob out, I then, having not had a moment to myself yesterday, sat down with my laptop and emailed John Fulshaw, detailing the events of Friday night.

That done – to my shock, almost an hour had now passed – I set about getting prepared for breakfast. I'd decided on a fry-up as we had a long way to go, and with the hospital visit still an unknown quantity lunch might not end up happening at all.

There was no sign of Kieron by the time I'd started on the bacon, but Mike and Sophia had obviously both been drawn down by the smell of it.

'God, there's nothing like the smell of bacon frying,' said Mike, coming up behind me to give me a hug. 'Hungry, are you, love?' he finished, turning to Sophia, who had already sat down at the table.

She nodded, but, half-way through an enormous great yawn, couldn't answer.

'Gawd,' said Mike. 'Is that the Mersey Tunnel?'

'Oh, funny ha-ha,' she said, pulling a face at him. But in a nice way. I exhaled mentally. She seemed in an okay mood.

And she certainly had an appetite, as she cleared her plate in no time, and even leapt up with it, offering to wash up. I shook my head. 'No, you go upstairs and get ready, love. Mike'll wash up. We've got to be away in half an hour, now.'

'You can't judge her moods at all, can you?' said Mike once she'd gone back to her room to get dressed. 'She's so chirpy. It's like she's completely shut off from where we're going today.'

'I know,' I said. 'Defence mechanism, maybe? Or perhaps she just refuses to accept the finality of it. Maybe she really does cling on to the hope that her mum's going to wake up. I mean, it does happen, doesn't it? Occasionally. I think, if I were her, that's what I'd be concentrating on thinking.'

'*Is* it likely, though?' Mike said. 'What are the odds? From what John said, it doesn't sound like anyone else thinks that. Anyway,' he added, as he slid the last of the plates into the drainer, 'I'm off to jump under the shower.' He grimaced. 'Sooner we go, sooner we're home.'

The journey itself was pleasant enough. Sophia's mother was in a specialist hospice in Derbyshire, about ninety miles south of us. It was attached to a big hospital, and catered for the terminally ill, but also people in vegetative states and long-term comas. The time flew by, in fact, Mike and I listening to Radio 2, which was our favourite, and doing what we often liked to do on long car journeys – playing our own version of 'Name That Tune', trying to be quickest to guess what each new track was. Sophia had plugged herself into her iPod as soon as we'd set off, and stayed that way, half-dozing, for the duration. We did stop for a quick comfort break half-way (mostly so I could have a sneaky cigarette) but were still there in good time for our 10 a.m. appointment.

From the outside, it was a welcoming, cottagey sort of place, tucked snugly beneath the clinical bulk of the hospital behind. It had extensive gardens, too, which, in the summer, I could tell would be full of flowers, and another with a duck pond and picnic tables. Even so, as I'd already anticipated, it was still somewhere you could tell most people wouldn't want to spend time. They did such wonderful work but you could never escape the reality that this was somewhere people went to die.

It wasn't a nice place for a 12-year-old to have to keep coming back to, I thought, as we introduced ourselves at the reception desk and waited while the receptionist wrote on our visitors' passes. Inside it was as clinical as any hospital.

'Good morning,' the woman said to Sophia, somewhat belatedly, I thought. 'Are you well?' I got the impression she didn't much like her.

'I'm fine, thank you,' Sophia said politely. 'Is mother ready for us?'

I winced slightly. That 'mother' sounded all wrong. Like an affectation. My bet was that they too probably had her tagged as a little madam, just like pretty much everyone else we'd spoken to. Yet the fact that she seemed to rub everyone up the wrong way made me even more determined to see beneath the surface.

'Yes, she is,' the receptionist answered. 'All bathed and smelling sweetly. You could give her hair a bit of a brush though, if you'd like.'

'Thanks,' said Sophia, still sounding clipped and formal. 'Come on, Casey, come on, Mike. Follow me.'

I glanced back at the receptionist as Sophia grabbed my arm and pulled me along. She was shaking her head. In sorrow? I couldn't tell.

Sophia's mother was in a private room, the last in a row of them, and like the rest of the interior it was painted off-white and was functional. Though two abstract paintings decorated one wall, and there was a good view of the gardens, there was little in there bar the bed – one of those pneumatic affairs that was air assisted and was designed to prevent bed sores – a chair, a bedside cabinet, with a CD player on it, and under the window a small table and two further plastic chairs. Unlike the other rooms we'd passed, there was no evidence of loving visitors. No cards, no flowers, no cuddly toys. The only homely feature was the floral-patterned duvet cover.

But I took these details in only vaguely at first, as all my attention was fixed on Sophia's mother. She lay on the bed, attached to some kind of machine, which I presumed must be the ventilator. She looked quite beautiful, lying there, with long flowing hair and flawless skin. In fact, she looked very much like Sophia, and only slightly older. No wonder people would comment that they looked like sisters – they did. And despite her apparent serenity, I could now visualise the two of them together, and the spectre of the rows about those boyfriends ... I wondered how old she had been when she'd had Sophia. Young, very young, was my guess. And how long had she been lying here, suspended in time? It sent a shiver down my spine, and also moved me. Such a tragedy. And this poor damaged child was now her legacy. In truth, I couldn't take my eyes off her at first. She looked so perfect, it was difficult to grasp the gravity of her condition. The only clue that she was actually ill, besides the machine, was that her limbs were strangely twisted. You could see that her legs were at odd angles under the sheet. Her arms, however, rested on top. And the palms of her hands were facing upwards and bent up, as if she was waiting to catch something in them.

Sophia must have caught me staring. 'She's gorgeous, isn't she? And don't be scared by her hands. They went like that ages ago. It's supposed to be quite a common thing.'

'Oh, I see,' I said, making a beeline for the chairs under the window. I felt uncomfortable suddenly, as if we were really intruding. This was obviously a very personal thing between them, and I felt we needed to make ourselves scarce. I grabbed Mike's hand and yanked him in the direction of the chairs. He'd said nothing yet. He was obviously as shocked as me.

'You just get on with whatever it is you usually do, love,' I said to Sophia as we sat down. 'I've got magazines for me and Mike. Just ignore us. Forget we're here.'

I bustled about in my bag and pulled out my gossip mags, handing one to Mike. 'Dear Deirdre and all those pop stars? Great,' he said.

I slapped his leg and gave him a 'don't start' look, before opening my magazine up and pretending to read. But I couldn't seem to concentrate. It was all just too weird. Sophia had by now put a CD on the CD player, at least giving us some welcome background noise, for which I was grateful. She was humming along to this as she leaned across the bed and brushed her mum's hair. Perhaps this was how they went, I thought, these visits. She stood and brushed her mum's hair, she hummed to the music. But I was soon to be proved very wrong.

It was the sound that caught my attention. I'd been reading, then I suddenly heard a slapping sound. I looked up and was shocked to see I hadn't misheard the first time. She'd just slapped her mum around the face. It was already reddening. Then she did it again. 'Wake up, you nasty bitch!' she hissed. 'Don't you think I've paid for long enough?'

'Sophia!' I said, startled. 'What on earth are you doing? Stop that now!'

She didn't seem to hear me. She just walked round to the other side of the bed and said, in a completely different voice now, one that sounded genuinely gentle, 'Oh, poor Mummy. You look so sad. *Please* wake up for me, Mummy. I love you.'

Mike looked at me, clearly uncomfortable. But I patted his knee. She'd gone quiet again. Maybe best not to inflame things.

'Let's just leave it for a moment,' I whispered. 'She looks okay now.'

Well, if not okay, at least more like you'd expect her to be. She'd started to cry now, in fact, very softly, but still audibly, and was stroking her mum's arms. 'Look at you,' she said. 'All twisted and broken. Oh, why did you let it come to this, Mummy?'

I was braced for another outburst and watching her intently, when out of the corner of my eye I saw movement. I turned to see the faces of an elderly couple, who were in the corridor and staring in through the glass panel in the door. I nudged Mike again, and seeing that, Sophia followed our gazes. She stared for a moment, then looked away. The couple didn't, though. They stayed, peering in for at least a minute longer.

'Who were those people, Sophia?' Mike asked once they'd gone. 'Do you know them?'

'No,' she said, shrugging. 'No idea.' She was massaging her mother's arms now, but seemed back in the room with us – no longer in that strange, trance-like state. So we got back to our reading, with just half an eye trained on what was happening, which, thankfully, seemed much more the sort of thing you'd expect. She wiped her mother's face with a damp sponge, then her arms and her hands, then pulled out nail polish, a nail file and clippers from her bag, and began giving her mother an impromptu manicure. She was just finishing this when a nurse put her head around the door.

'Sorry to interrupt,' she said, 'but it's time for Sophia's private time now.'

'Oh,' I said. 'Right ...'

'It's what we've always done for her. She likes to have the last ten minutes on her own, just the two of them ...'

'Of course,' I said, rising, along with Mike. I could tell he couldn't wait to get out of there.

'Perhaps you'd like to stroll around the gardens while you wait,' the nurse said brightly. 'It's still dry ... not too cold ...'

'Yes, of course,' I replied. Strange, I thought, as I stashed my magazines in my bag again. She could have had private time the whole time if she'd wanted to, surely? But, thinking about it, perhaps not. She was still only 12, after all. Perhaps that ten minutes, like the private time she spent with her consultant, was a concession she'd obtained only by asking. And why wouldn't she want that? It must feel, after all, that she had no control over her life now, whatsoever.

'Right, car park,' I said to Mike as we left. 'I need a cigarette.'

We went back out of the front door and, ignoring the gardens, headed to the car, where I'd left my supplies.

'Well, that was weird, wasn't it?' said Mike as I lit one.

'Tell me about it,' I answered. 'I'm finding the whole thing difficult to get my head round, to be honest. Aren't you? Oh, look –' I pointed across the car park. 'Getting into that blue car. Isn't that the couple who were looking through the door?'

'I think you're right,' Mike said. We stood and watched them pull out of their parking space. 'And it looks like they're headed over here.'

He was right. Moments later they'd pulled up alongside us, and the elderly man, who was driving, wound his window down. 'Are you two Sophia's new foster carers?' he asked Mike curtly. So they *did* know her.

'I'm sorry,' I said, shocked at his tone. 'And you are?'

'We're her grandparents,' he said. 'That's our daughter in there.'

'Oh,' began Mike.

The woman in the passenger seat leaned across now. 'Yes, and lying in that state thanks to *her*.'

'Thanks to her?' I said, stunned at the way she'd spat the words out. 'Whatever do you mean?'

'Oh, everyone will know. In the end, they will. It'll come out. You mark my words.'

I was still trying to take in that these were Sophia's grandparents. That she *did* have some family. And who looked perfectly respectable. Not at all like the families of some of the kids I'd dealt with. But why hadn't we been told about them? And why had Sophia blanked them? Maybe I'd misunderstood. Maybe the woman was speaking about one of the nurses, got her knickers in a twist about some aspect of her daughter's care.

I bent down so I could see her properly. 'Look,' I said. 'If you'd like to speak to Sophia, she'll be out in a few minutes. But if you're worried about anything, you really don't need to be. She's – 'what was I *saying* here?' – she's doing *fine*.'

The woman glared at me. 'You think we care about that? Let me tell you, young lady, that the only concern we have about that girl is that she is still allowed to walk this earth freely!' She looked slightly hysterical. 'What has she got on you?' she shouted. 'Come on, what is it?'

Her voice was turning into a shriek now, and getting louder, and her husband, looking agitated, placed an arm across her body, gently urging her back into her own seat. Then, saying nothing to either of us, he drove them both away.

We stood in the car park, stunned into speechlessness.

Mike finally spoke. 'What the ...?' He didn't need to finish. That had been my thought exactly.

Chapter 11

'John, I really do need some more information on this family. I feel we're scrabbling around in the pitch black here.'

It was mid-week – our fourth week, now – and I was getting more and more frustrated by the lack of any kind of progress. Where were Sophia's files, for goodness' sake? In a vault, somewhere, classified by MI5? I felt my hands were tied; without knowing what we were dealing with, it was impossible to know how best to make progress. For that reason, I'd held off having any sort of discussion with Sophia about the unsettling business at the hospital. For herself, she seemed entirely uninterested in it, trotting back to school on Monday and consigning it all to history. Which was great for the atmosphere at home, while it lasted, but got us no further in helping her.

'I know,' John said plaintively. 'I'm doing my best, Casey, really. But given what you've told me now, I'd better do better than my best, hadn't I?'

'Yes, you'd better!' I said. 'Better than that, even!'

We both laughed, but I knew John was well aware that I meant it. What was supposed to be a short interim placement for us was turning into a nightmare that was taking over our lives.

And our heads. We'd left the hospice with our minds full of questions, none of which we'd been able to discuss with Sophia in the car. She'd actually emerged from the building just as the elderly couple had driven off. She'd probably seen some of our bizarre exchange with them, even though we doubted she could have heard it. But she made no mention of it whatsoever when she climbed into the car, and by some unspoken pact – maybe all those years of marriage had made us telepathic – neither of us felt inclined to start bombarding her with questions.

But one thing was clear, as we discovered when we got to bed, and could at last talk freely: we'd both had the same dark ideas swirling round our heads. The grandparents, particularly the grandmother, had been clear in what they were trying to insinuate: that Sophia was responsible for what had happened to their daughter. So could it be true? Had Sophia put her mother in this dreadful state? Far from it being a suicide attempt, had Sophia pushed her down the stairs?

But while I tried to wait patiently – well, not *that* patiently – for John to come up with some more concrete information about Sophia's background, it seemed the here and now of our lives was going to hold incident enough.

It was the following Sunday, and after a blessedly uneventful week on the Sophia front Mike and I were in the kitchen, preparing breakfast. With the hospital visit done now (and perhaps Sophia would be back with Jean for the next one) the day stretched ahead invitingly, and I felt remarkably carefree. I should have known something bad was due to happen.

Leaving Mike in charge, and with the kids not yet down, I slipped off into the conservatory for a sneaky fag. Once Sophia had gone, I told myself as I lit it, I'd really make the effort. Get a new giving-up plan into action.

'Morning, Casey!' I turned to see Sophia in the doorway.

'Morning, lovey,' I replied. 'You want a coffee? Mike's got some brewing in the kitchen.'

'Yeah, I will, ta. Nice day, isn't it?'

I nodded my agreement. 'Still a bit cold to be coming down in those, though.' She was in her pyjama bottoms, but had reverted to a clingy little vest top, which, given the size of her top half, was rather in-yer-face. But softly, softly, I thought. That was the best way. 'Tell you what,' I said. 'Pop your dressing gown on and perhaps we could have breakfast out here.'

'It's okay, I'm not cold. I think I'll go and get that coffee. See you in a bit.' She headed back inside.

I finished my own coffee and cigarette and went back to the kitchen to take charge of my main job – frying the eggs. I was always in charge of eggs, because I was the expert at cracking them. Mike always seemed to break at least half of them. He was at the worktop by now, beginning to make and butter toast, having put everything in the oven to keep warm. Sophia was standing next to him, pouring herself a coffee, and humming along to a Rihanna song in the radio. I began cracking the eggs into my giant frying pan.

'Sophia, love,' I said, 'when you're done, can you go upstairs and give Kieron a shout, please?'

I had my back to her, concentrating on not breaking any yolks. I only turned round, moments later, as she hadn't replied, to see that she'd actually gone to fetch him. Instead it was to see that Mike had dropped a piece of buttered toast on the floor and was staring, mouth agape, at Sophia. I was puzzled. 'Clumsy, clumsy,' I joked, bending down to pick it up. He certainly didn't seem to be about to. And it seemed I was about to hear why.

'She just grabbed me from behind!' he managed to splutter, pointing at Sophia.

I looked at her. She grinned. 'Mike, that's a bit of an exaggeration! *Groped* you? I just poked you in the side!'

'I said *grabbed* me, not groped me. And you know damn well what you did! Now go and get Kieron, like Casey asked you.'

He turned back to the counter, and I could see that he was seething. But Sophia clearly couldn't – or wouldn't. She put down her coffee and then sauntered slowly over to him, where she came right up close behind him and coiled her arms around his chest. She then squashed herself right up against his back. Now it was me who was open-mouthed with shock.

'What the hell do you think you're doing!' Mike thundered, wrestling her arms from him and moving out of her way. He looked desperately towards me. 'How dare you behave like that in this house!' he railed at her. 'Now get out of here, go upstairs and get dressed. You can come down for breakfast when you're prepared to behave like a young lady. Go on! Get up those stairs! Now!'

Sophia rolled her eyes at him. 'Chill out, for fuck's sake! Can't I even give my foster daddy a hug for making breakfast for me?'

'No you damned well can't! Not at your bloody age!' He pointed to the door. 'Now just *go!*'

Sophia threw her hands in the air as if in exasperation. 'Fine,' she said. 'But you should know, Casey –' she turned her gaze to me now – 'that all men are the same. I know what they like.'

She then waltzed from the room and trotted off upstairs.

Mike pulled a chair out and sat down heavily. He was shaking. 'Casey, I swear, when you had your back turned to both of us she came at me from behind, hand between my legs, and ... well, she practically *cupped* me.' He looked horrified. 'It all happened so fast. One minute she was ...' He shook his head. 'She was so *brazen*. And next minute – next *second*, she's pouring the coffee, looking like butter wouldn't melt ... I can't *believe* it.'

I was mortified. 'I *know*. I honestly felt like slapping her – I couldn't help myself. But, God, Mike, I can hardly believe it, either. That she'd be so brazen as to *do* things like that? I mean, she's just a *kid* ...'

'Trust me, Casey,' he said. 'That girl is no kid. She knew *exactly* what she was doing.'

At that point Kieron came into the kitchen. 'Hey,' he said, 'what's all the shouting about?' He nodded towards the stairs. 'You know Sophia's up there talking to herself again, don't you? Calling herself names this time – bizarre. What's going on?'

Because I knew he'd do it in a more level-headed fashion than I would, I left Mike to explain while I went up to dress myself. I could hear Sophia myself now, muttering to herself in her bedroom, calling herself a 'stupid, fucking slut' and 'a bloody whore'. But before I tackled her I needed to shower and calm down and think for a bit. What on earth were we going to *do* with this child? We simply couldn't have things like this happening, and it threw everything else out of kilter. Was this the sort of thing she used to do with her mother's boyfriends? It didn't excuse anything on the part of the men, obviously – never, never – but talk about putting yourself in harm's way and making yourself vulnerable to exploitative, predatory men!

I was more concerned, however, about Kieron. Mike could handle most things, and we'd been trained in all this. The sort of kids we'd get – well, a lot would have been sexualised and brutalised from an early age. It was a part of what we had to be prepared to have to deal with, having damaged kids behave in scary and inappropriate ways. But Kieron had not asked for this, and shouldn't have to deal with it. And knowing what she'd done to Mike would spook him even more – it was him, after all, who had pointed out to me that we were vulnerable to her making sexual accusations.

I got in the shower and let the hot water stream over my face. Poor Kieron! He'd had so many traumas with Justin initially, and I knew he'd hoped it wouldn't be like that again. I just hoped I could reassure him that this was the pattern. That, in time, things almost always improved.

When I emerged from the bedroom, Sophia was still at it. 'Fucking slut! That's what you are, Sophia!' I heard her say. 'A dirty fucking whore. Look at yourself, go on, take a good look, slut!'

This was the aspect that threw me the most. Not so much the action itself as this. All this talking to herself all the time. This hadn't been covered anywhere in training. We were foster carers, not trained psychiatrists. And this seemed like their area of expertise, not mine and Mike's. I left her again, not yet having worked out what to do, and instead went downstairs to Mike and Kieron. 'Well, she's still at it,' I told them, adding a smile to attempt some levity. 'Chatting away to herself in the mirror!'

But Kieron was in no mood for jokes. 'Mum,' he said. 'What are we going to do? I've just told Dad – I didn't mention it before, because I didn't want to upset you, but she's been wandering about upstairs in just her underwear. She waits till she hears me coming out of my room and then acts like it's accidental. But it isn't. So now I just turn round and go back into my room till she's gone. Because she's doing it on purpose, I know she is.'

My heart hit my boots. 'I don't know what we're going to do, love. I wish I did but I don't. I have to speak to John about all this. He's supposed to be finding out more anyway. And in the meantime we're just going to have to be really careful – you two, especially – not to put ourselves in vulnerable situations.'

'Bloody hell, Casey!' Mike said with feeling. 'I wouldn't have said standing buttering toast in my own kitchen was putting myself in a vulnerable situation!'

'I know,' I said. Mike was right. It wasn't that simple. 'I wish I had some answers, but I don't. But I'll report the incident straight away and, as I say, speak to John, and ...'

'Well, well, well, isn't this just peachy?' It was Sophia. 'Little family meeting, is it? About me?'

No one had heard her come back downstairs. 'Sophia –' Mike started, his voice angry.

'No, let *me* speak, please, Mike. Casey may not have any answers, but I do. Keeping your pervert son out of my bedroom would be a start.'

'You lying little cow!' Kieron shouted. 'How dare you say that? Trust me, I don't want to go anywhere *near* you!'

She just grinned at him. 'I've seen you watching me. You can't keep your eyes off me. Have you never seen a pair of tits before, or what?'

'Sophia!' I practically screamed her name, to be sure of her full attention. I knew I had to stop her before Kieron lost his senses. 'I don't know what you think you're playing at, but it won't work in this house! Now I suggest you turn around, go right up those stairs and *stay there*, because I'm coming seriously close to *really* losing my temper!'

I glanced at Kieron. He looked like he could kill her on the spot. I'd never seen him so angry before. Sophia glared at us all, as if we were really something quite distasteful to look at, before leaving the kitchen, thundering back up the stairs, and slamming her bedroom door with such force it made the house shake. I thought fleetingly of how much abuse my internal doors took with this job of mine, but seeing Kieron's face jolted me. He now looked like he was about to cry.

'Pay no attention to her, babes,' I hurriedly reassured him. 'This is obviously a part of her *modus operandi*. I know it's upsetting, but as you can see she's badly damaged, and it's plain to see that she's just lashing out …'

'I don't care, Mum!' he said. 'I can't have her saying things like that. I mean, Lauren's so easygoing, but she'd still probably wonder …'

'Don't be daft, love,' I said firmly. 'Lauren knows the kind of kids we have. She'd know it was just rubbish.'

'She would, son,' added Mike. 'Lauren's not stupid.'

'But that's not the *point*,' he said. 'I can't bear it. It makes me so stressed. I feel I can't live in my own home without watching my back all the time! No, I've made my mind up. I'm going to go and stay at Lauren's for a bit. At least until Dad can put some locks on the doors or something.'

Mike nodded. 'He's absolutely right, Case,' he said. 'I know it's crap for us, but perhaps Kieron *should* go and stay at Lauren's for a bit. Just for a few days, till we've worked out with John how we're going to handle things. And in the meantime I'll sort out some locks for all the bedrooms. We can't be living like this, love, we really can't.'

I looked bleakly at my son and my husband. Was this what our lives had become because of my job? Us having to allow our own son to lock himself in his room for fear of what might happen if he didn't? A saying crossed my mind then, and it made for grim thinking. *The jailors were becoming the jailed*.

I tried to shake myself out of it, to get a sense of perspective. We weren't prison guards charged with keeping a criminal off the streets after all. We were carers, *trained* carers, of desperate kids. And she *was* a kid – no more, no less – just a kid. Just a deeply disturbed 12-year-old girl.

I felt so miserable when I woke up on Monday morning that I seriously doubted my own sanity. I was a morning person. Always had been. A dyed in the wool lark. Always first up, radio blaring, breakfast on the go. But my first thought on waking had been such a grim one. Last night my dear son had packed his bags and left home. Not for ever, I knew that – and he would one day soon anyway – but it was the circumstances of the leaving that hurt; that he'd left because I'd forced him to. I knew it wasn't as straight-forwardly damning as that, but it was still my fault, my choice to bring kids like Sophia into his life.

I dragged myself from my bed anyway – Mike had already left for work – and went downstairs, hoping that the watery February sunshine might go some way towards lifting my mood. I also had to remember it wasn't Sophia's fault either. She hadn't asked to come to us, either, had she? She'd been happy (though 'happy' wasn't the right word – far from it) to stay with Jean, in whose care she had clearly felt safe. And what *of* Jean? What was that all about really? I had so much to discuss with John Fulshaw this morning that I had half a mind to make myself a list.

I was carefully removing poached eggs from the pan when Sophia came down. I'd put them on when I'd heard the shower pump go off. To her credit, she wasn't generally any bother on a school morning. Always got up with her alarm, was dressed and ready on time. How many parents would give their left arm for that luxury?

'Eggs this morning,' I said, my back to her as I dished them up. 'All right with you, love?'

I got only a mumble in reply and turned to see her rummaging in her school bag at the kitchen table. I noticed she looked drawn and slightly dishevelled compared to her usual, carefully pulled-together appearance. 'You feeling okay, Sophia?' I asked her. 'Taken your pills yet?'

'Oh for Christ's sake, can't you leave me alone for five minutes?' she barked irritably at me. 'No, I haven't taken them yet, okay? Because I feel sick.'

I racked my brains for some memory of what the literature said about nausea. 'But doesn't that mean you need to take them?'

She rolled her eyes. 'Oh, we're the expert now, are we?'

I decided to ignore the rudeness and focus on the Addison's. I still didn't know anything like enough about her illness. Whether I was right or not, I simply didn't know. 'Look, love,' I said. 'If that's the case then I think I should ring school and tell them you won't be in till later. Let's wait till you're feeling well enough to go.'

She looked world weary. 'I'm fine, Casey, really. I just get like this sometimes. Look, I'll take them when I get to school. I promise. Just as soon as I know I'll be able to keep them down.'

I made a mental note to call her consultant, or someone at the hospital, at any rate, so that I could get advice from a real expert about what should happen if she felt sick. There was just so much information and so many different aspects to her condition that I felt I needed to take a flipping GCSE in it. 'Okay, love,' I said, as I placed her breakfast in front of her anyway. 'Sorry you're feeling rough. Perhaps if you try a nibble of something you'll feel better. Could it be your blood sugar?'

'Perhaps,' she said. 'I hope so.'

She ate very little, but I couldn't force it down her. So I just made sure I reminded her to eat a bag of peanuts if she needed them. Then I went out into the hall with her to wave her off and wish her a nice day, as had become my habit. I knew these little rituals mattered, even if she didn't. They all helped to give her a sense of security that I suspected she'd had little of in her young life.

She surprised me by hovering in the doorway, and I sensed a mood change. 'I'm so sorry about yesterday, Casey,' she said, confirming it. 'I really am. Are you still angry at me?'

'No, love. I'm not. I'm just confused. You see, I know Mike and Kieron as well as I know myself, and the things you said, well, they were just upsetting for them. We're just not like that in our family, that's the thing, love. And it hurts when people make those sorts of remarks.'

She chewed on her lip and nodded. 'I'm really sorry. It was only supposed to be a joke. That's how it started. But it went too far, didn't it?'

'I'm afraid it did, love. And it wasn't a very funny joke, was it?'

'No, it wasn't.'

'But listen, you're going to be late for registration if you don't get off now. How about we have another chat about all this when you get home? Like I say, I'm not angry, and

135

I'm so glad you've apologised. That was very mature of you.'

This seemed to cheer her up. 'Okey dokey,' she said, grinning. 'See you in a bit then.'

And then she was off, now happy as Larry again, it seemed like. Case closed. I returned her last wave before closing the door and watched her trot off down the road looking every inch the innocent schoolgirl. This child really was such an enigma, I thought, one minute coming on as this voracious sultry temptress, the next this angelic little girl. Did even *she* know who she was? I didn't think so.

I ignored the washing up and headed straight for the phone. Time to get back on to John Fulshaw. Make his Monday.

Chapter 12

John listened patiently while I described the events of the previous day.

'And it's not so much the sexual impropriety,' I told him. 'I've plenty of experience with kids who've been sexually precocious. It's all the other stuff she does. All that talking to herself. It's as if she goes into this trance; I'm not sure she even realises she's doing it. But you can flip a switch, almost, and she becomes someone else. I think she needs help, John. Psychiatric help, I mean. Anyway, have you managed to find anything else out?'

'Nothing specific about the abuse allegation, sadly. Not as yet. But I have at least been able to establish a bit more family background.'

'Brilliant,' I said, sitting down on the bottom stair. 'Shoot.'

'Sad story,' he began. 'Aren't they all? But essentially, her mum had her at 16.'

'That doesn't surprise me. She looked hardly any older than Riley when I saw her.'

'Because she wasn't. What would she be now, 28? Anyway, the father, as you know, has never been in the picture. Never seen or heard of again after that one-night stand, far as I know. May not have even known Grace was pregnant. What we do know, however, is that the parents were mortified. They lived in another part of the country altogether when their daughter fell pregnant, but moved the whole family, lock, stock and barrel, up here. Including the younger brother – this is the guy who fostered Sophia originally, her Uncle James – who was by all accounts none too happy about the move. Seems he married young and moved his wife well away from it all.'

'Away from what?'

'From the parents, is what I've been told by social services. They were very controlling, apparently. Particularly the mother. Not short of a bob or two either. Quite well to do. Which fits, because they apparently installed Grace and little Sophia in a flat and, financially, she wanted for nothing.'

'Bit odd.'

'I thought so too. But apparently that was the set-up. As far as we know, she never really had any sort of job. Just lived off the bank of her mum and dad. Sophia had pretty much anything she wanted as well … hmmm, well, materially, at least. Which would obviously explain why she comes across as being so spoilt. As you say, a strange sort of set-up. And of course then Sophia's Addison's disease was diagnosed – not sure quite when that was, but quite young – so that dominated things a fair bit.'

'And with such a young mother, and a lone one ...' The picture was becoming clearer now. 'I wonder how supportive the parents were? They certainly seemed in bits – particularly the grandmother – when they accosted us.'

'Well, the impression social services had, having spoken to the uncle, was that the daughter was something of a shameful secret – hence that move two hundred miles away. And though she and Sophia were financially supported, she never had much of a life. Pretty young girl, whole life in front of her and everything ... but completely without direction, and single-handedly looking after a sick child. My instincts tell me Sophia's mum was something of a mummy's little princess herself, who rather tarnished her crown by getting pregnant. And you know, Casey, of course you do, how throwing money at a kid with problems often just makes them worse. Had she had to fend for herself a bit more, maybe she would have been more motivated. Got a job, got a life.'

Got over herself and perhaps focused on her child, for that matter. 'You are so right,' I agreed.

'But as it was, it seems she was mostly directionless – and by all accounts highly promiscuous, too. Pretty girl. Constant stream of boyfriends coming and going. And the consensus, and certainly the brother would seem to corroborate this, was that she resented Sophia greatly, for having ruined her life. As did the grandparents.' John sighed. 'I know we see this sort of thing all the time, but it never gets any less upsetting, does it? These poor kids. Anyway, that's why the brother took her in when her mum had her accident. No choice. Because the grandparents pretty much disowned her.'

'That's so shocking. And then he did as well.'

'It wasn't that so much. I don't think he wanted to. He just couldn't handle her. Big difference. Wife pregnant, this sick child, all the baggage with his parents ...'

'I suppose. And, if current form's anything to go by, she was one hell of a lot to take on. And speaking of which, how *is* Jean doing?'

'Um, not entirely sure, to be honest. Okay, I think. I've not heard anything to the contrary, certainly. How are *you* doing, that's the main point. Are you coping?'

'Just about,' I said. 'Though I'm not at all happy about the thing with Kieron.'

'I know,' he said. 'And I'm so sorry to put you through all this, Casey. I know it's hard ... But be reassured. You have your safe care agreement in place, and –'

'John, you know as well as I do that's just a piece of paper in a file. Means nothing when things like happened yesterday happen.'

'I know, Casey. Look, here's a thought. Do you think it would be helpful if I came round and had a chat with Sophia myself? You know, just ran through what's acceptable and what's not with her, pretty damned firmly?'

'I don't think it'll make any difference at all, John. She's already apologised for yesterday and I've told her that's the end of the matter. The problem is that I honestly don't think she wants to do and say these things. It's just like it's instinctive with her. Like a learned behaviour. Which, after what you've told me, would seem to fit. And there's also the

Addison's. Do you know much about it?' John admitted that he didn't. 'Well, I do. I've been reading up on it big time, as you can imagine. And there's this symptom of "brain fog" – well, that seems to fit, doesn't it? But I also read that in a few cases – when there's extreme stress of some kind – patients can develop mental health problems. Depression, even psychosis.'

'That sounds serious.'

'Exactly.' I glanced at the clock on the hall wall. The morning was disappearing fast. 'Look, don't worry, okay?' I said. 'I just want you to be aware, really. We're coping okay. It's just good to know you're at the end of a phone, John. And it's great to have a fuller picture of her background now. That helps.'

'Well, I'm still on it. They're still tracking down the files from the night of the accident. We'll see what that throws up. And, well, in the meantime …'

'I'll hang in there, John. Don't worry.'

I felt a lot more positive after speaking to John. Hearing Sophia's background put flesh on some bones, and what I'd learned from him certainly put some of her behaviours into perspective. What a start in life! And wasn't that always the case? Being born into a heap of problems, not of her making, had created a near monster out of this poor child. No wonder she had issues that needed resolving.

I decided then and there that from now on I would focus on the positives. Soon, in a few weeks, perhaps, she'd be reunited with her long-term carer. In the meantime, I would do my very best for her.

I got up from the stairs, stretched out my legs and rolled both my sleeves up. An early spring clean was in order. For me, there was nothing quite as cathartic as getting stuck into some serious grime-fighting. I turned the radio right up – well, there was no one there to be annoyed by it, was there? – and set about making the house really sparkle.

I was about two hours into it when I heard the phone ring. I was in the conservatory by now, having a quick break for a glass of milk, and had to sprint back into the hall to catch it before it rang off. I was hot and sticky, despite the season, as I'd been giving it so much welly, and had to wipe sweat from my forehead as I snatched up the phone.

'Mrs Watson? Casey? It's Tina Williams here …'

Oh, God. That meant school. Tina was the school secretary and I knew her well from when I'd worked there.

'Oh, dear,' I said. 'That sounds ominous, Tina. What's happened?

'She's had some sort of fit, we think. Or a collapse. We're not sure. We've phoned for an ambulance, of course, but we don't know how long it will be, so we'd really like you to come up too, as there's no one here who can administer her emergency medication.'

'Of course,' I said, my heart once again in my boots. 'I'm on my way. Give me ten minutes, okay?'

'Sure,' said Tina. 'See you in a few minutes.'

As I dashed around, pulling off my pinny and grabbing my handbag and car keys, I remembered that I had planned to call her specialist this morning, and had completely forgotten. Sidetracked by John, I thought, then too busy polishing. *Stupid woman!* I berated myself angrily.

As I drove towards school I felt increasingly nervous. All that talk about how it would probably never happen, and here it was, happening – it was real! She might slip into unconsciousness. And unless the ambulance got there first, this was my bag. I might have to inject the steroid medicine into her myself, and the idea made me queasy. It was one thing to be told how straightforward it would be, but quite another to actually have to do it to a person.

But that might not be necessary in any case. I racked my brain for the correct course of action, hoping all those sessions poring over the leaflets in bed would come back to me now that I needed them. I had to take the syringe out, push the plunger down, insert it into the little bottle, draw up the liquid up, push out any air bubbles, then jab it in her thigh. I must do it quickly, do it decisively, push the plunger fast and firmly. The drug should kick in within ten or fifteen minutes. Was that it? Give or take? Yes, that was it. That was the order. I could do this. I could do this. I could do this.

But when I drove through the school gates I felt a surge of relief. The ambulance was already there. I grabbed my bag and jumped out and ran in through the front doors. With any luck, someone would have done it all already.

I was signed in, and Tina took me down to the medical area, where I was met by a smiling paramedic. Where would the world be without people like that, I thought gratefully.

'Is she okay?' I asked.

'She's just fine, Mrs Watson. My colleague is in there now,' he said, nodding towards the adjoining medical room.

'Giving her a bit of a dressing down, actually. She knows exactly how to control her condition – been very vocal about it – and seemed quite proud, in fact, to tell us that she knew this would happen if she had a bout of vomiting and didn't take action.'

'She was sick? I'm so sorry,' I said. 'That's really my fault. She refused to take her pills this morning because she said she was feeling ill. I should have kept her at home, shouldn't I? Called the doctor. But she promised me she'd take them when she got to school, and she didn't seem *that* bad, so … God, I'm such an idiot!'

The paramedic was really sweet and sympathetic. 'I tell you, I've only spoken to her for ten minutes,' he reassured me, 'and I can already see that she's stubborn as well as manipulative. You shouldn't feel guilty. A lot of kids with chronic conditions like this get, shall we say, a bit arsey at this age. It's their way of trying to control their condition, rather than it controlling them. But they grow out of it, don't worry. They soon realise that it's much easier to try and find a way of living *with* it.'

It made sense, what he said, and, for probably the first time, I had a real feeling for the enormity of what Sophia had to live with on a daily basis. She must feel so different from the other kids, having to monitor her body so closely all the time, and at an age when a child is supposed to be carefree.

It was with this in mind that I joined Sophia in the medical room. I immediately went across and hugged her. 'Oh, love,' I said. 'I was so worried. How are you feeling?'

She wrapped her arms around me and started to cry. 'I'm sorry, Casey,' she sobbed. 'Can we go home, please. I'm so tired.'

I glanced over at the paramedic, who nodded. 'Fine to go,' he confirmed. 'And lots of fluids for the rest of the day. But we've made it clear – haven't we, young lady? – that next time she's sick she needs to let someone know. Because next time she might not be so lucky.'

I felt Sophia stiffen in my arms as he said this. She carefully withdrew from me, wiped her eyes and then looked directly at the paramedic. 'Yes, thank you for that, Andrew,' she said icily. 'But think I understand how my hormones work. Job done, boys. Bye-bye. See you soon.'

'Sophia!' I gasped, shocked by the venom in her voice. 'That was completely uncalled for! Those men came here to help you!'

The paramedics seemed relaxed, however. With 'seen it all before' expressions, they nodded a goodbye to me and left, leaving me stunned by how Sophia could be so rude to them.

Sophia herself simply flopped back into my arms. 'Please can we go home now?' she said in a small, pleading voice. 'I really do feel tired. Really awful.'

Tina gave me a look too – a clear 'Oh my God, poor old you!' one – as she duly led me out, armed with more paperwork. This was the ambulance report, to go in my file, and as I tucked it away, having put Sophia to bed, I mused. For a short-term placement, hers was positively bulging.

I spent much of that afternoon musing, in fact. While Sophia slept and I finished my housework, I thought again of her jaw-dropping discourtesy. Was this really just spoilt brat behaviour, was this manipulative, or something more? It seemed so unplanned, so random, so unexpected when it happened. And so often, straight afterwards she seemed genuinely unaware. Unaware, for sure, about quite how inappropriate it was, as was clear every time she apologised for what she'd done. Yes, she was sorry, but she never seemed to have any clear sense of just *how* wrong it was. I began to wonder if we weren't all too fixated on throwing our hands up in shock and horror to really hear what was happening with this strange and challenging young girl.

Was this a cry for help? And were none of us listening?

Chapter 13

The next couple of weeks seemed to go by in a fog. Living with Sophia was like riding on an unfamiliar rollercoaster; we never knew when the next white-knuckle bit was going to happen. When she was in a sunny mood she was a joy to be around, now she'd settled in – funny and giggly and sweet. But when she got into one of her dark moods she was really quite venomous, slamming doors – my poor doors! – shouting and swearing, and storming off, enraged, to her room. She could swear like a navvy, and she seemed to relish doing so when she was like that, sometimes at all of us, and sometimes at herself. There seemed no triggers to all this, and no warning signs either. The only time I had a clue that she was about to switch personas was if she failed to take her medication at the right time. At those times she would become flushed and unsteady and speak gibberish. And I was becoming adept at spotting the signs now, which was a relief. But her mood swings and violent temper weren't just about her condition. And now I knew so much more about how she'd come to be here, I knew it would take much more than a couple of pills to get her right.

But in the short term things were looking up. Mike had fitted locks to the bedroom doors, as he'd promised, and as *he'd* promised Kieron had come home. By mid-March he'd been home for a couple of weeks, and on this particular Saturday had asked Sophia if she'd like to go bowling with him and Lauren. I think he was trying to rebuild his relationship with Sophia for my sake, which was a kind gesture, and made me so proud of him.

Sophia seemed genuinely thrilled to have been asked, too. 'So can I go, Casey?' she asked me.

'Of course you can,' I told her.

'And it'll be nice for you too,' she added, grinning at me impishly. 'Give you a chance to think what we're going to do for my birthday.'

'Hey,' admonished Kieron, 'one treat at a time, missy! When's your birthday anyway? Not soon is it?'

'*Kieron!*' she cried. 'You know *exactly* when my birthday is! It's written in giant letters all over the calendar!'

This was true. She had written it there, at my invitation, in big swirly shocking pink felt pen. And it was good to see that she was just as over-excited about her birthday as any other 12-year-old girl. 'He's just winding you up, love,' I said. 'Take no notice. And you're right. Better get my thinking cap on about that, hadn't I?'

I reached into my handbag for my purse so I could give her some money for the outing. And as I pulled it out she surprised me by coming up behind me and planting a kiss on my cheek. 'Thanks, Casey,' she said. 'You're the best.'

I smiled as I waved them off, pleased to see everyone happy, but as I shut the door I felt a wave of sadness wash over me. Because it was a veneer. As the experiences of the last few weeks had proven, days like this couldn't be the norm. Not with all the underlying problems Sophia had. You couldn't put band aids over such big psychological wounds. But days like this did at least show me how they *could* be, if only we could tap into the past properly and help her to put it right.

I went back into the kitchen and thought about cleaning it. Mike had been called in to work and wouldn't be back for hours yet. No, I thought, today I would resist the urge to don my Marigolds. I'd phone Riley and see if she was free instead. I did need to think about what to do for Sophia's birthday, and being a Saturday, there was a good chance David would be around to look after Levi, so Riley could come into town with me for a couple of hours.

Even with all the traumas and horrors of the last few weeks, it was unlike me to have left planning for Sophia's birthday so late. I loved birthdays – liked any kind of family celebration really, and anyone who had the good (or bad!) fortune to come into our circle could rely on their special day being Casey-fied. I particularly loved putting on kids' parties – with all that cutting and sticking and paint and glitter, they were my forte – and I had last year treated Justin to the party of his life – a full-on *Little Mermaid*-themed pool party in the garden, complete with hired giant paddling pool and real sandy beach. If there were awards going for completely mad, ridiculously OTT parties, I would definitely be in for a shot at it.

'So what's the theme for this one?' Riley wanted to know, once we'd got ourselves settled in our favourite café and were tucking into French onion soup and Welsh rarebit. 'What sort of thing were you thinking? What sort of things is she into?'

'Hmm,' I said thoughtfully. 'You know, that's quite a hard one, as it happens.'

'Come on, think, Mum. There must be *something*.'

'Yeah, *boys*!' I said with feeling. 'But aside from that …'

'So it's simple. We do a hunk party. Round up a bunch of Kieron's mates from college. Dress them up like Chippendales, have them all dance to that Tom Jones song … Or then again, hmm. Maybe not.'

But joking aside, it was a poser to know what to do for her. With so much focus on the difficulties brought about by her physical illness and her emotional instability, there'd been precious time for just plain old getting to know this child, really. She'd asked for a mobile phone for her present, and her team had allowed it. Which was unusual. Kids in care aren't generally allowed them, as contact with birth families often needs to be closely monitored for their own wellbeing. Not the case for Sophia, sadly, which was probably why they'd agreed to it. She could hardly go and secretly call her mother, after all.

But then I remembered something. On the form she'd filled in for us she had put down that she really liked musicals. 'She's even been to London a few times,' I told Riley now. 'To see some of the big West End shows.'

'So that's it, then,' said Riley, beginning to warm to the task. 'Yep. I can see this, Mum. The bright lights, the costumes, the greasepaint, the soundtrack ... We can transform your downstairs to the Moulin Rouge theatre, or maybe the *Phantom of the Opera* one – where's that? Or the slums of Victorian London, and do *Oliver*. I'll be Nancy, and Kieron can be Bill Sykes – he'd be good at that ...'

'*Wicked!*' I said.

'Yes, I know. It will be.'

'No, *Wicked*. Wicked as in the *musical* called *Wicked*. That's her favourite one. She's been to see it. I remember her telling me. Her uncle and aunt took her when they were fostering her. Yes, that's right.'

Riley looked thoughtful. She frowned. 'Such a tragedy her family abandoned her, isn't it?'

'It really is,' I agreed. But I really didn't want to quash my happy mood. Chances were that it wouldn't last terribly long anyway, so I intended to enjoy it while it lasted. 'Let's not dwell on that now,' I said. 'Let's think positive.'

'You're absolutely right, Mum,' Riley said. 'Let's think party. Whatever happens we can't let her out of our clutches without a Watson-style bash to her name, can we?'

Before heading off to the party shop, however, I first had to drag her to the mobile-phone shop down the road so she could do what I couldn't – talk sensibly to the man there about what to buy. To a cave-woman like me, at least, a phone was a phone was a phone, a thing you used to make calls and send messages. But apparently not; what we left with both looked good – girly pink, encrusted with diamante – and, more importantly, did all the other things a phone had to do, like take pictures, make videos and do 'apps'. It was all Greek to me (and it probably did do Greek translations) but Riley assured me that in this day and age it was a bargain, despite the price almost giving me a heart attack.

But if my bank card wasn't done for the day at least the next bit of spending was more my natural territory. I knew the party accessories shop like the back of my hand. As did Riley. Like mother, like daughter. 'So,' she said, '*Wicked*. We need to think colours. Green, black and white, mainly. Yes, that's what we'll go with. Green, black and white balloons, green, black and white face paints ... then we're going to need witch stuff and wizard stuff ...'

'You make it sound like a Halloween party!'

'Mum, do you actually know what the musical's about?'

'It's about *The Wizard of Oz*, isn't it?'

'Well, not quite. It's about the witches. The good witch, the bad witch, and this very handsome wizard. And the wizard ends up falling for the bad witch, who really *wasn't* bad and ... Oh, I'll tell you the plot later. Just trust me, okay? The main thing's that she's green. It's the green theme that's key here. Come on, let's start getting stuff in our basket, shall we. I can't be too late because David will be suffering from nappy fatigue.'

And so it was that an hour later, and laden down with all our green stuff, we returned home, feeling very pleased with ourselves. We were just upstairs, stashing all our purchases out of sight in my bedroom wardrobe, when we heard the sound of the others coming in.

'That's good timing!' I called down, as Riley and I started down the stairs. 'We've just got back ourselves, this very minute.'

I walked into the kitchen then, expecting a sea of smiles and a reply, but was met with an uncomfortable silence. 'Is everything okay?' I asked, looking from one to another. Kieron raised his eyebrows and nodded towards Sophia.

'Everything's fine,' she said. 'Look at his face! *Honestly!* He's just annoyed 'cos he got beaten by a girl.' She giggled then and reached across to pull his ear.

'Yeah, that's right, Sophia,' he said, batting her hand away. '*Course* that's why I'm annoyed.' He reached for Lauren's hand and stomped off with her into the conservatory.

'Okaaay,' said Riley. 'So I think that's my cue to get off. David and Levi will be wondering where I've got to.'

'You want me to drop you?' I asked, conscious of the tension in the room still.

She shook her head. 'No, you're all right. I'll walk. I need the exercise.'

'So, love,' I said to Sophia once I'd seen Riley out and returned to the kitchen. She was still standing against the kitchen worktop, looking petulant. 'What really happened? Because I think it's pretty clear Kieron's not upset because you beat him at bowling.'

Now she glared at me. 'Well, if it's not that, how the hell would *I* know what's wrong with him? For God's *sake!* Why must everything be *my* fault?'

I was just about to give her an answer when she obviously decided she didn't want one. She marched past me and thundered off up the stairs. *Great*, I thought, as I waited for the inevitable door-slam. *Bye-bye happy mood for today, then*.

I followed Kieron and Lauren into the conservatory to find that they'd opened the French door and gone out into the back garden. They were sitting at the table out there, looking glum.

'God, that little madam ...' I began, despite my best professional intentions. Sometimes, it was just a knee-jerk. Didn't matter how much you understood all the underlying reasons, didn't matter that you cared. Sometimes you just couldn't help it.

'Mum,' Kieron said, 'she is *impossible*. She blatantly grabbed my bum while I was bowling. Just grabbed it. In front of *everyone*. I was so embarrassed. And when I told her to knock it off she just laughed in my face! Said was I only saying that because Lauren was about! I mean, as *if*!'

'She did, Casey,' Lauren confirmed. 'And I did try to have a word with her about it – Kieron was really upset – but she just laughed at me as well and called me a jealous bitch.'

'Oh, I'm so sorry, love,' I said, pulling out a chair for myself and sitting down. 'She's just a nightmare when she's like that. And when the two of you have been so kind, and taken her out and everything. I'll speak to her, I promise. We can't have her doing this.'

'Oh, what's the point, Mum?' said Kieron. 'She's not going to stop it, is she? But that's the last time *I* take her anywhere. So embarrassing. And there were people we *knew* there, as well.'

I was just about to apologise again – I so felt for them both – but as I was about to open my mouth to do so a hairbrush suddenly crash-landed on the garden table.

Startled, we all looked up to see the source of the projectile, to find Sophia grinning down at us from her bedroom window.

'All talking about me again, are you?' she shouted down, her tone cocky, her expression self-righteous. 'Fucking losers, the lot of you!'

'Sophia!' I shouted back. 'Get inside now! And don't you dare speak like that! We have neighbours next door!'

'Fuck the neighbours as well!' she yelled, ramping up the volume. Then she popped her head back in and banged the window shut.

Thank God for safety glass, I thought, as I pushed my chair back and got up to go in and remonstrate with her. Kieron stopped me. 'Don't, Mum,' he said. 'Stay here. Let her have her little rant. She knows we told you the truth and all she's trying to do now is to give you something else to be angry about.'

He was right, of course. I needed to remain focused on the original incident, not dance to the strings she was now trying to pull. So easy to fail to see the wood for the trees. Thank heavens for my clear-thinking Asperger's son, who saw everything in a much simpler light!

We headed inside now, in any case, as time was moving on, and Mike would soon be home and hungry for tea. I didn't go up and speak to Sophia – Kieron was right. Best to leave her – and instead took my frustrations out on the chops we were having. Not that I'd noticed. It was only the fact that Kieron and Lauren were laughing that made me realise I was being a bit heavy handed in my pounding. 'Hmm,' said Kieron, grinning from ear to ear as he watched me. 'I *definitely* wouldn't like to be that lamb.'

'Nor would I!' Mike agreed once he was home from work and I'd filled him in on the day and the latest Sophia drama. Kieron had popped to the bus stop to see Lauren safely on her bus. I was so glad she'd turned out to be such a generous-minded girl. It couldn't be easy for her having a boyfriend with a family like ours. We were enough of a culture shock on our own, I thought ruefully, but with the fostering – well, there was certainly never a dull moment.

'But I'm going to do as Kieron suggested, and ignore the outburst,' I said. 'Kind of play her at her own game and pretend everything's all right. Perhaps if we start ignoring all the outbursts, she'll feel less inclined to have them in the first place.'

'Good idea,' said Mike, as Kieron returned. 'Be nice to have a meal without some woman causing a hysterical hoo-hah, eh, son?' he winked at me. 'Now, shall I make the mint sauce?'

And the meal did actually go without a hitch. I called Sophia down, and she smiled sweetly, and helped me dish up, was polite and cheerful, and couldn't have been more different. It really was as if she was just an everyday 12-year-old girl – having a flounce and a tantrum one minute, sweetness and light the next. It also seemed that, just as I'd said to Mike earlier, by the miracle of just ignoring bad behaviour – as a psychologist would tell you to do with a toddler – it really could be spirited away.

Like magic. But that was precisely what we didn't have. And however appealing it was to think that simple behaviour modification would work, putting her on the points system that was central to our fostering programme would be, I was becoming increasingly sure, just a plaster on a big gaping wound.

But I did want to talk to her. Talk was what was needed; it was the only way to try and understand her better. So I suggested as we cleared the tea things that, while the men watched their football, she and I watch a DVD in the conservatory together, which she agreed to both readily and meekly. She even ran in and tidied it, plumped up the sofa cushions and got a throw from her bedroom for us to snuggle in.

'*Mama Mia*,' she said. 'Can you stand that again, Casey?'

I nodded. I could recite the script in my sleep. She'd already had it on three or four times since she'd been with us, and I'd already seen it a couple of times myself. But that didn't matter. I was more concerned with getting her out here, just the two of us, in the hopes she'd open up to me some more.

We watched for about forty minutes, when I suggested we take a 'commercial break' so I could rustle up two hot chocolates and nibbles. In her case they were a bag of crisps – like most people with her condition, she craved and needed salt – and in mine, a couple of my favourite chocolate biscuits. 'And a quick chin-wag, I thought,' I added, as I passed her her drink.

She frowned. 'Is this about earlier in the garden? Because I'm so sorry, Casey, I really *am*. I just lost my temper. I promise I won't do it again.'

'No, it's not about that,' I said. 'Though that was immature of you, and you know that. We just don't speak to one another like that in this house, and while you're with us you mustn't either.' She looked chastened. 'No,' I went on. 'It's about what happened when you were bowling. Kieron and Lauren told me, and they have no reason to tell me anything but the truth. And I just need to know, lovey, what were you thinking?'

'It was just a joke, all that, Casey. I swear it was. I just thought – well, that Kieron would find it funny.'

'Sophia,' I said gently. 'You have to understand. There is *no way* Kieron would find something like that funny. He is a grown man, and you are 12. Much too young to be touching him like that. But you are also old enough, I think, to know that, don't you? All this touching men – well, it's not right, is it?' I almost asked her to reflect on how she had felt about it when the tables were turned and she was being molested by those grown men. But something held me back. Something told me that now wasn't the moment to go there. I wanted her to reflect on her own behaviour. Here and now. She looked on the edge of tears.

'I'm so sorry,' she said, her chin wobbling. 'I do know that. I just didn't think about it. I just did it. I don't *know* why. And then Lauren looked at me as if I was a piece of dirt, and – I dunno. It just made me so angry. And when I get like that I just don't seem to know how to stop it.'

Her tears were spilling over now, and I put my arm around her. 'Sweetheart, you've lived with us for over two months now. You must know that we all care about you very much. We're here for you. That's why we do what we do – and that includes Kieron and Lauren – to help you and support you through a bad time in your life. So you need to think about him the way he wants you to think about him – like a big brother. Not some boy at school you fancy. Not a conquest.'

She wiped the tears from her cheeks with the back of her hand. 'I do think of him that way. I do, honest, Casey. It's just like, well, it's just like I can't stop myself. I wouldn't have done it if had just been me and him, honest I wouldn't. It's just like Lauren tries to keep him all to herself, and I feel left out.'

Never a truer word, I thought. *Never a truer word has she yet spoken*. This was surely the nub of it, this instinctive behaviour. Learned, no doubt, at her mother's knee. Only metaphorically, maybe, but wasn't that the crux of it? That she knew no different than to compete for male attention in this way? To compete with her mother for the attention of the apparently countless boyfriends, and to play up to them too – to punish her mother for her lack of love by focusing that male attention on herself instead? I was no psychologist, but this was hardly rocket science, was it?

'You are a silly sausage,' I said, pulling her close. 'First off, Lauren's entitled to keep Kieron to herself – she is his girlfriend, after all! And you're all wrong about that anyway – it was *her* idea to take you bowling! She wants to be friends with you. They both do! Which is why you must try to think before you act. And as I've said before, there's plenty of time for you to be having boyfriends. Ones your *own* age. Not wrinkly old guys like my Kieron. That a deal?'

'That's a deal.'

'So shall we get back to that movie?'

In answer she clicked the remote and snuggled in even closer. And for the next hour, bar my dead arm pinioned under her, you could almost believe that just by talking and cuddling and being patient and really listening, you could fix all the ills in the world. Which you could, in many cases. I did actually believe that.

But this child, I'd soon learn, was just too broken.

Chapter 14

Predictably, the next few days passed without incident. A pattern of behaviour seemed to be emerging. We would have an outrageous tantrum or outburst, which Sophia would then try to explain away or ignore, and then she'd be especially good for a few days. Until the next event, anyway (which we rarely could predict with any certainty), when the cycle would start up again.

Both the agency and Sophia's social worker deemed this a good thing. That there was a pattern at all – all this repeated blowing up and then reining in – was seen to be evidence of 'progress'. In time, they felt, we would learn to read her and expose her 'triggers': which events or interactions (the illness aside) caused her to lose control, upon which 'we' could set about tackling them. That 'we', however, felt very much a royal 'you'. It was me and Mike, our whole family in fact, that would be at the sharp end of all this. *Great*, I thought. *We'll just keep on being emotionally battered – just as long as you've decided it's a 'good' thing.*

Casey Watson

Privately I wasn't so sure. I felt the pattern was just evidence of a structured routine, no more, no less, and that while we might make some progress with Sophia's behaviours it wasn't actually addressing the root problem.

But it wasn't for me to play psychiatrist, was it? I'd told John my concerns and that was all I could do. My job was to care for her, not treat her – I wasn't qualified, so best I get on with doing the stuff I *was* qualified for – giving our little lady an unforgettable thirteenth birthday.

By the time we reached the Wednesday before the big day I had pretty much got everything organised. I'd also asked Riley to come round and help me with some of the decorations while Sophia was at school.

Well, I say help me, but in reality it was me who was the helper. Ever since she became old enough to display her talents as an artist, it was Riley who became the family's creative consultant. She'd been on the internet and printed several photos she could work from, and soon had me busy cutting out all the giant witches and wizards she'd drawn. But then it came to the painting, and I was never much good at painting. Emulsion, yes, works of art, no.

I looked out of the window – it was a beautiful spring morning. Cold but clear. And Levi was getting fractious, which gave me an idea.

'Listen, love,' I said. 'Now we've got everything cut out ready, d'you mind if I go for a walk with Levi? He'd probably enjoy an hour in the fresh air and I'll just be a spare part watching you do all this, won't I?'

Riley grinned. 'Skiver! But no, be my guest, Mum. You'll only be under my feet hanging around here, anyway.'

'Charming!' I chided, pulling my coat on. But we both knew I'd be more hindrance than help if I stayed. As well as being artistic, Riley had a real artist's temperament – i.e. she'd trash my nice clean kitchen in no time, splattering it with poster paint and strewing bits of card and globs of glue everywhere. And I'd be bustling around then, trying to clear everything up, wiping surfaces that were due to get splattered again shortly, and generally getting on her nerves. I bundled the buggy out of the house before she changed her mind.

Levi was five months old now, and really beginning to notice the world around him. We walked down to our local duck pond and he laughed in delight as I tried to imitate their quacking noises for him. And as I sat there, my gorgeous grandson gurgling happily on my lap, I wondered how my life would be now if I didn't foster. It was like being in another world, sitting there with Levi. And another time, too, surrounded only by nature. No cars speeding by, no modern buildings, no hustle and bustle; just trees and dappled sunshine and early daffodils and crocuses. And the newest member of our family, who couldn't have made me happier. I sighed wistfully as I thought of life ever being that simple for me, of not always feeling pushed to do more. But it wouldn't happen. I knew fostering *was* me. And it was something I needed to do. All the years working with troubled kids in school had simply served to lead me to my vocation.

'Ah well, baby,' I said to Levi, 'better start heading back now. Don't want you catching a cold, do we?' He smiled lovingly up at me and dutifully clapped his hands – his new trick. And as we retraced our steps to home I found myself thinking just how lucky most children were, to have loving families, who would do anything to protect them and care for them. I felt a surge of love for my own two, who I knew I'd always feel proud of. I was so lucky. And I knew for certain that I would *always* foster, and no matter how bad things seemed we'd get through it – all of us as a family, I knew, would do our very best for the sad kids, the damaged kids, the unloved kids, the hurt kids – *any* child that came to us could be sure of that.

I couldn't believe how much Riley had accomplished by the time we got home. She'd painted two life-size witches and a wizard already, and laid them out on the conservatory floor to dry. They would make quite an impact when up on the walls – she was so clever. And better still, she'd even started clearing up.

'Leave that, love,' I said. 'I'll see to it. You put the kettle on.'

'Mum,' Riley grinned at me, 'don't think I didn't see your face when you left. You were itching to follow me round with the dustpan. I'm almost done, anyway. Go on, *you* put the kettle on.'

I laughed. My children knew me so well.

Five minutes later we were both out in the garden with coffees, while Levi slept soundly after our small adventure.

'I have just one problem,' I said, as we ran through the party plans. 'And that's what I'm going to do with Sophia while we get the place ready. I know it's only for a couple of hours, but I don't feel I can ask Kieron to take her out, not with how delicate things have been between them. And I need you here to help me, of course, to do your creative magic.'

'I know,' said Riley. 'Why don't you ask Lauren if she'll do it?'

'What?' I said, shocked. 'I can't see that happening. I don't think there's much love lost there, either.'

'No, listen. It might be the perfect way to help smooth things over. If Lauren agrees to it, it will prove an important point to Sophia – that adults don't hold grudges against kids about stuff. And also prove to her that Lauren does want to be her friend. Go on, ask her. I bet she says yes.'

Riley, it turned out, had been spot on. Not only was Lauren delighted to be able to help out, she even went one better and invited Sophia over to hers for a birthday sleepover. And as Lauren was a dance and arts student at college, she also knew exactly what to do with her.

'I thought we could start the evening off with some beauty treatments,' she told Sophia, once she'd put the suggestion to her. 'And then we could get into our PJs – gotta do that, haven't we? As it's a sleepover – and then I thought I could show you some of the stuff I've been learning for our end-of-year performance. I'm playing the part of Sandy in *Grease*.'

'Oh, my gosh!' Sophia squealed. 'I *love Grease*. Oh, I'm so jealous, Lauren! I know all the moves and everything!' She turned to me now. 'I can go, Casey, can't I? Please say yes!'

I was pleased to see that she was remembering her manners and asking for permission. Such a huge change from the imperious manner of her early days with us. 'Of course you can, love,' I said, laughing at her enthusiasm. All her doubts about Lauren seemed to be gone now. 'You can consider it one of your birthday treats, can't you?'

She lunged at me then, giving me an impromptu hug, and almost knocking me over in the process. 'Oh, thank you! Thank you, Lauren! Oh, it'll be just like *Grease*, won't it? Like that bit when all the girls are in Frenchy's bedroom, singing about Sandra Dee, won't it?'

I loved to see Sophia like this. But it was funny. When she acted older she seemed so much older than her years, and when she acted younger she really did seem like a much younger child; more like a 10-year-old than a high-school-hardened 12-year-old. Seeing her like this, you'd find it hard to believe she was going to be a teenager in just a couple of days – that event that all kids think will magically transform their lives. Such a paradox, she was. Such a conundrum.

So everything now was in place. Lauren would pick her up on Friday evening, then, after their girlie sleepover, would take her into town on the Saturday morning, where she'd treat her to breakfast. They'd then go shopping, so Sophia could choose her own birthday present from her and Kieron, now that she was 'going to be so grown up'. Odd, it occurred to me, and also rather sad, that we were busy reclaiming her childhood in order to help her leave it behind.

* * *

It was a great help having Sophia away at Lauren's on the Friday evening, not just because it meant we could get the decorating under way earlier, but also because it gave Mike and me a precious evening to ourselves, which was something we both badly needed. And that meant that I woke up feeling refreshed rather than frazzled, and looking forward to the special day ahead.

Not everyone shared my serenity, however. I came into the living room to find Riley, having put the finishing touches to the decorations, transforming a very reluctant Kieron into a wizard.

'Riley, please,' he whined. 'Can't Dad be the wizard? I wanted to be the prince,' he added petulantly.

'Oh, stop moaning, Kieron! The prince stuff is too big for you, I told you! Besides, the wizard is the *real* star of the show.'

'Riley,' he huffed. 'I'm not eight years old now. You can't con me like you used to, so don't try.'

I smiled to myself. There were many downsides to fostering for my 'apparently' adult children. But the upside was the chance to continue their own childhoods by dressing up in silly outfits and squabbling like little kids. It was enriching in the most unexpected ways. For me anyway – I loved hearing them together.

'Hey, you two,' I called to them, from my precarious perch on the step-ladder in the conservatory, 'once you've finished bickering you can come in here and help me pin up all these goats and munchkins, or whatever they bloody are!'

I really needed Mike with me, so he could pin up the high bits, but by now he was off upstairs transforming himself into a handsome prince. Riley, too, was all done – she made a brilliant bad witch Elphaba – so it was just me all behind, undressed and unpainted. I really needed to get a move on.

Upstairs all was ready for Sophia. We'd got her a Glinda costume, Glinda being the beautiful Good Witch of the North, which we knew would be the costume she'd most want for herself, and the best suited with her pretty face and blonde locks. That said, now that I'd at last familiarised myself with the story, I couldn't help thinking she was more of an Elphaba, the witch that didn't start out bad, never wanted to *be* bad, but the one who ended up bad – the tragic product of her circumstances. The one who, by the end of *Wicked* (which was before *The Wizard of Oz* story started) had become the witch we all knew and loved to hate. I got down from the step-ladder and had a moment of sad reflection. I could only hope Sophia's future wasn't so certain.

But this wasn't the day for negative thoughts or amateur philosophy, so I popped 'Defying Gravity' on the CD player – my favourite song from the musical – which shook off my melancholic musings about the birthday girl and put me in a party frame of mind again. We had quite a lot of people coming and they'd soon be arriving: my eldest brother, who was visiting from Ireland and his children, my sister and hers, plus my mum and dad, of course, and Jack Boyd, Sophia's social worker. He was clearly her favourite and seemed genuinely fond of her, and was keen to make the effort to come and join us for an hour.

I'd also managed to invite three mates from her school. Despite her protestations that all the girls hated her, it seemed Sophia had made a few friends, and fortunately I already knew the mothers of three of them. So I'd secretly invited Mollie, Corin and Dannika, and had them promise to keep things quiet till the big day.

Which was fast disappearing, I thought, as I bolted upstairs to get myself ready. A quick five-minute transformation and I was finally good to go, and Riley and I could lay out the buffet. I'd gone overboard, as always, and Mike's two pasting tables were groaning with food. We had sandwiches, sausage rolls and all the usual savouries, plus lots of themed stuff – green cupcakes, green jellies with bugs in and a green trifle, as well as a big green-and-black birthday cake, in the shape of a witch's hat, which came courtesy of my very clever mum. Riley was just finishing filling the gaps between the plates with plastic spiders when Mike came down to help us finish off.

'This looks great, Case – you've surpassed yourselves as usual, girls,' he told us.

'And so have you, Dad,' Riley answered. 'You almost look handsome.'

'And you,' he came back, quick as you like, 'darling daughter, look like the little witch I always knew you were!'

'Ahem!' I coughed, doing a little twirl. 'And *moi*?'

Father and daughter both shrugged and pretended they hadn't heard, which earned the pair of them a friendly slap on their rears.

'You look gorgeous, love,' Mike said eventually, laughing. 'No matter how many warts you start to grow. But listen, it's nearly one, and Jack Boyd will be here any minute. How about I go make us all a quick coffee?'

He was just pouring them when the doorbell rang. Kieron answered. It *was* Jack. 'Hello, young man!' he said, in his booming Irish brogue. Sophia's favourite social worker was nothing if not a character. 'Look at you!' he exclaimed. 'I wish I'd known you were all going to be dressing up. I'd have brought my own witch along, so I would!' Kieron ushered him into the kitchen and Mike got another mug down for coffee. 'But as it happens,' Jack continued, 'she's taken the kids shopping ...'

'I'd like to see you say that to her face!' Mike laughed.

Jack grinned. 'You're into blood sports, then, Mike?'

So far so good, I thought. This was going to be a great party. Just as long as the birthday girl was having a good day as well. And it seemed, when she arrived, that she was. I'd had everyone hide in the living room for her arrival, and, bang on cue, they all leapt out. 'Surprise!'

And she seemed genuinely thrilled. 'Oh, my gosh! Oh, you guys! Oh, Casey, I don't know what to say! And oh my *God*! It's all *Wicked*! And you're Elphaba, Riley! Oh, it's brilliant!' She was practically jumping up and down.

'And you're Glinda,' I told her. 'Or you will be, in a minute. Just as soon as you pop upstairs and put on your costume ...'

She clapped her hands together. 'Oh, that's brilliant!' she cried, needing no further encouragement. Screaming her delight, she shot straight off upstairs.

I turned to the assembled guests. 'Yup, I think she's happy, don't you? So let the party start. Kieron? Music, maestro, please!'

Sophia's second entrance was equally dramatic. She really did look beautiful in her costume. She was also in her element with all the compliments she was getting, and dutiful – I noticed how she went round every guest individually, thanking them personally for coming and for all the gifts she was given. She was thrilled to bits with her new mobile, and once again threw her arms around me, and though she once again nearly decked me – she was just so much taller than I was – I was quietly thrilled myself to see how tactile she was becoming and, most of all, in a non-sexual way. 'Oh, I just love it,' she said. 'And I promise to save plenty of pocket money for credit. I'll never ask you for credit for it, honest. Ooh, my friends are going to be soooo jealous. It's wicked!' With which she skipped off to find them, bright eyed and beaming.

Jack Boyd had bought her a new leather handbag, which looked expensive, and perhaps a little over-extravagant, but it wasn't for me to comment, and she did look so thrilled with it. He too was the recipient of a giant bear hug. He had the grace to blush and gently extracted himself, even if, on this occasion, it looked entirely innocent.

He had to be on his way then, so I did take the opportunity to see him out. I'd barely spoken to him since Sophia's arrival and it would be good to have a word.

'Thanks for coming, Jack,' I said. 'It's so obvious how much it means to her.'

'I do try,' he said. 'I kind of feel I'm the closest link she has to her mother. I'm not really, of course, it's just that I've been there since the beginning. I like to think she sees me of one of her few "constants".'

'I'm sure she does,' I agreed. I paused. 'Jack, can I ask you something about Sophia?'

'For sure.'

'Well, it's just that she acts out around Kieron and Mike – in a really full-on way – and it's caused, well, a couple of dramas.' Gold medal for understatement there, I thought ruefully. 'And when she does it, it's almost like she becomes someone else. It's really marked, and, to be honest, a little scary – a little *spooky*. Do you have any experience of that sort of thing yourself?'

To my surprise, Jack's face coloured. You could see the blush so clearly. 'I'm afraid I know just what you mean,' he confessed. 'To be honest, for a while I was quite concerned about it. So much so that I stopped taking her out in my car unless there was another adult in there with us. It was uncomfortable, to say the least. But it stopped. After a couple of months she just stopped doing it. I don't know why – perhaps she realised it wasn't getting her anywhere ... But definitely unsettling. Especially for so young a girl. And of course I always had the business with the boyfriends on my mind. And then the family placement breaking down ... But you know the background ...'

'I do now,' I said, nodding. 'And it explains a great deal.'

'Terrible tragedy. Still, you seem to be doing a marvellous job with her.'

'We're doing our best,' I said. 'It's pretty challenging, but I'd like to think Jean will see a difference when we hand her back.'

'Um, well, yes ... Anyway, better let you get back to your party. Thanks for inviting me. Say goodbye to Mike. Speak soon.'

I went back inside. What did 'Um, well, yes' mean? Well, no matter. I was just pleased to find Sophia still in such fine fettle. She was now entertaining her friends with some funny quotes from *Wicked*. My nieces and nephews were with her too, and they all seemed to be having fun. Time to slip out into the back garden for a sneaky fag with Riley.

'Isn't it great to see her like this, Mum?' she said, gesturing to the chair beside her. 'It's so sad that she can't always be so happy.'

'Riley, love, *no* teenager ever stays this happy.'

'Oh, you know what I mean. I mean nobody would imagine, seeing her now, would they? No one would guess that she has so many problems – so much sadness in her life.'

I sighed. I knew exactly what she meant. It was tough, seeing the girl that she could be – that she *should* be – yet knowing the turmoil and distress of the girl inside. No family – well, no family that wanted anything to do with her, and having to spend her birthday in the company of virtual strangers. *No*, I thought. *Shake it off, Case. Just do the very best you can for her. Make sure the time she spends with you is at least as happy as it can be.* She would be safe, she would be cared for, she would be given all the guidance I could muster. Anything to help her move on and live a happy, productive life.

* * *

As I closed the door on the last of my guests that afternoon, I did so with renewed passion for my job. It was silly – perhaps unrealistic – for me to want to try and move mountains. But if I couldn't make a huge impact on every child that came my way, I could at least try to – and so often it was the little things that mattered. Helping them to trust again, to feel secure, to know they had a place of safety, would never be harmed here.

Mike was at the door with me, my very own handsome prince, and I knew he knew exactly what I was thinking. Perhaps he was thinking it himself, even. He certainly didn't seem to mind when I gave him a hug and a kiss and smeared green face paint all over him. I didn't have to say anything. I knew he understood the emotions I was feeling. I felt energised, motivated. Like I was doing what I was born to.

Which, unbeknown to me, was just as well. I'd soon need every ounce of those resources that I could muster.

Chapter 15

They say life is what happens when you've made other plans, don't they? A great expression, and particularly apt in my line of work. Because one thing you can always expect is the unexpected. But, high on a successful party, and flushed after an hour's cleaning, I think I took my eye off the ball.

The garden and conservatory clear now, I decided to pop up and have a quick shower before tackling the kitchen. We had plenty of green jelly, but inexplicably no milk, so while Kieron went to buy some, in order that we could all have a much-needed coffee, I thought I'd take the opportunity to scrub away my sticky green face. Not to mention the witch's hair, liberally coated in grey spray paint by my darling daughter, which had horrified me every time I'd glanced in a mirror. If this was what I was going to look like in old age, I decided, you could forget about growing old gracefully. Thank heavens for the miracle of hair dye.

I felt much better once I'd managed to restore my raven tresses, and having tied them back and pulled on a pair of trackies and an old T-shirt, I went down to join Mike in the kitchen.

Sophia was apparently up in her room, sorting her presents, but Kieron was with him, having returned with the milk. And as my lovely hubby had already made a sizeable dent in the washing up, the three of us spent a pleasant twenty minutes at the table, just chilling out and chatting about the success of the day. I loved those family moments, just relaxing, after an industrious but productive bout of team work. Though, in this case, it was the calm before the storm.

'Casey?' Sophia's voice. 'Can I borrow your curling tongs, please?'

We all had our backs to her and all turned as one. And, to my dismay, she was standing there, made up to the nines and wearing nothing bar a black lacy bra and minuscule matching thong. And the smirk on her face was equally revealing.

Kieron spoke first, his eyes blazing. 'Go and get some clothes on, you little idiot! What the hell d'you think you're doing?'

I stood up and pushed my chair back. 'Sophia,' I said calmly, anxious not to allow this to flare up. 'Room, please. You know the rules in this house about appropriate dressing. Go and get dressed, please, and then you and I shall have a little talk, and *then* I shall dig out my tongs for you.'

She took a step, but not out of the room – closer *to* us. 'What is *wrong* with you people?' she wanted to know. 'It's only underwear, for God's sake!' She turned to Kieron. 'And don't you come over all horrified with me, Kieron. I'm sure you've seen *Lauren* dressed like this.'

Mike, who had been silent up to now, was seething. I could see it. He practically launched his chair at the wall opposite as he stood up. He marched wordlessly past Sophia, out of the door and up the stairs.

Kieron, too, was pale faced with anger. 'Don't you dare,' he said to Sophia. 'Don't you *dare* talk about my girlfriend like that! Mum, I'm sorry, but I'm off. I'll be at Lauren's if you need me.' He too marched past Sophia, but as he did so he turned. 'No one wants to look at you like that,' he hissed at her, 'with your tarty underwear and your cheap permatan. Not me. Not Dad. Not *anyone*. You just have to go too far, don't you? *Pathetic.*'

'Oh, piss off, Kieron,' she said. 'You little wimp. You probably don't even know what a woman looks like!' And with this, to my consternation and horror, she put her hands on her hips and began to gyrate them, thrusting her pelvis out provocatively. Kieron's words all those weeks ago came back to me, then. It *was* like *The Exorcist*. It was like she was possessed. Where'd the sweet girl of just an hour ago disappeared to? It was horrible to watch. Just horrible.

'Sophia!' I yelled at her. 'Stop that right now! Get up to your room, do you hear me? I mean it!'

Kieron had already marched off to the front door and I felt tears well in my eyes as he slammed it. What the hell was going on? This was just awful.

'I'll go to my room when I'm good and ready!' she shouted, spit flying from her mouth towards me. 'And you can tell that pathetic son of yours that this is not a "perma-tan". It's fucking melatonin, okay? And I can't fucking help it!'

I gaped, unable to think of a single thing to say to her. But she hadn't finished anyway. 'And,' she continued, 'I am 13 years old and can wear what I fucking well like!'

'Not in this house, young lady!'

Mike. Back from upstairs. He threw a bathrobe towards her. 'Put that on right this minute! And fasten it! How many times do we have to tell you, eh? Eh? If you're only wearing underwear then the decent thing's to *cover yourself up*!'

'Piss off!' she said again. 'You can't make me!' Sophia was looking scarily angry now, almost out of control, her stance rigid, her expression hard. She wasn't so much speaking to as snarling at Mike. She'd ignored the bathrobe and it had fallen to the floor. He retrieved it, then slung it unceremoniously over her shoulders. 'Room!' he then bellowed at her. '*Now!*'

'No!' she screamed at him. 'You want me to move, then *you'll* have to *fucking move me*!'

I couldn't quite believe what happened next. To my horror, Mike simply picked her up from behind, and, holding her by the elbows, carried her out into the hall and up the stairs. I followed him out of the kitchen and gazed on in shock as she screamed at him, kicked him and head-butted him all the way. He's a big man, my husband, but Sophia was a big girl, and, in her fury, fired up with so much adrenalin, she was fearfully strong, too. It must have hurt him.

'Put me down, you fucking animal! I fucking *hate* you! You old bastard!' She never stopped screaming abuse at him, not once, all the way to the unintended return journey to her room. I felt sick as I watched the scene unravel. How had our lovely day managed to turn into this?

I felt helpless as well. This didn't feel right, was not right. He had no choice, he was angry, he was only human. Only *human*. But Mike had laid hands on her. He had physically removed her. This was not supposed to happen. All our training had taught us that. De-escalate a confrontation. Defuse anger. Deflect violence. Walk away. Walk away until everything calms down.

But I didn't blame him. Training was fine, but all the training in the world couldn't prepare you for the real thing, the here and now. Not for a situation such as this, where no matter how hard you try to keep things calm, you just know it's still going to get worse. And I did know that. I'd known it the minute she'd arrived in the kitchen, near-naked, just as soon as I'd seen the expression on her face. Sophia was ready for a fight. Spoiling for one. And wasn't going to stop until she got one.

I thought, desperately. Why? What was the bloody 'trigger' here? Was it the contrast? As she sat in her room amid her presents, did the contrast between her day – all the fun, all the gifts – just prove too much, when set against her real life, to bear? I tried to put myself in her shoes, walk the proverbial mile in them. Was that it? She just had to let her anger out? Justin, her predecessor, would attack his own body, would sit with a knife and tear off his own toenails. Was this Sophia's version of exactly the same process? Look – I'm a monster! Look how easily I can make you hate me!

I heard a door slam upstairs, followed by more bangs and screams, then Mike appeared at the top of the staircase, looking ashen and dishevelled. He started down them. God, I thought, he looks ten years older! And bizarrely, a stray thought popped into my head, that perhaps I'd better dye his hair too.

He reached the bottom and tried to flatten it down. 'She can stay up there for the rest of the night. I've had it,' he said.

'Are you okay, love?'

'No, I'm raging.' He shook his head and touched my shoulder. 'I'm not hurt, love, if that's what you mean. She's bloody strong, though, I'll give her that. Jesus. Don't ever take her on at martial arts, love, I mean it. She'd be bloody lethal, I tell you!'

It sort of defused the tension, him saying that. But this was serious.

'I'm going to have to call EDT, aren't I?' I said.

EDT are the emergency duty team, a service you could access if you had a crisis at the weekend or out of hours. You told an unknown – and therefore uninvolved – social worker the problem and they logged all the details for you. They would then decide what to do according to the specific situation. For example, if you were reporting a child who had run away, they would take a description, log the details and then call the police. Going through the EDT was an important first step for a carer, as it not only supported you, but also created a formal record of events.

And in this case it was important that we involved them right now, in case things got worse and the situation escalated, or Sophia put in a complaint with her own version of events. This did happen from time to time, so it was made clear to us in training that we must be very thorough about recording all incidents like this, particularly if actual physical contact had taken place. And, truth be known, I also wanted my thoughts on her mental instability to be recorded in as many places as possible. Her team might be keen to make light of her 'behaviours', but no one who had witnessed what we had just witnessed could be in any doubt that this wasn't just a particularly ranty teenage tantrum but clear evidence that her mind was all over the place. When would someone else accept that this child was *ill*?

I phoned EDT while Mike made more coffee. This was going to be a long night – we both felt sure of that – and we wanted to feel we were prepared. I spoke to a really nice, sympathetic social worker, who assured me I'd done the right thing. Her name was Christine and she promised me she'd get everything logged and be at the end of the line, any time, all night.

But as it turned out I didn't need to call Christine again, as the rest of the evening was quiet. Sophia did as she was told and remained in her room, only coming down, at around ten, to get a drink. None of us spoke; she clearly felt as disinclined as us to engage. And after making a big huffy show of banging around the kitchen, she went back up to bed, and I, for one, was grateful. I did sleep eventually, Mike too – we were both shattered. But I woke on Sunday morning with that horrible sinking feeling as the events of the previous day immediately clamoured for my attention. I gently shook Mike.

'Are you going to get up and come down with me, love?' I didn't feel able to face the day – and potentially Sophia – on my own yet.

'Course, love,' he said, stretching and then gathering me close for a cuddle. 'But let's give it ten minutes first, eh? I've been thinking about last night.' He gave me a squeeze. 'You and me both, eh? And it's so obvious – Sophia is a lot more disturbed than anyone thought. I mean, she was scary to watch. That wasn't just a show of temper, was it? It was horrendous. And we're just not equipped to deal with that sort of stuff. I think she's mentally ill, and I think it needs dealing with. But not by us. By the right people.'

I nodded. 'I agree. I was thinking the same. When I speak to John tomorrow I'm going to ask him if we can enlist the help of CAMHS or something.'

CAMHS was the child and adolescent mental health service. Social services used it as a first port of call when a child displayed the sort of disturbing behaviours Sophia had. The only snag was that I knew from my time in school that they always had a long waiting list. And they were very particular about who they'd work with, too. Their rules generally allowed for them to work only with children in long-term, settled placements. The reasoning was simple – that their input would not then be interrupted by things like a move or a change to a new school.

But it had to be worth a shot. This needed addressing as a matter of urgency. I was more convinced than ever that this child needed help we couldn't give her.

'Right, that's settled, then,' Mike said, swinging his legs out of bed. 'Come on, shorty, let's get going. But an easy day for you, today. Starting with food. No cooking dinner. We're going out for Sunday lunch. And treating Riley and David as well, I think, yes? They deserve a treat after all the hard work they put in yesterday. And we need to get some normality back into our bloody lives.' He frowned then. 'But best leave Kieron and Lauren out of the mix, eh? I think he'll need a couple of days away from it all, you know, to calm down.'

I felt wretched all over again, thinking of my poor son. And also unsure about taking Sophia anywhere today.

'You think that's wise?' I said, pulling on my dressing gown. 'Us all going out? I'm not sure I have the energy to deal with her here, let alone take her out in public.'

Mike sat down on the bed. 'I think that's *exactly* what we need to do, Case. Take control of the situation, not let it control us.'

I smiled then. 'That's what you used to say when Riley was a baby and she was off on one – d'you remember?'

'Oh, yes,' he said. 'And the same applies here.' He nodded towards the direction of Sophia's room. 'I reckon she's going to be in there *dreading* facing us today, don't you? So the best we can do is to play everything down. We've got a plan on now, we've logged what happened, we're dealing with it. No point in ranting. It'll just fall on deaf ears. Today we just accept her apology – and I'm sure there'll be one – and get on with the business of having a normal happy family Sunday. Agreed?'

I nodded. He was right. 'Agreed.'

'Though if I'm wrong, and she comes out all guns blazing, like Paul Newman and Robert Redford at the end of *Butch Cassidy* ...'

'Then what?'

He winked. 'Then I'm packing a bag and leaving home.'

But as it turned out he didn't need to. No sooner had we got downstairs and brewed the coffee than Sophia arrived in the kitchen. She was belted up tight in her PJs and dressing gown, her eyes looking like she'd gone ten rounds with a cage fighter. She must have been crying for hours.

'Oh, Mike,' she said in such a tiny voice. 'Oh, Casey.'

And then she sat down and promptly burst into tears.

Chapter 16

I'd purposely not told Riley about the night before when I called her, but between then and now she'd obviously spoken to Kieron. And he'd obviously filled her in on all the details.

'Well, if it isn't little Miss Wonderbra,' was how she greeted my young charge when we arrived at the pub. I winced as I watched Sophia's face redden.

'I'm sorry, Riley,' she said. 'I didn't mean any harm, honest. I just kind of had a funny turn, I think.' She lowered her gaze and began fiddling with her cutlery. I interjected.

'Yes, she certainly did have a funny turn, love, that's for sure. But as your gran used to say, least said soonest mended. Come on, let's have that baby off you. Come and sit down. So. Which is it to be, everyone? Beef or pork?'

Mike had been right. It had been a good idea to get out. The house felt closed in after so much shouting and upset, and luckily our favourite pub, in the next village to our one, had a big enough table free to accommodate us all.

Following the drama of Saturday night, Sunday morning had been a surprisingly calm aftermath. We'd just sat down with Sophia, and while I hugged her and tried to comfort her Mike had calmly told her that we were a little worried about these 'funny turns' of hers, and that we were going to see if we could get some proper help for her. She was meek and acquiescent – clearly as shattered as she looked – and agreed that she didn't understand why these rages overtook her. Or this urge to be so provocative all the time.

And then we told her that was the end of it, and that we were going out for a big roast lunch, and she immediately brightened, before us mentioning that Riley and David would be there too.

'You won't tell them?'

'No,' I said. 'As Mike says, it's all done with. Now why don't you take your medicine, have a quick bite to eat, then perhaps go back to bed for a couple of hours?'

It was a shame, then, that Riley had felt the need to have a dig, but I completely understood – sibling loyalty ran deep with my children. And because of his Asperger's, Riley felt particularly protective towards her little brother, so I knew how enraged she'd probably have been.

But lunch was fine; perfectly pleasant, not least because Levi stole the show, taking pride of place in his high chair, which I'd parked next to Sophia, keeping everyone's minds otherwise occupied. And, once we were done with the main course, and Sophia asked if she could take him out into the pub garden for a push around in his buggy, I was only too happy to say yes. Riley and I could join her, in fact, and cram in a sneaky cigarette while she did so.

We waited till Sophia was out of earshot, at the play area, before discussing what was uppermost in both of our minds. 'But, Mum,' said Riley, once I'd explained how we wanted to play it, 'surely you turning a blind eye isn't going to help her. If you do that, how's she going to know the things she does are wrong?'

In many other circumstances Riley would have been right. But not this one. 'That's just it, love. She already knows it's wrong. I know she does. The problem is that she doesn't seem to be able to control herself. She's like a completely different person when she acts out in that way.'

'So just ignore it, then? Is that what you're saying?'

'Well, no. We still have to acknowledge what she does. But it's becoming increasingly obvious that telling her off gets us nowhere. No, this is the long game, I think, love. We have to cry for help ourselves this time, and loudly. And not stop until we actually get some.'

I could see Mike gesturing from inside the pub, poking his finger towards his open mouth. 'C'mon, love,' I said, putting out my cigarette. 'I think Dad wants to order desserts.' I waved to Sophia and beckoned her back as well. 'And, look, thanks, love. It's a trial, I know, but I really think she's ill.'

Riley frowned. 'Just as long as she doesn't make *you* ill, that's all. Or Dad.'

'We're fine, love,' I reassured her. 'I promise.'

And that was exactly how I did feel. A new Monday, and I was full of a new determination to make progress. I was intent on getting the support Sophia needed and, just as I'd said to Riley, I wasn't going to stop until I got her some. I was feeling better in all senses. We'd had a peaceful afternoon, I'd had a much better night's sleep, and best of all was that Kieron had called on Sunday evening and promised to come home again after college this evening, provided we had settled Sophia down.

But once Sophia had left for school and Mike for work, I still took some time to get my facts in order, going through my log and listing each occurrence separately, so I could present a coherent case for more support. I really needed to paint a clear picture of how things were escalating, making it clear that her medical condition, initially deemed to be the main challenge, was now secondary to the stability of her mind.

'I think you're right, Casey,' John conceded after I'd read my list out to him. 'It does seem like she's unravelling emotionally, doesn't it? This obviously runs deeper than we've been led to believe. And I'm sorry. Sorry that you and Mike are having to go through all this upset.' He sighed. 'Victims of your own success, you two, I think. We all just assume that you're dealing with everything. We've not been very supportive here, have we?'

'We don't feel like that, John,' I said. 'We know you're there if we need you. I just feel very strongly that this needs to be flagged up as urgent – we need to access appropriate help for her.'

Happily, John promised me that's what we'd get. He would, he said, get in touch with social services for me, plus contact CAMHS and see what could be sorted. 'And I'll call you later,' he finished, 'so we can arrange for us all to meet up.'

Ah, meetings, I thought, as I put down the phone. There was always the promise of a meeting to hang on to. Nothing immediate, of course. Just another meeting. That was the way it was in social work, miles of red tape that couldn't be cut. And, great as social services were – and they were – there was rarely a sense of any urgency to make or break lives at these meetings. Perhaps the real trick would be to kindly ask these poor kids if they could just put their emotional breakdowns on hold for a couple of weeks.

I went into the kitchen to make some toast. I felt frustrated. There was nothing I could do now but wait. But in the meantime I could perhaps go and shop for a new handbag. Now that would cheer me up, I thought. A brilliant idea. And then I smiled to myself at the way my mind worked. Here I was, almost at breaking point, my poor son struggling with living in his own home, and all I could think about was buying handbags!

I didn't rush, however, and John was back on the phone before I left, with the news that CAMHS had agreed to see Sophia as a one-off and that he would speak to all involved *re* the timings. No promises, as she would still need to fulfil their criteria, but at least it was a start.

I went off to the shops in happier mood. One which sadly, however, wasn't to last. It was around 1 p.m. by the time I'd scratched my handbag itch sufficiently, buying a beautiful, shiny, red patent number, that was gorgeous and perfect but still not so costly that it would need to spend time hidden from Mike at the back of the wardrobe. I was just thinking about some lunch when my phone rang.

'Hellooo!' I answered chirpily, not even glancing at the display, as I'd fully expected it to be Riley.

'Mrs Watson? Casey? It's Mr Barker. Sorry to disturb you, but can you talk?'

My heart sank. Mr Barker as in Sophia's head of year. 'Yes, of course,' I said. 'Is she ill again?'

'Not this time,' he answered. 'Though it's rather serious even so. Were you aware she brought a mobile phone into school this morning?'

Shit, I thought. *I didn't even think about that.*

'No, I wasn't,' I said, thinking privately that he was going a bit overboard. Loads of kids took their phones into school. 'But listen,' I went on. 'That's my fault. It was a birthday present and I never thought about telling her they weren't allowed in school.'

'It's not the fact that she brought it in,' Mr Barker said. 'It's what she's been doing with it that's the problem.'

'I don't understand.'

'We've just had a visit from a very angry parent. Jake Enfield's mum just brought him back in from lunch, complaining about some disturbing pictures on his phone that had apparently been sent to him by Sophia.'

Oh, no … 'What kind of photos?'

'Naked photos, essentially. And I gather from Jake that quite a few of the boys have had them.'

'Oh good Lord! I'll come straight up. Assuming you want me to. Is she in class at the moment?'

'No, we've got her in the medical room. She's refusing to hand over her phone to us, and we were hoping you might be able to persuade her. We need to know who else has the pictures so we can be sure they're all deleted.'

I felt both angry and dismayed as I left town and drove to the school. After all we'd said yesterday! What on earth had possessed her? But what point was there in trying to fathom her out? That was the problem. You couldn't try to rationalise such unfathomable behaviour. That was precisely why we needed the mental health team.

When I arrived in the medical room she was sitting stubbornly in the corner, clutching her school bag as if her life depended on it. Think, Casey, think. How to play this.

I sat opposite her, trying to focus her attention on me, rather than the angry-looking teacher who'd followed me in there. Mr Barker was there too, standing to one side of her.

'You okay, love?' I said gently. 'I've just been saying to Mr Barker that this is partly my fault for forgetting to tell you this morning. Mobiles aren't allowed in school.'

Sophia just stared incredulously. '*Everyone* brings their phones into school, Casey.'

'I dare say,' I agreed. 'But now you've been caught with yours, you're not going to be allowed to bring it in again.'

'Fine!' she snapped. 'So I'm being sent home now, right? In which case, can we just leave now?'

'In a minute, sweetheart. I just need to delete those silly pictures first. We don't want everyone looking at them, do we?'

'I've already deleted them,' she said, looking daggers at the other teacher. 'You think I wanted these pervs gawping at me?'

'Don't be rude,' I said mildly. 'And I still need the phone. It's not just that they're gone, it's who else already has them. You don't want a load of other parents seeing them, do you?'

It seemed to dawn on her, then, that this was now out of her control. She undid the zip on her bag and practically threw the phone at me, and we soon had, even with my limited phone skills, the numbers of six other boys she'd sent the pictures to.

Thankfully, the school were happy to leave things at that, even though I knew that they had their own view on my softly-softly approach to disciplining her. But I was reticent about mentioning the mental health team as yet, because I didn't want to destabilise her life further by having them get involved and 'label' her. At least not until I knew where we were going.

As for Sophia, we were going nowhere fast. On the way home she simply made good use of her right to silence and doggedly refused to answer any of my questions. Which did the trick. I decided to give up trying.

I kept the phone, though. If she refused to play ball, then so did I. Perhaps it would at least make her reflect on the consequences of her actions. But what I didn't expect was that it would do exactly that – while Sophia reflected on the consequences of *her* actions, I'd be reflecting on the possible consequences of Mike's.

It was Thursday when it happened. Around 9 p.m. Mike and I were sitting watching the news when the phone rang in the hall. Kieron was in his room and Sophia was asleep in bed, and my first thought – my only thought – was that it must be my mum. She often called at this time, when she knew we could chat in peace and, like many her age, she didn't much do mobiles.

But it wasn't my mum, it was Jean, Sophia's previous carer.

'Oh, hello,' I said, once she'd introduced herself to me and I'd had that whole '*Jean? Jean who?*' thing run quickly through my mind. I'd only met her once, after all. 'How are you?' I said, conscious of how ill she'd been.

'Oh, *I'm* fine,' she said, her voice clipped and curt. 'Thank you very much. Although I can't say the same for Sophia.'

Both the words and the tone did two things. One was to get my hackles up. Who'd speak to a near stranger in such an aggressive way? And the other was to make me do a double take. How would *she* know how Sophia was? We were the ones looking after her. Very odd. Then I had a thought. Had John said something to her? I doubted it. But even if he had, what was with the sarcasm?

'I'm afraid you've lost me, Jean,' I answered pleasantly, albeit with gritted teeth. 'What about Sophia?'

'She hasn't rung me for three days, so I know something's wrong.' Again, that accusatory tone. 'I've been trying her mobile,' she continued, 'and it's going straight to voicemail. Now why would that be?'

Now I was confused as well as irritated. Three days? What did she mean? When had she been speaking to Sophia?

'I don't understand,' I said. 'Have you been on the phone to Sophia?'

Mike had turned down the TV and come out into the hall. He was watching me, puzzled, making a '*what*?' face.

'Yes, of course, 'Jean replied. 'She phones me often. Well, when she can get to the phone and have some privacy, that is … I had hoped that with her mobile it would get a little easier, but it seems you've put a stop to that too, have you?'

Had it been long enough, my jaw would have hit the floor about now.

'What?' I said. 'Jean, Sophia has no business phoning you. Not without our permission, anyway. And the mobile we bought her is none of your business. And, frankly, I don't like your tone.'

'Oh, I'll bet you don't,' she barked back at me, almost shouting now. 'Were you afraid she might tell me all about how she was dragged bodily up the stairs by your husband? Well, you're too late, because …'

Now it was my turn to raise my voice. I couldn't help it. I was furious. 'How dare you speak to me like that!' I replied. 'I'm going to hang up now and I suggest that you don't ring my house again, okay?'

Whatever she said in reply I didn't hear, because I slammed the receiver straight down. 'Oh. My. God!' I seethed.

'What?' Mike said. 'What was all *that* about? Who the hell was it?'

I had started crying now, as you do when you've been upset out of the blue. And shaking, too. 'God! That bloody woman! I'm so mad, Mike, I could scream!'

'But what did she say?'

'Sophia's been ringing her, apparently, and since she's been here, presumably. Giving her updates on how we're treating her – well, that would seem to be the gist of it. God, I can't believe it! Who the hell does she think she is?'

'But what did she *say*?'

'She was cross that her mobile's going to voicemail. The cheek of it! The mobile *we* bought her!'

I tried hard to mentally gather myself together. I didn't want to tell Mike what she'd said about him. That wouldn't help. But, God, I felt betrayed. And also terrible. Why had she done this? No, that was stupid. Why did Sophia do anything? But even so I still felt like I'd been slapped in the face. We were trying so hard, but she was clearly unhappy with us all. Why else would she go behind our backs like that?

It took a massive effort of will not to confront Sophia the following morning, fruitless though the act would probably be anyway. I'd doubtless be met with another bout of sullen silence, which in my current mood I wouldn't have taken quite so gently as I had earlier in the week. But Mike was firm. We must try to avoid escalating another outburst. And the fault lay not with Sophia, not really. Despite my pique, her feelings about us – me – were her own affair. It was the subterfuge I couldn't stand – that and Jean's tone. How dare she stand in judgement based on the complaints of an unstable 13-year-old child? She'd been trained as a foster carer, hadn't she? So she bloody well should have used some judgement of her own!

No, it was John that I needed to speak to. Right now. I called him as soon as I had the house to myself and spent five minutes trying to keep from losing my temper as I related the conversation.

'So I hung up on her,' I said. 'And I'm still seething. What makes her think she had a right to do this? I tell you, I feel totally undermined.'

'I do understand,' he soothed. 'It must have been a dreadful shock. No matter what you think, though, I'm quite sure this isn't born out of malice. She really does just have Sophia's best interests at heart. No, she shouldn't have done what she did. Of course not. But I think she carries a lot of guilt about abandoning her, and ...'

'John, she hardly abandoned her, for goodness' sake. She was ill. It's not like she won't be having her back soon ...'

There was an uncomfortable silence, then John cleared his throat. Uh-oh. I knew that noise of old.

'Well, that's the thing. I was going to wait till I came up for our meeting so I could tell you and Mike face to face ...'

I felt a chill pass through me. What had been said? Had Jean encouraged Sophia to put in a complaint? *What*? 'What's happened?' I said. 'Is she still ill? She did sound a bit wired ...'

'Actually, no. It's not that. And please don't breathe a *word* to Sophia, obviously, but, well, she doesn't want her back. Casey, she's resigned.'

'Oh, God, John,' I said. 'Really?'

He sighed. 'I'm afraid so.'

Chapter 17

My mind was in turmoil now. How was this going to affect everything? How was Sophia going to take it? And where did it leave us, exactly? I felt anger, too. That she'd wimped out on everything. I tried to rein it in – I didn't know the circumstances around it all, did I? But after the way she'd spoken to me it was hard to feel charitable.

'It's been a shock to us all, Casey,' John went on. 'No one expected this. But it seems Jean's not terribly resilient, I'm afraid. Quite the opposite, in fact. Off the record, she's something of a delicate soul and it seems fostering's been a bit of a shock to her system.'

It had been a shock to mine too, I thought, so I could certainly understand that. But even so, it wasn't something you took on lightly. Surely someone during her training would have counselled her thoroughly and recognised she wouldn't be cut out for it? Our kind of fostering, at any rate. I said so.

'Maybe it was just too much like being thrown in at the deep end,' John mused. Then he cleared his throat.

'Actually, I found something else out about that. She's not a specialist, Casey. I had that wrong. She was just a main-stream foster carer who they turned to in an emergency situation. The uncle had practically landed Sophia on the doorstep of social services. She probably shouldn't have been taking on a child like Sophia for her first placement. But then, no one knew what we do now, did they?' He sighed. 'Jean's also now saying that the reason for her breakdown *was* Sophia. Well, a big contributory factor at any rate. It's all been too much for her, basically.'

'But what happens now?'

'Well, you can rest assured that we're busy looking for a new long-term placement for Sophia, but there's no point in me fudging this – it could take time. Which means that you and Mike might have to have her for a bit longer. But, as I say, it's important we don't tell Sophia this right now.'

'No, obviously, but, God! How is this all going to impact on her when she *is* told? She's clearly very attached to Jean – she's obviously been phoning her pretty regularly ...'

'Which is why we'd be really grateful if you'd allow them to remain in contact. Organised, this time, of course. Jean's very keen on that – still wants to play some part in Sophia's life, if that's workable. And that can't be a bad thing, can it?'

'No,' I admitted. 'I guess not.'

'Exactly. Give her access to a larger support network.'

I thought back to my parting words to Jean and felt guilty. Yes, she'd provoked them, and her manner had been inexcusable. But perhaps I should feel less cross and more sympathetic towards her. It can't have been easy for her;

she must be feeling dreadful about Sophia. 'I'll call her,' I said to John. 'Smooth things over. And I'll see what we can get organised about that contact.'

'Thanks for being so understanding, Casey. I appreciate it, I really do. And I'm sorry we didn't keep you in the loop in all this. It's just that Jean's link worker was so sure she'd reconsider and change her mind. But listen.' His tone was immediately brighter. 'Good news as well, which I was going to call you about anyway. I've got my hands on the police report from the day of Grace's accident.'

'*Finally*. And?'

'And it's certainly illuminating. And there's also a psychiatric evaluation for you to look at. How are you and Mike fixed? I'm quite clear later this week.'

'Can't be too soon, John, it really can't.'

The police report was in the form of a big manila file, across the front of which, in red letters, was written 'CONFIDENTIAL'. John pushed it across the dining table towards me and Mike. 'I warn you, Casey,' he said, 'it's pretty grim stuff. I've read it all twice now, and if this is what Sophia's been bottling up, then no wonder she's having psychological problems.'

I opened the folder. At least I knew that after hearing Justin's story – not to mention the kids in school – it would take a lot to shock me these days. And I was right. Sophia's wasn't so much shocking as tragic. She'd simply been born to the wrong mother at the wrong time.

Mike and I started to read. There was a lot of jargon on the first page, giving details of this officer and that officer and who did what, then it went on to record a transcript of a phone conversation between Sophia and the emergency services.

999 OPERATOR – *'Police emergency. Can I help you?'*
YOUNG GIRL – *'It's my mum. I think she's dead.'*
OPERATOR – *'Can I have your name and address, lovey?'*
YOUNG GIRL – *'Yes, I'm Sophia, I live at [address given].'*
OPERATOR – *'Okay, sweetheart. That's great. Now, how old are you?'*
SOPHIA – *'I'm almost eleven.'*
OPERATOR – *'Thank you, Sophia. Now, listen – there are some police officers on their way to your house now, so you just stay on the phone talking to me until they get to you, okay? Then you must let them come in. Okay, lovey? You understand that?'*
SOPHIA – *'Yes, okay. But she's dead. I think she must be. [Pauses.] She's fallen down the stairs, I think, and there's blood. She's very cold.'*

The unemotional nature of the typewritten transcript made the facts seem, if anything, more chilling. I read to the end of the conversation with the operator, and tried to imagine how it must feel to take such a call.

The report then went on to describe the scene. It said that officers had found two young girls in school uniform downstairs in the property. At the foot of the stairs they found Grace Johnson lying unconscious, with a head wound. Breathing was shallow, her pulse was weak and she had suspected fractures to two limbs. Paramedics had apparently arrived at 08.30, and she had been taken to nearby St Luke's Hospital. An empty container labelled as containing diazepam had been found on the table by Ms Johnson's bed.

The report went on to say that both girls had been questioned about when they had last seen Ms Johnson, and Sophia had told them that she'd last seen her at 7.30 the previous evening. She'd gone in to kiss her mother goodnight as she'd told Sophia she was ill and needed to go to sleep. Caitlyn had said that she hadn't seen Ms Johnson at all, neither the previous evening nor that day. When asked if she had heard anything – the noise of a fall in the night – Sophia had started to cry, and apparently told the police officer, 'She told me she'd do this.' A family liaison officer had apparently then arrived at 08.50, and taken both the girls back to headquarters.

'God,' I said to John, once I'd finished reading the report. 'Set out like this ... well, it really brings it home to you, doesn't it? What sort of a state must Sophia have been in?'

'That's not all of it,' he said. 'If you turn over you'll see that there's more. The pills *had* been taken by Grace, some time before the fall, and then a few pages on it says that apparently when Sophia is told her mum is still alive she acts really strangely, just shrugging and saying, 'She'll probably die, though, right?' They question her again, following that, because they suspect she knows more than she's letting on. At the next interview, however, she refuses to speak at all, and in the end they put it down to her being in shock about what appears to be her mother's attempted suicide.

'This is mad,' said Mike. 'How come we never knew anything about this? How come social services weren't onto this? Seems pretty clear to me that the police thought there was a question mark hanging over the whole thing!'

John gave Mike a long look. 'You know what I think?' he said. 'My gut instinct? My hunch is that nobody wanted to go there, so no one asked. Attempted suicide or accident. Case closed. It wasn't that difficult for me to get hold of this, in the end. Two phone calls. That was all. And here it is.'

'But that's terrible,' I said, once again revisiting the notion that we might have a would-be murderer in our midst.

'And what do you think, John?' Mike added pointedly. 'It doesn't seem as though much was done as far as the police were concerned. They just accepted it, did they? That Sophia's mother did it to herself? That was that?'

'I know, Mike,' John answered. 'I'm with you, mate. It's down as a probable suicide attempt, and, as I said, the case has been closed.' He pushed another file across the table. 'But there's also a psychiatric evaluation in there that you both might like to read, which seems fairly unequivocal that Sophia didn't try to kill her mother. But read it yourselves. I think you'll reach the same conclusion as me – that whatever did or didn't happen, this child should never have been just farmed out to foster care without some sort of proper psychological support in place. It beggars belief, really, that she was just given to us – to *you two* – without everyone concerned knowing the full facts.'

'You're certainly right there,' Mike agreed. He turned to me. 'And it's at least reassuring to know that the consensus seems to be that she's not about to kill us in our beds, eh, love?'

He smiled. But it was entirely without humour.

John had been right. Reading the psychiatric report had been illuminating. And once again, it seemed crazy that this child had been with us for almost four months, and we'd only just clapped eyes on this stuff.

After it was established that Sophia's mother's injuries meant she was unlikely to ever recover consciousness, Sophia herself had been offered counselling. By now she was living with her uncle and his wife, and it seemed all the rest of the family had been for sessions too. There had been a rift in the family from the outset, as John had already told us, the grandparents – Grace's parents – having disowned her. But it seemed that this wasn't just because they resented her existence – it was because they really did believe that if it hadn't been for Sophia, Grace would never have been driven to try and kill herself. Indeed, the grandmother, apparently, was still unconvinced that Sophia hadn't pushed her down the stairs. The uncle, as we already knew, had strongly refuted this, causing a breakdown in relations between the various factions, the grandparents disowning their granddaughter at that point and also breaking off contact with their son.

From what the report said, Sophia herself seemed to get little from the counselling. Initially, it seemed she had on a couple of occasions 'confessed' to an attempted murder, but the psychiatrist felt strongly that this was not the case. She had issues around the difficulties in her relationship with her mother, and he felt these 'confessions' were actually more attention seeking – that cry for help – and fuelled by both guilt and distress. It seemed she felt totally responsible for her mother wanting to die – her very existence being the cause of her mum's unhappiness. The report concluded that this constituted an ongoing problem, as it was something that could never now be fixed.

'And we'll never know now, will we? Not really,' I said to Mike. 'That's the crux of it. We'll never know what was going through Grace's mind at any point. How she felt about her daughter, whether she loved her at all. Oh, the poor, poor child. It's just so sad, Mike. And shame on those grandparents. *Shame* on them.'

We were reading independently, Mike passing the sheets to me as he finished them. He nudged me now. 'Hey, and look at this,' he said. He handed me another piece of paper. This was something that had been recorded by the police too, it looked like: a separate handwritten account, following up an abuse allegation. But it wasn't what I expected – something to do with Grace's boyfriends. It was an allegation made against Sophia's uncle.

Sophia had told a school friend, by all accounts, that he'd been touching her inappropriately, and the school friend had alerted their teacher. It had then been investigated, clearly, but the case had been dropped. There was no evidence, and he had apparently denied it from the outset. I looked at the date; this would have been a good while after she'd moved in with them – just a couple of months before she'd gone into care. There was no mention of what Sophia might or might not have said about it. But did that even matter now? The damage had been done.

'No wonder,' I said to Mike. 'No wonder he didn't keep her.'

'And it makes you think, doesn't it? About just how vulnerable we really are. What d'you think, Case?'

'I don't know *what* to think now, love. And that's the honest to God truth. On the one hand, it makes me think about all the things she told me about her mother's boyfriends, but at the same time ... well, the way she's been with you, and especially Kieron ...'

'Well, I know what *I* think. I think it's like you said to me before. She's in a mess. She hates herself. She's lashing out. Asking for trouble ...'

'And clearly getting it. She might have had a chance with the uncle, mightn't she?'

'But then again, if he *did* touch her ...'

'Do you believe that? I don't.' I stood up. My back was aching. 'I need a coffee and a cigarette. And you don't either, do you? Tell you what, though – it makes not a jot of difference really, does it? Whether it's true or in her head, it's no bloody wonder she's in a mess. And she *is* – this isn't the stuff of spoilt brats or badly behaved teenagers. This is actually scary, don't you think?'

Mike stood too. 'You're telling me, love. And it's not like we're doctors. Should we really be continuing to be involved in all this? I mean, if it's going to take time to place her, do we really want to keep her in the meantime? And "place her"? With who, exactly? If not us, who else? I don't know, love. I think we might just have to pull out of this one ...'

'But we can't, Mike. I don't think I could have that on my conscience. What kind of damage might we do if we shipped out on her as well?'

'Love, this is way beyond our job description, it really is. Just think about it, is all I'm saying. Think about all of us in this.'

And I did. I thought of all of us, and how much of a toll this was taking. I worried about Mike and I worried about Kieron, especially. Was it fair of me to put this complicated child's needs before theirs?

I was still wrestling with my responsibilities as I went to bed that evening. Little did I know that, within less than a week, the problems we'd had so far would fade into insignificance.

Chapter 18

'Sophia, love. Come on! It's time to get up!'

It was Friday morning, the last day of school before Easter, and I was down in the kitchen putting eggs on for breakfast. All was suspiciously quiet upstairs. I tried again, this time heading up the stairs as I called to her. 'Sophia! Come on! You'll be late if you don't move it!'

Once again, though, no answer was forthcoming.

Typical, I thought, as I trudged the rest of the way up to the landing. We'd already had words about school the night before, Sophia plaintively whining about having to go at all. 'It's the last day,' she kept repeating. 'No one bothers going in on the last day. There's no point. We don't actually *do* anything.'

But I'd been adamant, just as I'd always been with my own two. 'I don't care what everyone else does,' I told her firmly. 'You are going to school and that's that.'

I'd had no hint that she'd do anything but accept that when I'd woken, my alarm going off at 7 a.m. as usual, and

hers at her regular time of 7.15. That was generally my cue
to get up. While she went and showered I'd go down and
start breakfast, and while she dressed and got ready I'd
invariably nip out into the conservatory for a quick cup of
coffee and a cigarette. Today, it being so mild, I'd taken
both into the garden, relishing the peace and solitude –
only Bob kept me company – and enjoying five uninter-
rupted minutes to myself. It was a beautiful spring morning
and the sun was already shining, sending dappled shade
through the pink bower of my blossom tree.

But this morning, when I'd come back into the kitchen,
she hadn't appeared. I reached her bedroom door now.
'Sophia,' I said, knocking. 'You awake, love?'

Not getting an answer, and feeling the first tinge of worry
about her Addison's, I turned the handle and opened the
door. She was lying in bed, the duvet pulled right up under
her chin, but she wasn't asleep – far from it. She looked very
much awake. Awake and looking stonily right through me.

'Sophia!' I said, shocked. 'What on earth are you playing
at! Have you seen the time? Come on, love. Up!'

'I told you last night,' she replied, her tone sullen. 'I
won't be getting up, because I'm *not* going to school.'

I almost laughed out loud at her insolence, her complete
conviction in the matter. 'And I told *you*, young lady, that
you *are* going to school,' I said. 'Now stop playing silly
beggars and go and jump in that shower. Come on, or
you're going to be late.'

She sat up in bed then, and flicked her blonde hair
behind her. Then raised her arm and jabbed a finger in my
direction.

'*You* don't tell me what to do,' she said. 'I thought I made that clear last night. Now get out of here, *little* woman, and next time you want to come in here, kindly wait to be invited, okay?'

I don't know if it was that 'little' or just the jaw-dropping cheek of her, but I felt as furious as I'd felt in a long time. A 13-year-old, barking orders, in *my* house?

I don't think so! I thought, as I raised my own finger. All the outbursts, her instability, our fears for her sanity notwithstanding, this statement sounded like nothing more complicated than the petulant, bare-faced defiance of a spoilt adolescent. 'Don't you dare speak to me like that!' I rounded on her. 'Who the *hell* do you think you are? Get out of that bed, right now, before I really lose my temper. Two minutes!' I marched out and slammed the door.

I needed to calm down, I realised, as I headed back downstairs again. Slamming doors was a teenager's department, not mine. But Jesus! This girl would try the patience of a saint!

Almost as if on cue, then, I heard the door slam again, and turned to see her coming down the stairs behind me, her face contorted, her eyes wild, her whole demeanour scary.

'You fucking bitch!' she screamed at me. 'You ugly fucking bitch! I'm going to fucking kill you when I get my hands on you!'

I was shocked to the core now, but some instinct seemed to kick in and instead of continuing to the bottom I turned and, facing her now, spoke clearly and calmly. 'I suggest that you stop right there, Sophia,' I told her. 'Think about your next move and what its consequences might be.' I licked dry lips. 'I think you know I'm not joking now.'

I stood my ground, but I knew I was out of my depth here. I had never encountered such a venomous outburst. I'd come across violence and threats many times from kids over the years – Justin, early on, had even threatened me with a kitchen knife. But there was something about Sophia that felt in a different league. I knew I had to tread carefully here, for my own protection as much as her sanity.

I was immensely relieved, then, to watch her turn and walk slowly back up the stairs. Perhaps, I thought gratefully, this would be the end of it.

It wasn't. 'I'm still not going to school,' she said, back now on the landing. 'You sad cow. Why don't you just go and fuck yourself?'

Oh my God, I thought, as I mentally regrouped to respond to this. I knew I could walk away now, and that might be the best course, but I also knew that if I did, this scenario could get really ugly – I felt Sophia was capable of anything right now, and I knew she was certainly not ready to concede. And if I let that happen, the monster inside her would have won. Which would simply confirm to her that she was indeed a monster. No, the hard course was the only course; I must assert my authority. Take control. She had nothing to attack me with here, after all.

I walked back up the stairs again, never taking my eyes from her. And it was then that it occurred to me that my position was quite precarious. Three steps lower than her, Sophia literally towered over me. 'Sophia, love,' I said quietly. 'Let's just calm down and stop this silliness, shall we? You know full well it's wrong to speak to adults like that, don't you? Come on, love. What's brought this on?'

She looked down at me and laughed. It went through me. 'Do you know what a silly little woman you are?' she spat at me. 'You don't get it, do you? If I don't want to do something, what the hell do you think *you* can do about it?'

I felt the anger surge again in me and fought to press it down. 'Look,' I said. 'I've had just about enough of this now. You're the child, I'm the grown-up.' I paused so she could digest this. 'Now bloody well get dressed before I dress you myself. Do not underestimate me, Sophia!'

What happened next was all a blur but will remain with me for ever. Because, sudden though it was, it all seemed to happen in slow motion. One minute I was preparing to take a step and march her back to her bedroom, and the next I saw her grin – and it was a grin of pure malevolence – as she raised her hand and shoved me in the chest.

I was falling now, and instinctively tried to grab something. Flailing wildly, I was able to wrap my hand around the banister, but such was the force of her hand slamming into me that in doing so I was violently twisted around, which arrested my fall to the bottom of the staircase, but wrenched my arm and slammed me hard against the wall.

From there I could only look on in shocked horror as her hand flew to her mouth and she let out a shriek. 'Oh my *God*!' she started screaming at me. 'Oh, my God, Casey, I'm so sorry! I'm so sorry! What have I done? Oh my God!'

She ran back into her room then, still shouting apologies, and I could hear her huge convulsive sobs even as I stumbled back downstairs.

Right away, listening to her, I was in my own turmoil. What had I done wrong? What could I have done differently to defuse things? What other course of action should I have considered in all this that might have had a less damning outcome? I was all too aware of what *could* have happened. Had my fingers not managed to get a grip on that banister, I could be lying on the hall floor right now, badly hurt.

Or worse … I thought of Grace and swallowed. I realised I was shaking, so I reached for my cigarettes and cold coffee, and, almost on autopilot, went back into the garden. I wasn't sure what to do next. Didn't have a clue, in fact. My head was empty. All I could think of was my own uselessness, my own complete lack of foresight in going back up those stairs, my lack of memory about the demons that must haunt Sophia about what happened to her own mother, how her losing control – and its subsequent consequences – would surely colour everything now. God, I thought. This was *terrible*. Why was I failing so badly with this girl?

I started crying then, crying at the contrast of my warm sunny garden with what had happened, *in my own home*, just minutes before. I pinched my cheeks in an effort to stop myself weeping, trying to re-channel my emotions down a less self-pitying route. But I felt wretched. What kind of a foster carer was I if I couldn't control a girl who'd just turned 13?

I didn't hear Sophia when she came through the conservatory, but as I rubbed at my cheeks angrily and puffed furiously on my cigarette, there she was, suddenly, all dressed for school.

'Right, I'm off now,' she said, her expression still hard-faced and angry. I wasn't sure if she was spoiling for further conflict. I wasn't.

'Good,' I said. '*Go*. We will speak about this later.'

She turned on her heel then and stalked back inside, slamming each door she went through, one by one. First the glass conservatory door, which rattled in its frame alarmingly, then the kitchen door – bang – then the front door, a loud thud. It was only when I heard that, that I left my safe haven. I needed more coffee – a very big mug of coffee. I felt like I'd gone five rounds with Mike Tyson.

It was still early – much too early to hope to get hold of John Fulshaw – but I needed to speak to someone, two someones, in fact. I first called Riley, who I knew would be up and about with Levi, and then Mike, who'd had an early start, and might by now be on a break at work. Both were understandably concerned and also furious, and both wanted to come straight home and check I was okay.

I held them off, though, grateful as I was for my family. There was no point in either of them rushing home to me. The storm had passed now. Its perpetrator had gone to school, and the house was now empty. I'd just needed to vent my feelings, that was all.

It was John I needed really, so I could log this latest incident, and once it was past nine I dialled his number. I must be his favourite caller, I mused ironically, as I listened to the ring tone. Always calling him with bad news, these days. Never good. Even so, I couldn't help feeling a surge of irritation at getting his answerphone.

Had he known it was me? I also hated talking to the wretched things at the best of times, and this was definitely not the best of times. I left what probably sounded like a very garbled message, finishing with a heartfelt request that he ring me back.

Right, I thought, that done, *now you have to cheer up, Case.* So I flicked the switch on the kettle – at times like this, you couldn't ever have too much coffee – and ramped the volume on the radio up to max. Then I turned it down just a little, so I could still hear the phone, and forced myself to sing along to the Three Degrees.

And after around fifteen minutes the phone did indeed ring. Assuming it would be John, I ran to get it.

But it wasn't john. It was Edith Thomas, the school nurse.

'Mrs Watson?' she said. 'I'm so sorry to bother you, but we need you to come to school as soon as you can.'

I listened, dumbstruck. *What now?* Silly question. 'We've called an ambulance,' she was saying. 'But if you could come as soon as possible, we'd appreciate it. We think Sophia has had some sort of collapse. She's unconscious ...'

'Oh, Christ,' I said. 'I'll be there as soon as I can. You do have the emergency kit in school, though, so ...'

'Yes, we know,' she said patiently. 'But there's no one here who can administer it. It must be either you or a paramedic.'

Why? I thought. Why? Suppose I'd been unavailable? Would they have just sat there and done nothing? God! Where were the protocols for this? Surely they could give it! I mentally re-focused. This wasn't the time to row with her. Hopefully the ambulance would beat me anyway. 'Okay,' I said. 'Ten minutes, okay?'

As I raced upstairs to dress – I was still in my pyjamas – I couldn't shift the nagging doubt that had lodged in my mind. She'd caved in so easily, in the end, after all. Still angry, yes, but at least she'd gone to school. Was this development just a tactic, of the kind Kieron had mentioned, to draw attention from what she'd already done?

I was dreading the thought of injecting her. I'd got away with it the last time, but would I strike lucky again? I just had this sense that my luck had run out. I wasn't a nurse or a doctor, and I was terrible with needles, but I just knew I would have to do it, that the buck stopped right here. With all this in my mind I was beginning to feel completely frazzled. And even more so when I pulled into the school car park to find no reassuring ambulance was already parked. *Please just get here*, I thought, as I ran down the school corridor to the medical room and Sophia. *Please, please just get here.*

Chapter 19

Sophia was lying face down on the medical bench, her face turned to one side and her cheek pressed against the mattress. There was a teacher sitting beside her, one I didn't recognise, who was rhythmically stroking her hair back from her brow. Her eyes were closed. She did indeed look as if she might be unconscious, but, equally, she could have just been asleep.

Nearby, Edith, the school nurse, was standing with a clipboard, writing notes. She looked up as I entered. 'Ah, Casey,' she said smiling a weak, troubled smile. 'Sorry to have to ruin your morning like this, but it looks as though we are going to need you to inject Sophia with her medicine. She's been like this for a good ten minutes now.'

The ten minutes it had taken me to get there, in fact. I looked closely at Sophia. I felt sure I could see her mouth twitch. The trace of a smile, perhaps? I just couldn't seem to shift the idea that this was all part of an elaborate grand plan. I felt like a puppet having my strings jerked.

'Oh, dear,' I said, frowning at Edith. 'I'd hoped the paramedics would have been here by now. You know I've never done anything like this before, don't you?'

'You'll be fine,' she soothed. 'There's nothing to it, really there isn't.'

Then why couldn't she do it, then? I thought crossly, even though I already knew the answer. I fumbled in the emergency bag, my fingers beginning to quiver, and prepared the syringe as I'd been shown to. I then took one last hopeful glance through the still open medical room door, willing the paramedics to come belting down the corridor and save me. But there was nothing. *Nope!* I thought, trying to still the shakes. *You're on your own.*

I took a deep breath, to steady myself. This really wasn't complicated. All that was required was for me to jab the needle into her leg and to push the plunger till the contents had gone in. Simple, at least in theory. But, in practice, still quite difficult. It was all I could do not to close my eyes as I jabbed the needle into her – just the idea of wilfully sticking a needle into another person felt wrong, even though I well knew how silly I was being.

I winced as I pushed on the plunger to deliver the vital hydrocortisone, and then sighed as I heard the sound of boots in the corridor. Typical, I thought. The paramedics had arrived now. I pulled the needle out of Sophia's thigh just as they entered the room.

She had, almost immediately, come round. She rolled onto her side now, and then pulled herself upright. Her face, though, was a shock. It was a picture of anger. 'I bet you fucking loved doing that, didn't you?' she snarled at me. 'Couldn't wait to stick the needle in, eh? Bitch!'

I felt a rush of heat in my cheeks. 'Don't be silly, Sophia,' I answered. 'I was just doing what had to be done. You were unconscious.'

I was confused then – hang on, I thought, if she'd been unconscious, how had she even felt that? I also felt embarrassed, because I could sense the shock in the room at the way she'd spoken to me. And what the hell was I doing, defending myself to her? I bent down a little. I was not having this. Not again. 'Anyway,' I said solicitously, maternally, patting her. 'How are you feeling, love? Better?'

One of the paramedics was now getting some background from Edith, making his own notes about what had happened. The second now came over to speak to Sophia, who was sitting there, doggedly ignoring me.

'Now then, missy,' he said, getting down on his haunches. 'What d'you think happened?'

Sophia slowly looked him up and down before answering. 'Aren't you a little young to be a paramedic?' she asked him. 'And I had an Addisonian crisis – heard of them, have you?'

'Yes, I have,' he said, seeming completely unruffled. 'And I also see we have a little madam on our hands. Sophia, I think we both know that you haven't had a crisis, because if you had, that would have been the fastest recovery in history – *Guinness World Records* kind of fast. Come on,' he said, rising again. 'Let's check your blood pressure.'

Scowling, she rolled her sleeve up so he could get the cuff around her, and said nothing while he pumped it up and took the reading. He smiled and shook his head then, and glanced across at me. 'I think you've been giving your mum the run around,' he told her. 'Your vital signs look perfectly fine to me.'

'She not my mother,' she barked at him. 'She's just a *carer*. And I'm telling you, I *did* have a crisis, okay? I know my own body, thank you very much!'

'Sophia!' I interjected. 'That's quite enough, thank *you* very much! This man knows his own job, too!'

The nurse, who'd watched all this, beckoned to me then, and I followed her and the other paramedic outside. He introduced himself as Phil and led me a little way down the corridor.

'My colleague's right,' he said. 'That sort of recovery doesn't happen, Mrs Watson. Just so you know for the future, it normally takes some time for the hydrocortisone to take effect. And you'd know it. Right now we'd be rushing her to hospital and putting her on a drip. But as you can see, she's just fine. Seems like young Sophia's leading everyone a merry dance here.'

I felt stupid, then, but also quite angry. My first instinct had obviously been right. 'But what do I do?' I said. 'How am I supposed to know the difference? I can't *not* follow the procedure for a crisis, can I?'

He shook his head. 'There's the rub. You can't, I'm afraid. It's a tough one. You can always try to shake her and get a reaction. But if she wants to play dead ... well, then, you're right. You have no choice. An unnecessary injection of steroid won't do anything terrible in the short term – not if it's only occasional, anyway, whereas, if it *is* a crisis, the consequences of *not* giving it are very dangerous.'

'I'm just so glad you got here,' I said, 'and know what you're doing!'

'Stroke of luck,' he said. 'Colleague of mine's the expert – not me. He genned me up on the way over.'

So there was a God, after all. I nodded. 'I think I've met him.'

He nodded sympathetically at me, having obviously spoken to Edith, now, as well. 'Quite a handful you've got on your hands with that one, eh? On all fronts ...'

And that, of course, was the problem. Every day that went by it was just hammering itself home to me. I was just so woefully ill-equipped to help Sophia. I listened quietly as the other paramedic lectured her on the dangers of 'crying wolf' and also about how wrong it was to use emergency resources when they had other real emergencies to deal with. I knew it was important that they do this, but I was listening half-heartedly, pretty certain that she'd heard all this many times before, and that not a bit of it was even sinking in. It also occurred to me that, from what I'd read, these crises were really rare – how likely was it that she'd have had two in as many months? And if she had, she'd be really very ill. And the vomiting, too. I realised that it had never been confirmed that she had *actually* been sick that previous time in school. We'd only had her word for it, after all.

God, this child was so ravaged, so bent out of shape by her wretched life, that her anger at the world seemed to take precedence over everything, causing her to lash out at anyone and everyone – no matter the cost to her own health. It was almost as if she couldn't allow herself happiness; every instance of pleasure had to be immediately expunged, beaten off by her self-imposed punishments. It was as if she really did want everyone to hate her.

I took her home in silence. She didn't speak, not a word. And I was perfectly happy with that state of affairs, as I felt perilously on the edge of tears now. I needed to get her off to bed; crisis or no crisis, a lie-down wouldn't hurt her, and I needed her and her demons out of my sight for a while, at least till I felt strong enough to face them.

It was this sense that I was in the presence of such anger, I imagine, which left me totally unprepared for what happened next.

I had just stepped out of the hall and into the living room when she seemed to fall, literally, at my feet. Where she'd been standing, she was now lying in a miserable, crumpled heap, grabbing my ankles and sobbing uncontrollably. My first thought was *Shit, now she really has collapsed!* But it was soon apparent that her problem wasn't physical.

'Oh, Casey,' she sobbed up at me. 'What's *wrong* with me? Why do I feel like this all the time? I can't bear it. *Why?*'

Shocked, and also shackled, all I could do was shuffle slightly, so I was perched against the arm of my sofa.

'I can't bear it,' she sobbed again. 'I hate my life. I *hate* it. I just want to die. I swear to you. Why can't I just die?'

The events in school suddenly took on a chilling new complexion. But against that sat my now almost knee-jerk reaction. *Crying wolf*, I thought, as I leaned down to soothe her and stroke her hair. Was this more of the same? Was she crying wolf now? She was such a good actress. I'd more than ample evidence of her skill at it. And yet … and yet … this didn't *feel* like it was acting. 'It's okay,' I said softly. 'It will all be okay.'

But would it? To be honest, I didn't think so. We were currently living such a yo-yo existence, us two, neither of us, it seemed, knowing what was coming next. She couldn't control herself and I couldn't control her. And how exactly was that state of affairs going to change?

Perhaps I was wrong. Perhaps Sophia knew exactly what she was doing. Perhaps even now she was engineering what would happen. But what difference did that make? If it were true then perhaps that was worse. I was so confused, but one thing I knew above all else was that this child – this desperate young girl – needed me.

I shuffled down then and joined her on the floor of my living room, and, forgetting the events of what had already seemed a very long day, I lay beside her and gathered her into my arms. I then gently rocked her as she cried her little heart out, tears sliding down my own cheeks as I listened to her strings of apologies – for what she'd put me through, and Mike through and Kieron through and Riley through, her wish – and here her clarity of speech and logic chilled me – that she could just die, so that she didn't have to hurt any more. Saddest of all, though, was her desperate, plaintive crying for her lost mother, about which no one could do anything at all.

It felt like hours – in reality about one hour, perhaps longer – before she stopped crying, and, even then, her chest and shoulders still continued to heave spasmodically. It was longer still before she was able to pull herself up beside me and agree with my suggestion that she could perhaps do with a sleep.

I took her up to her room and she crawled into bed fully clothed.

It was all I could do not to take half a dozen steps across the landing and crawl under the duvet myself.

When Mike and Kieron got home I was still feeling like a zombie, and though I had managed to speak to John (keeping myself calm through sheer willpower; I couldn't bear the thought of snivelling down the phone at him) I had achieved nothing in the way of dinner. Mike was, of course, still angry at the events of first thing in the morning, and emotionally in a completely different place to me. As was Kieron, once Mike had filled him in. I wearily brought them up to speed with everything that had happened subsequently, reflecting, as I did so, that if you wanted a definition of the phrase 'rollercoaster of emotions' you could take our day, wholesale, and just use it.

This was the reality of having such a badly damaged girl in our lives. All the normal emotions you'd apply to a situation – anger, frustration, irritability, exasperation – had to be taken out, shaken out, inspected and put back again; the usual rules just didn't apply. It was one thing to sit in a psychiatrist's office and accept intellectually that Sophia wasn't responsible for her actions, but actually living with it … now that was a whole different kettle of fish. I knew my arm would ache tomorrow, from the wrenching it had suffered, but it was the constant snapping of nerves that was becoming the real issue. I felt drained. Wrung out.

'Go and have a lie down, love,' Mike counselled, once I'd finished. 'You look exhausted. Go on. I can rustle something up for me and Kieron. I'd rather have a rubbish dinner than have my wife in this state. Please, love, just allow yourself to down tools for a change, okay?'

The concerned looks on Mike and Kieron's faces made me feel even more wretched. Eyes once again threatening tears, I fled the kitchen before they noticed.

I slept all the way through to Saturday morning.

I woke to the smell of breakfast cooking. Bacon. Mushrooms. And, hmm. Those delicious herby sausages? And for a moment I couldn't work out which day it was. Saturday, that was it. So Mike would have popped in to work by now, wouldn't he? So was Kieron cooking breakfast? He was many, many good things, my darling son, but no chef. I pushed the covers away, got out of bed and pulled on my dressing gown, feeling guilty for having deserted all my loved ones the night before.

But it wasn't Kieron standing proprietorially over the frying pan, it was Mike.

'Oh, love,' I said wrapping my arms around him. 'You should have woken me. I'd have done that. Besides, shouldn't you be at work?'

He shook his head. 'I called the office. I've officially taken the whole weekend off.'

This was a rare treat, and I felt grateful.

'Where's Kieron?' I said. 'I'd have thought his nose would have already dragged him down here. And Sophia –' Just saying her name aloud lit a small flame of anxiety. What would be next in this ever-changing drama?

Mike nodded towards the window. 'Take a look,' he said.

I followed his gaze, to see the pair of them outside in the garden, both tucking into their breakfasts at the table and chatting away nine to the dozen. I noticed they even had Kieron's CD player out there. I could hear the tinny sound through the open window.

I was stunned. He'd been so angry about what had happened. Could it be that he'd decided to accept my belief that she really wasn't quite responsible for some of the things she did? 'Well, I …' I began.

'Don't stop to analyse, just enjoy,' Mike said, grinning. 'Go on, sit down. Breakfast is imminent.'

It took no encouragement whatsoever for me to do exactly that, and within minutes I was wolfing it down like a woman possessed – having gone without dinner, I was ravenous.

I was just clearing the last mouthfuls when Sophia appeared in the kitchen, balancing plates and mugs precariously in front of her and still giggling about something Kieron must have said. She smiled when she saw me. 'Hi, Casey,' she said brightly. 'Boy, you had a long sleep. You must have been tired! Did Mike tell you about my belated birthday card?'

I was too busy digesting her first statement to really note her second. Once again, had the previous day completely disappeared from her memory? Wiped like an old DVD?

Mike was shaking his head, though. 'Not yet, lovey, no. Sophia had a belated birthday card in the post today, love. From her grandparents.'

'Really?' I mentally caught up. Perhaps this was the best way. Stick rigidly to the present. Press 'erase'.

'Well, from Granddad,' she corrected now. 'He was the one who signed it. He wrote *her* name on it, but it was really from him. And guess what else?'

'What?'

'He put a hundred pounds in it.'

I raised my eyebrows at Mike. 'Wow,' I said. 'That's a lot of money! What are you going to do with it?'

She shrugged. 'I dunno yet. Maybe get a new iPod or something. Anyway, I've given Mike the money to look after till I decide.'

'D'you think we should tell social services about this?' I asked Mike, once she'd skipped back outside into the garden. 'It's a bit out of the blue, after all, isn't it?'

'I'd say so,' he said. 'Anyway, John's calling later, isn't he? Run it past him. Maybe there's stuff going on with the family we don't know.'

'Well, wouldn't *that* make a change, love,' I said wryly.

John called, as he'd promised he would, mid-way through that afternoon, by which time Sophia was engrossed in a DVD in the living room, Kieron and Mike having gone off to football. I took the phone off to the conservatory to speak to him.

'Funny you should mention that,' he told me when I filled him in about the card, 'because there have been some developments with the family. Not particularly edifying ones, sadly. There's still a big rift between son and mother, not helped, by all accounts, by Grace's consultant's recommendation that they should perhaps consider withdrawing life support. They don't expect anything in terms of a recovery at this stage, and it seems both grandfather and her uncle are in agreement, but gran – well, it's her daughter isn't it? By the grace of God and all that ... She's not budging.'

'Oh, God,' I sighed heavily. This was just all so sad and tragic. 'And what about Sophia? How's she going to react to all this?'

And just when are CAMHS going to get around to seeing her? I thought but didn't say. Some time before her whole world implodes might be nice.

'Oh, there's no need to say anything to her yet,' John said quickly. 'All undecided. Nothing's concrete at this stage. And if they do ... well, there'll need to be a visit arranged first, won't there? So she can say goodbye properly to her mum. And let's face it, might be the best thing. You know. Allow her to move on.'

Yes, John was right. In the long term, perhaps. But she'd still have to *deal* with it, I thought, as I put the phone back in the hall. It would be huge. It would be horrible. It could tip her right over the edge. And it would be us who'd have to deal with the fall-out.

'God, it's just one thing after another!' Mike said, when I told him later. 'When's that lass going to cop a break, eh?'

Not yet, I thought. What were the chances she was going to get that lucky? This was real life. No magic wands to wave around.

Chapter 20

Though the news about Sophia's mother weighed heavily on my mind, the remainder of the weekend went surprisingly peacefully. I was bemused by this sudden contact from the granddad, but also pleased. Perhaps some lasting reconciliation could be achieved within the family, even if it would take the form of coming together in grief if and when they decided to withdraw Grace's life support.

In the meantime, however, I was just glad of the calm and as happy as everyone else to make the most of it. I was particularly touched by the way Kieron was handling things. Despite everything – and he'd borne the brunt of so much since Sophia had been with us – it was as if he'd decided to do his level best to form a bond with her, putting aside all that had happened in the past.

Bar Sophia's quiet demeanour, I had no evidence to support that, but by Monday I'd decided that perhaps the events of last Friday had marked some sort of pinnacle. Perhaps they were a watershed we'd reached and could now move past. The idea was ridiculous, and, in hindsight, I think I just willed myself to think that. But it was the Easter break from school now, which meant Sophia was home full time, and the prospect of being in an environment so racked with tension – hard enough in term time – was an alternative I simply couldn't contemplate.

And with the school holidays came more sun, which made everything feel better. For me, particularly, as it meant I could spend more time in my garden, and with a baby in the family, this meant a return to the simple outdoor pleasures I'd enjoyed when my own two were tiny.

'Let's fill the little paddling pool,' I said to Sophia on the Monday morning. Riley was bringing Levi over and, since the temperature was so balmy, we'd planned to spend much of the day doing absolutely nothing in the sunshine.

Sophia jumped to it, seeming as infected by spring fever as I was, helping me to lay blankets on the grass, inflate and fill the little pool, and get out all the baby toys from the cupboard in the conservatory. Levi was not only sitting up now, but rolling as well, so it would be good to give him some outdoor space to explore.

By the time Riley arrived the garden looked like a nursery-school playground, but instead of the whoops of laughter and cries of 'What are you like, Mum!' I'd anticipated, Riley's expression when she arrived was pinched and drawn.

'What's up, love?' I asked her, because it was so obvious that something was.

'Oh, Mum, look at him,' she said. 'Look at his poor little face! He's got chickenpox. We've hardly slept a wink!'

It didn't take much of a look to confirm it, either. Some get it mildly, others aren't so lucky. Both of my two had suffered badly with chickenpox – I'd got through bottle after bottle of calamine lotion. And it looked like poor Levi was following suit. He was liberally plastered with the tiny pink blisters – he even had them inside his eyelids. 'Oh, you poor little thing!' I cried, reaching in to lift him from his pram. Levi, however, was having none of it. He screamed immediately and began squirming and kicking to be put down, big tears running down his cheeks and irritating his face even further. Riley lifted him back from me and laid him back down.

'It's no good, Mum. He's been like this all night. I think he just wants to be left alone, to be honest. It's like he's angry with us because we can't do anything to help him.'

'And it must hurt, being held, when your skin is so sore.'

'Exactly. But he'll be so much better out here in the garden. He always seems to settle better outside.' She smiled a tired smile. 'And I could definitely use some down time. Hopefully he'll drop off to sleep in his pram and we can enjoy a spot of girlie sunbathing and gossip, eh, Sophia?'

So, having already done my housework for the day, and seen my 'boys' off to their respective weekday places, I got out three sun loungers, made up a batch of drinks and sandwiches, and the three of us then spent an enjoyable hour doing just that.

It really was a gorgeous day, far warmer than was usual for the time of year, and there was a delicious pleasure in doing absolutely nothing for a while, bar chatting about the latest celebrity gossip and half-listening to the radio:

Sophia had switched on the one in the conservatory and relocated it to the open French doors so we could hear it. Even Bob, normally so energetic, seemed content to lie and slumber, his eyes half closed and his tail giving only the occasional flick.

I should have known the peace and tranquillity wouldn't last, though. After an hour or so, Levi, all done with napping, woke up. Instantly reminded of his wretched condition, he began grizzling again, plaintively and miserably. It made it all the worse that he was generally such a happy, contented baby. We just weren't used to seeing him, or hearing him, so sad.

Sophia put her magazine down. 'Shall I wheel him around the garden for a bit, Riley?'

I was touched by her gesture. It was sweet of her.

'Thanks, love,' said Riley. 'I don't know that it'll help any, but, yes, why not. He might at least be distracted by the change in scenery.'

Sophia jumped up and then spent the next ten minutes duly pushing the pram around the perimeter of the garden, but, as Riley predicted, it didn't seem to be helping. If anything, Levi's cries were getting even louder, and I could tell this was beginning to upset Sophia.

'Sophia, love, just fetch him back here and sit down. He's just poorly, love. Nothing we can do. Don't worry, he'll be okay.'

Sophia wheeled the pram back and Riley stood up, then pulled a bottle of liquid paracetamol out of her baby bag and began to shake it. She passed Sophia Levi's dummy with her free hand.

Casey Watson

'Here, love. Can you take this? And when I give Levi his medicine, do you think you could pop it straight into his mouth after so he doesn't try to spit it straight back out again?'

'Okay,' Sophia said, nodding, and, seeming pleased to have been given the responsibility, she then knelt close beside the pram ready to do as asked. But when she did, it was obvious that Levi was not happy – furiously spitting medicine, he immediately struck out, throwing his dummy way across the lawn and accidentally scratching Sophia's nose as he did so.

She looked shocked, but not half as much as we were about to be, because Sophia's reaction was as fierce as it was instant. She immediately slapped him on the leg, really hard.

Riley dropped the medicine bottle and yanked her away by the shoulder. 'What the hell are you *doing*!' she yelled in her face, her maternal rage rising. 'You don't hit babies! What the hell did you think you were *doing*?'

I had jumped up from my sun lounger now. 'Sophia! Are you mad?' I jabbed a finger towards Levi, who was now really screaming, the weal on his tiny leg reddening even as we watched. 'Look!' I snapped. 'Look what you've done! What were you *thinking*?!'

Thinking nothing, I realised, even as I shouted. She just did it. An instinct as natural to her as breathing. Hit. Lash out at someone. Hurt.

Riley had by now snatched Levi up from his pram. She was almost beside herself, I could tell. She looked straight at me, perhaps sensing my hesitation about how best to handle this. Because I *did* hesitate. The only thing certain right now was that our nice girlie day in the garden was over.

'Don't you *dare*, Mum. Don't try to pacify her, okay?' She turned to Sophia. 'Go on. Get out of my sight! I can't even bear to look at you!'

Sophia's own expression had now morphed from shock to defiance. Or, perhaps worse, to that glazed, look-right-through-you mask she had. 'Fuck you!' she spat at Riley. 'Fuck you both! You fucking hate me!'

'Sophia!' I shot back at her, matching her decibel for decibel. 'Go to your room *now*! Don't you dare start all that again!'

I could feel my anger building to unmanageable levels. In contrast to Friday, when I'd felt the stuffing had been knocked out of me, here, just like Riley, I felt pure maternal rage. This was my daughter and my grandson and it was my job to protect them. If she defied me again now, I knew I might not be responsible for my actions. I needed to calm everything down, fast.

'*Go!*' I yelled again. 'Just *go!*'

And, to my relief, she must have seen something in my expression. 'Oh, don't worry,' she answered. 'I'm going, all right!'

She ran inside then, but even before I could feel my pulse slowing she was back in the conservatory doorway, waving her packets of pills and emergency steroid injection kit in front of her. 'And I'm locking this lot in my room with me!' she called to us. 'You like that kid more than you like me, do you, Casey? Well, let's see how you feel when I'm *dead*!'

With that, she ran inside again, and even from the garden both of us could hear the sound of her thundering up the stairs. I looked at Riley, whose face was immobilised by shock. Even Levi had stopped crying now, transfixed. Then it hit me, and hard. This was serious. This was potentially fatal. I had no idea what an overdose of all those drugs could do to her, but I certainly had enough imagination to guess, and I wasn't about to take any chances.

'Oh, God …' I said, springing into action and racing inside after her. I took the stairs two at a time and was at her door in moments. I knocked loudly. 'Sophia! Open this door right now!'

'*Fuck off!*' her voice cracked, she yelled so loud. It was almost unrecognisable. 'I'm going the same way my mother did, I swear to you! I'm doing it! Now *fuck off and leave me alone!*'

I inhaled slowly. I was still breathless. There was sweat beading on my forehead. 'Look, Sophia,' I said. 'What you did was wrong, and you know that. But it isn't *the end of the world!*' I struggled then, trying to come up with the best things to say, the image of her sitting on her bed, popping pill after pill … how many did she have of them, for God's sake? I knew Riley'd said not to pacify her, but this was serious. I did not want to have a dead child on my hands. Or my conscience. Oh, God …

'Just come out, love,' I tried. 'Riley's calmed down now. She was just shocked. As she would be, but it's all going to be …'

'*Fuck off!!!*' she screamed again, though she was becoming incoherent. She just kept repeating the words, over and over and over, intermittently screaming and laughing hysterically. God only knew what was going on in that room. I wished desperately for Mike. He would know what to do here. At the very least he'd be able to barge the bloody door open.

'Sophia!' I called again, trying to break through the cacophony. 'If you don't come out now, I'm going to have to call for an ambulance!'

As threats went, this was hardly a big one, I knew. But at least they would be able to get into the room with her. They *had* to.

'Ambulance!' she screamed back at me. 'You think I need a fucking ambulance? Well, go on, and while you're at it, call the fucking police as well! Because, I swear to you, I'm going to murder the fucking lot of you! When you're all tucked up in bed asleep, just you wait! I fucking will! I've done it before, you fucking bitch, and I'll do it again, you hear? *Fuck you!*'

'Mum!' Riley's voice. She was at the bottom of the stairs, holding Levi, beckoning me down. 'Mum, come on. Come down. This is pointless.'

I could see just how shocked she was – she'd obviously heard everything. She beckoned again, and I realised she was right. It *was* pointless. I rattled down the stairs and followed her into the kitchen. Sophia was still ranting and screaming upstairs, so at least I knew she wasn't slipping into unconsciousness.

Riley passed me the phone. 'Go on. Call that ambulance. Do it now.'

I took the phone from her, feeling a chill running through me. *I've done it before and I'll do it again*, she'd said.

And the suicide attempts. She'd made previous suicide attempts. I didn't know what or who to believe any more.

Riley put Levi back in his pram – he'd now been stunned into silence – then made coffee as I called 999 and gave the details. I also phoned John and gave him a brief résumé, promising to call him back and update him once the paramedics had arrived.

We then went into the conservatory, and I lit a much-needed, calm-before-the-certain-storm cigarette. It felt bizarre but the noise above us was comforting. All the while she was making it, I knew she was conscious. And, unable to get in, there was nothing else I *could* do but wait for the sound of the sirens.

'Oh, God, Mum,' said Riley. 'I had no idea things were this bad. This is madness. Utter madness. How do you cope with all this stuff?'

I didn't know, so I couldn't answer. So I just shrugged instead. 'How's Levi? I'm so sorry, love, I really am. That was just horrible.'

'He'll be fine,' she said. 'His leg is a bit red, but he'll survive. I just can't believe that she *did* that, you know? How could anyone hit a tiny, defenceless baby like that?'

I nodded. Though I knew, in truth, that the answer was 'all too easily'. In the real world, some people hit babies. A tragic fact.

She trailed off. We both did. We just sat there in silence as upstairs the bangs and crashes and screams and rants continued. As Riley said, the whole thing felt like madness.

But it was only minutes, thankfully, before an ambulance arrived, and on the doorstep there soon stood two capable-looking paramedics, one of whom, I was pleased to note, was Phil, whom I'd met on Friday at the high school.

'Here we are again, then!' he said, cheerfully, which calmed me greatly. At least, I thought, he knows what he's dealing with. Up to a point.

The other paramedic was a woman, who introduced herself as Bev.

'Right,' she said, as Phil headed straight off up the stairs. 'What's the history to all this kerfuffle, then?'

Riley and I exchanged a look. I hardly knew where to start.

Chapter 21

In the end, Sophia didn't put up much of a fight with Phil, the paramedic. No sooner had he gone upstairs than the racket had ceased, his rap on the bedroom door and their subsequent exchange of words being replaced by the low murmur of calm conversation and then, eventually, a reassuring silence. From downstairs in the kitchen, in my still-raddled state, he had made subduing Sophia all seem ridiculously easy and I wondered why he'd succeeded where I'd failed.

'I'm so sorry to have called you out again,' I said, when he came back downstairs and I'd seen off a now-reassured Riley. 'You must think I'm hopeless.'

He shook his head. 'Absolutely not,' he reassured me, accepting a cup of tea from Bev. Somehow, in the midst of everything, she had made a pot for us all. It was some measure of the kind of state I must be in that I accepted one too. I can't stand tea.

'You did the right thing,' Phil said with conviction. 'That's what we're here for.'

Bev had said as much when I'd outlined some of the background to the outburst, and had reminded me that it wasn't in any sense silly to have called them. I should – indeed, must – take all her threats seriously. She had the means with which to kill herself, and having stated her intention it would be irresponsible if I *hadn't* made the 999 call.

'Anyway, it's all calm up there now, love, so don't worry. I've given her a mild sedative – had to, to calm her down, and get her to take her medication. She was adamant she was never taking any, ever again – well, at least till she real-ised that I wasn't taking "no" for an answer, that is.'

'So she hadn't taken any pills then?'

Phil shook his head. 'She said not, and I believe her. Here.' He spread a haul of drugs onto the table for me to look at, including the emergency injection kit. 'Not unless she has some other secret stash squirrelled away.'

I felt relief flood through me. 'She can't have more. I can only get a limited amount on repeat prescription, and it looks like it's all there.'

'Nothing to worry about anyway. Well, obviously, you'll want to speak to her doctor about the whole *situation*, of course –' he said, grimacing. 'But an overdose of hydrocor-tisone isn't life-threatening anyway. Not in the short term. Hugely harmful if done over the long term, as you probably already knew, but, as a one-off it's not a goer if you want to be a goner.'

I couldn't help smiling. But the smile didn't stay on my face long. She was still up there, after all. Still very much my problem. And Phil's sympathetic expression told me he understood. 'Thanks so much,' I said gratefully. 'So she's sleeping now, is she?'

'Like a baby. And I doubt she'll stir till morning now, so you can enjoy a bit of breathing space. Keep an eye on her, obviously, but don't be surprised if you don't hear a peep till tomorrow. Not after the fight she put up, and that sedative.'

I looked at my watch. It was still only 3.30 in the afternoon. Yet the morning suddenly seemed a lifetime ago. I felt very tired.

'I could do with one of those myself,' I joked, as I let them out. But the smile left my lips again as soon as they drove away. Alone with Sophia now, I recognised a new feeling building, one that I'd never experienced to quite the degree I did now, not in my professional capacity, at any rate. I felt frightened. Of her. Of being in the house alone with her. I hoped Phil was right. I really hoped she didn't wake.

I had plenty to keep me occupied for the rest of the afternoon, at least. First, I had to record everything in my journal, which I did, sitting at the dining-room table, a large mug of coffee at my elbow, carefully including every tiny detail I could remember. I then called John Fulshaw and updated him similarly, repeating what Phil had said about getting her to see our GP to discuss her Addison's management and restating my case for the urgent need to get her that psychiatric assessment, too.

John was predictably reassuring, but had nothing new to say. Yes, it was in hand with CAMHS; no, he'd heard nothing further; yes, he would give them another chase.

Finally, I called Mike, and simply poured my heart out to him – the very last thing he needed in the middle of his working day. He listened patiently and sympathetically but I felt really bad when I put the phone down. What on earth had I been *thinking*? It was so unlike me to burden him like that. Not while he was at work. That was all wrong.

But it did make me feel better. And with Sophia asleep upstairs, I decided to end the day the same way I'd started it. I threw some chicken fillets and vegetables into a casserole for dinner, then went back outside to enjoy the last of the spring sunshine, hoping I could absorb something of the sun's strength and warmth.

The contrast I found there struck me forcibly. Here the garden, with all the toys strewn over it and with its playful, happy look, seemed so at odds with what was happening both in the house and in our lives. While the sun spangled prettily on the grassy water in the little paddling pool, upstairs, snoring softly, was a child in such a mess – and one seemingly hell-bent on self-destruction. Did I really have any hope of pulling her back? I was seriously beginning to doubt it.

When I woke the next morning, and the events of the previous day came flooding back to me, I experienced that same sense of fear I'd had yesterday, and I stretched out across the duvet to find Mike. Kieron had slept over at Lauren's the night before, and taken Bob, and I felt almost panicky to think Mike might already have gone to work, leaving Sophia and me in the house alone.

But I needn't have worried. Just as I began berating myself for my stupidity, he was in the open bedroom doorway, bearing coffee and toast.

'Treat,' he said, grinning. 'For the lady of the house. Since it's the school holidays I thought you could have a bit of a lie-in.' He placed the tray on the bedside table and bent down to kiss my forehead.

'Oh, thanks so much, love,' I said, shuffling up to a sitting position. 'What's the time?'

'Almost eight, so I really do need to get my skates on. But listen, love, you know where I am if you need me. So if you want to call me, don't you worry about it. I've told them what's happening, they know we've got some problems, so …'

'Not today, fingers crossed,' I said, willing myself to believe it. 'Going by past experience there's usually a couple of days of calm after a big blow-out, so I'm hoping today will be a good one.'

'That's the spirit,' he said. 'She's up and about, by the way.'

'Have you spoken to her?'

He shook his head. 'No, but I could hear her pottering about in her room, humming to herself. I dare say she'll be down, suitably contrite, when she's ready.'

I nodded. 'Contrite would be good. Anyway, Riley'll be over later to give me moral support. Don't worry. You get off, love. I'll be fine.'

Mike kissed me goodbye, and then went off to work, and in the ensuing silence I too could hear Sophia pottering in her room. Despite my optimistic words, I still felt anxious about facing her. I was glad when I remembered that Kieron was off from college. Glad that I'd have him around all this week, too. I hoped he wouldn't be too long in coming home from Lauren's, but I forced myself not to ring and check.

Chickening out of looking in on Sophia right away, I then went straight down to the kitchen and felt immediately brighter to see Mike had already brewed me a full pot of coffee. '*To cheer you up!* ☺' a post-it stuck to it declared. I poured myself a second mug and set about a spate of light cleaning; anything, I realised, as I wiped already-wiped kitchen surfaces, to put off the moment when I would have to go up and see her.

Yet I *would* have to, I realised, when the clock showed it was way past ten and she'd yet to emerge from her bedroom. No, there was no school, but at the very least I needed to get food and medicine down her. Either that, or make another call to Phil.

Get your act together, Casey! I chided myself, as I headed up the stairs on heavy legs. It was so unlike me to be reluctant to engage in a situation. Taking bulls by their horns was what I'd always been best at – wimping out, I told myself, was for wimps. She was probably hiding away in her room for exactly the same reason that I had been hiding away in the kitchen downstairs – in truth, perhaps we couldn't face each other.

But I was wrong. I could sense it in the way the hairs rose on my neck as I pushed the bedroom door fully open.

I knocked as I entered, not wishing to startle her. She was sitting sideways on to me, at her dressing table, rhythmically brushing her hair. 'Sophia, love,' I started. 'It's way past breakfast time – are you coming downstairs?'

She was staring into her mirror. Though not at it, but through it. She wasn't looking at her reflection. That was obvious. She was staring sightlessly into the far distance. She made no response. Didn't even twitch. 'Love?' I said, a sense of foreboding building in me. 'Are you okay? Come on, come down and let's get you something to eat, eh? You must be starving.'

Still she said nothing, but now she did stand and, still brushing her hair, began walking towards me. At first it was as if she was sleepwalking, oblivious, but then I realised she was just doing what I'd asked her to do, so I turned and, sure enough, she followed me placidly down to the kitchen, where she sat at her usual place at the table and went back to brushing her hair.

This isn't right, I thought anxiously. *This is scary*. What the hell was wrong with her? I'd never seen her like this. Ranting, yes, raving, yes, throwing her toys out of the pram, double yes. But this strange vacant state was altogether more frightening. Was this the beginning of a real crisis or was it all in her head? *Please, Kieron*, I thought. *Hurry home*.

'Sophia?' I tried again, placing a hand on her shoulder. 'Sophia, love. You don't seem very well. You need to take your meds and you need some food inside you.' This time, to my relief, she seemed to register that I was speaking. She didn't reply to what I said, but at least she nodded.

Relieved, I hurried over to the cupboard and pulled out the pills Phil had brought down last night. I was further reassured to see her calmly take both drugs, while I scurried across the room to make some toast. Still, she didn't speak – she was back brushing her hair again – but when the toast was done and I'd buttered it she ate both slices obediently, even passing her empty plate to me when done. At least that was one thing I no longer had to worry about, I thought, taking it. But this was serious. It was like she was in the middle of an extended trance and I didn't have the first idea what to do next. What I really needed to do was to call for help.

Leaving her to it – she seemed engrossed only in her hair, and showed no sign of moving – I took the house phone and my phone book out into the garden. So what did I do? Call an ambulance? Call John? What made most sense? Some instinct, however, led me to the number of her consultant, the man with whom she seemed to have this peculiarly intense relationship. If I was going to call anyone, it might as well be him. Of all the numbers I had, his was the one that made most sense. He knew her, knew her well. The others didn't.

I was stunned, even so, to get through to him immediately. Despite my determination to speak to him, it had occurred to me while dialling that there'd probably be layers of administration to get through before being granted access to the expert himself.

But he was happy to speak to me. And he sounded concerned. Especially when I told him about the suicide threats. Which made them suddenly seem very real. It was one thing to read on a file from social services 'has attempted suicide', quite another to have a child in your care who might at any moment try, and perhaps succeed in, taking their own life.

'She very nearly has,' he told me gravely, 'on several occasions. And I'm not just talking about since she's been in the care of social services either. Sophia's been with me since she was quite young – five or six – and she's attempted suicide, by refusing her meds, several times – and on at least two she very nearly succeeded.'

'Well, that's great!' I said, stung into anger instead of fear now. 'So none of this is recent, is what you're saying? Wouldn't it have been helpful for us to have known all this when we started fostering her?'

'It's a fine line,' he said, obviously unwilling to be brow-beaten by me. 'And, to my knowledge, social services did have access to her files. But you must understand that patient confidentiality is something I am obliged to take seriously …'

'I understand that. But I'm obliged to take the wellbeing of the children in my care *equally* seriously. And that's only possible if I know the full picture! We've clearly been look-ing after a child with longstanding psychological problems – problems that neither myself or my husband are qualified to deal with. Don't you think it might have been helpful for us to have been told all this stuff when we first saw you?'

Once again, a familiar phrase stuck in my head. *If we'd known all this stuff would we have ever considered taking her?* No, of course we wouldn't. We weren't qualified … no foster carer would have been. But it was too late to think about that now. I said so. She was clearly in a very bad place.

'I agree,' said her consultant. 'And perhaps you should take that up *with* social services. But, as a priority, I suggest you get in touch with your GP immediately. I'm too far away to be of much immediate use to you, but perhaps they can assess her and then liaise with me after that.'

Yup, I thought. Too far away. So no use. And though I knew my GP would be helpful and understanding, it was odds on that her medical notes hadn't even reached him yet, either. Though, like all GPs, he had a duty of care to take on children in the care system, in practice, we'd been told, a child's medical records could be very slow in following. I got Sophia's meds from him, obviously, but as to the chequered nature of her past – well, he would be none the wiser, would he? I decided to call John for advice first.

Frustratingly, I got his answerphone, so was forced to leave a message. Which I did, making it clear that both Mike and I, and her consultant, felt she was having some sort of breakdown and that I was now going to get the GP out. Failing that, I'd have to phone 999 again. I was just finishing relating this into the machine when I heard a clear voice – Sophia's – from behind me.

'Who the fuck was that?' she said. I swivelled in my seat to find her standing in the conservatory doorway, the faraway expression having been replaced by one I knew: that terrible twisted mask of rage and loathing.

'Please don't swear like that, Sophia,' I said, trying to keep my eyes fixed on hers. She looked almost deranged with fury. 'And that was a private phone call,' I added, albeit pointlessly. She'd obviously heard at least the end of it. Heard her name.

'No it wasn't. It was about me,' she said, confirming it. 'You fucking liar.'

I felt my mouth go dry, and licked my lips. 'I said stop that!' I continued. 'And yes, as it happens, it was about you. We're all very worried about you. You're …'

She thumped the door with her fist. It made me jump, it was so sudden. 'Fuck you! I'm not having any doctors coming here sticking me with needles again. Got that? *Got that?*'

I stood up now, but was acutely aware that I couldn't get back inside the house without passing her. I was trapped out here. 'Sophia, don't be silly,' I began. 'No one is going to come here and inject you. You've just taken your meds, haven't you? So why would anybody have to do that? I just need a doctor to come here and see you. To try to under-stand why you've been getting so unwell, that's all.'

'*You're the one making me unwell!!*' she screamed at me. She took a step towards me, and I felt myself stiffen. '*Why can't you just keep your big nose out?!*'

There was no point in just standing there. I had to act. I walked towards her, trying to look dismissive of her outburst as I placed a hand on the door jamb. 'Come on, Sophia, out of my way now,' I snapped. 'Let's get inside, put the kettle on and talk about this.'

But it seemed she had other ideas. She didn't move a muscle. She was no longer just standing in the doorway to the conservatory, but actively blocking my path. If I was going anywhere I really *would* first have to shift her, and the difference in our height and strength fully hit home.

Just then, however, I heard another door bang. Kieron! Oh, thank God, I thought. Kieron. It must be Kieron! He was in the conservatory seconds later, calling, 'Mum! Mum, you there?'

He then looked at the pair of us – Sophia had swivelled her head when she'd heard him – and his expression became puzzled. 'Hiya, Sophia,' he said. 'Mum, is everything okay?'

Sophia had fully turned now, giving me the opportunity to squeeze past her. I took it.

'*Mum, is everything okay?*' she mimicked. 'No, Kieron,' she spat then. 'It's fucking not! The bitch –' she jabbed a finger in my direction – 'thinks it's funny to have me stuck with needles to knock me out!'

I watched Kieron's jaw drop before he regained his composure. 'Hey,' he said, 'don't you dare speak to my mother like that! Get to your room, *now!*'

In the midst of everything, some part of me found a moment to observe that this business of my kids sending my foster kids to their rooms was becoming something of a regular occurrence.

'Do as he says,' I chipped in. 'And I *will* speak to the doctor. This isn't you, Sophia. I *know* it isn't. This might all be down to your medication. I think it is. Maybe your dosage needs looking at again.'

And maybe, I thought, recalling the notes about mental health side-effects, this is partly an effect *of* the illness. '*Do as he says!*' she parroted again, ignoring me. 'Casey's kids are always right. Perfect fucking Casey. Perfect fucking Casey and her perfect fucking kids!' She was hysterical now, spitting the words with real venom, and then

– shocking both of us – she launched herself at Kieron, who only just managed to jump out of the way. She lunged again. 'Okay, let's see how you like *this*, then, Mr Fucking Perfect!' But this time, as Kieron sidestepped, she simply swept past him, then ran back upstairs, laughing manically.

'What the hell was all *that* about?' he asked me, dumbfounded.

'Oh, love,' I said. 'I can't even *begin* to explain. I just need to ring the doctors. And I need to do it *now*.' I ran back outside to grab the house phone and brought it inside. It was late morning. With any luck I would be able to get a house call. And if not, well, I'd just ring for yet another ambulance. We absolutely, definitely, could not go on like this.

I went into the kitchen and dialled the GP's number with shaking fingers. Typically, I got the engaged tone three times before eventually hearing the sound of the mechanical menu. *Press one for appointment, press two for prescriptions, press three for home visits …*

I pressed three and willed my heart to stop thumping quite so hard. I then crossed my fingers as I explained to the receptionist who I was, and my concerns for Sophia's current condition. Luckily, she was able to offer me an afternoon slot, though, even as I disconnected, I worried whether I was doing the right thing. Should I have just called for an ambulance, after all? No, I thought, it was ridiculous to call an ambulance. There was nothing here that the GP couldn't handle. I couldn't keep whistling up ambulances willy-nilly, after all.

Crying for Help

But Sophia wasn't done yet with testing us. As I put down the phone I could hear Kieron calling the dog. 'Mum,' he said, coming in. 'Did you see Bob go out into the garden? I've lost him ...'

I shook my head. 'Lost him? How could you have lost him? Have you checked your room?'

'Mum, I just brought him back from Lauren's. And he's starving. I think my room would be the last place he'd go. He wants breakfast.'

'No,' I said, distracted, my mind focused elsewhere. 'No, I don't think so. No, he didn't come past me. He'll be *somewhere*. Keep looking. Right now I have rather a lot on my mind ...'

'But where could he *be*, Mum? He can't just have disappeared into thin air!'

I think we both thought the same thing at exactly the same instant. *See how you like this, then, Mr Fucking Perfect* ... Oh, God, I thought. Bob. *She* must have him. In any event, neither of us said anything more – just turned around, the pair of us, and thundered up the stairs.

Kieron beat me, and thundered into Sophia's bedroom. It was empty. He then marched out again and went across the landing to the bathroom, the door of which – as wasn't generally the case – was closed. He tried the handle. The door was locked. He began banging on it furiously. 'Sophia!' he was yelling. 'You've got my dog in there, haven't you? I know you have! Let him out! Let him out *right now*!'

'Fuck off!' she screeched back, just as I got there. 'The dog hates you! And if I'm going, the dog's coming with me!'

Kieron had tears in his eyes now, I could see, as he beseeched me – 'What's she doing to him, Mum? What does she *mean*? Mum, get Bob out! You have to get Bob out! *Please* get Bob out!' his voice, too, was now becoming hysterical.

I banged at the door with all the force I could muster. 'Sophia, you have ten seconds. Ten seconds, do you hear? You can lock yourself in there for all time, if you want to, but the dog comes out, you hear? The dog comes out *right now!*'

Silence. I put my head to the door, listening, despairing. I simply didn't know what she was capable of. I really didn't. And I was terrified. All these empty bloody useless words! All so pointless! And then I heard a thump – a solid 'thunk' sound, followed by a loud yelp. Kieron did too, and we could both all too readily visualise the image of our cherished pet being slammed into a wall.

'*Sophia!*' he screamed at her. 'I am going to *break this bloody door down!*'

He had just raised his fists to it when it did indeed open. Just a crack, just enough for poor Bob to wriggle through it, before slamming shut again, only narrowly missing mincing his tail. But my sigh of relief at seeing him was short-lived. Bob shot past us on trembling legs, skittering wildly across the landing, before half-running, half-falling, all the way down the stairs, coming to rest, whimpering and staggering, on the hall carpet.

Kieron let out a cry of anguish and immediately thundered after him and, by the time I reached the bottom, had already gathered Bob in his arms, his tears making twin shiny tracks down his cheeks, as he watched his beloved pet twitch in terror. I had not seen my son cry for close on ten years, and seeing him cry now broke my heart. *Oh, God*, I prayed. *Please let poor Bob be okay.*

Chapter 22

Looking at Kieron's anguished face made me feel terrible.

'Oh, God, Mum, look at him! Do you think he's broken anything? Oh, *God*!' I carefully felt all Bob's limbs, with shaking hands, and was relieved to find that all seemed in order. He didn't flinch or whimper, and I felt a surge of relief. He was just terrified and traumatised. He'd be okay.

But I wasn't. God, I was so *angry*. We had been here already – last year, when Justin, during a particularly dark time, had been viciously cruel to the poor animal. This wasn't fair. This wasn't right. This wasn't *on*.

'I think he's fine, love,' I reassured Kieron. 'She's obviously kicked him, or hit him or thrown him or something, but he's a tough little fella. He's fine, I think. Just fine.'

Even so, I thought suddenly, even as I consoled my fraught son, I would have to keep a very close eye on him. If she had thrown him – and that sickening sound seemed to suggest it – he might have internal injuries, ones I couldn't see. But for now I was reassured. He seemed to brighten by the moment. 'Why don't you feed him?' I suggested to Kieron. 'Get some food inside him, bless him.'

Nodding mutely, Kieron took him off to the kitchen, where Bob encouraged both of us that, actually, he was recovering by the moment, by wolfing down a huge bowl of dog food. 'I'm going to take him to Lauren's,' Kieron told me as Bob finished. 'And I'm not bringing him home until *she's* sorted out.'

The 'she' in question, Sophia, had now returned to her bedroom – we had both heard the thunk of her bedroom door slamming. Which was fine by me. Rather than confront her again, I took the opportunity to gather my thoughts. The GP was due now in less than half an hour. I filled it by updating my journal. I left nothing out, detailing every little thing I could think of. The only thing I omitted as I recapped my pen was, *'We are, literally, living in a madhouse ...'*

Our GP, Dr Shackleton, had been our family doctor for about fifteen years. He knew the whole family and was a jovial, no-nonsense sort. He'd seen everything during his long years in practice, including Addison's, so I felt confident he'd be able to enlighten me.

When I took him upstairs, it was to find Sophia lying placidly on her bed, reading a magazine, and perfectly happy (though she spoke very little, just nodded) to submit to a thorough examination. He checked her pupils, he checked her blood pressure, he checked her reflexes and pulse, he checked things what weren't obvious to me – vision and balance, perhaps, I wasn't sure – he palpated her stomach, and he percussed her chest. He asked her questions about how she was, and about how she'd felt earlier, and her response, overwhelmingly, was subdued and polite. She didn't remember anything about the events of the morning, and looked genuinely mortified when he very gently probed her about whether she might have been violent towards the family dog.

Eventually, his tests done, he suggested she get some rest, and, once again, she meekly acquiesced. She even pulled the bedspread over her to indicate the fact, and by the time we left the bedroom she'd closed her eyes.

'So what do you think?' I asked him, once we were again downstairs, in the kitchen. I spoke quietly, out of habit, and I also shut the door. I couldn't shake off the feeling that she might appear out of nowhere and start raving at us all over again.

'I think she's quite poorly,' he said. 'And it's possibly related to her condition. Possibly not. She certainly seems to be having some psychotic episodes. And from what you've said, it sounds like they're increasing, which is worrying.'

I explained that we were waiting for a referral to CAMHS, so she could have her mental health properly assessed. 'But you're right,' I said. 'It *is* getting worse, and more frequent. I'm beginning to be really frightened about what she might do next. Especially given her history of suicide attempts, and all the traumas and distress she's been through this past year. It's like living with a ticking bomb, to be honest,' I admitted. 'And, well … I don't mind telling you, I'm getting to the end of my tether.'

He smiled reassuringly. 'Leave it to me,' he said. And to my immense relief he rang the hospital then and there, to refer Sophia as a matter of urgency, and though the Easter Bank Holidays would hold things up a little we were promised an appointment for the following week.

'But as I'm sure everyone keeps telling you,' he said as I showed him out, 'don't just keep thinking you have to soldier on, Casey. If you're worried, or frightened, just call 999. As I'm sure you know –'

'– that's what they're there for,' I finished for him. 'I *know*,' I said, smiling ruefully. 'And I will.'

I popped up to check on Sophia straight after he'd left, mostly to reassure myself she really was asleep before embarking on all the housework I'd not had time to do. Where had the day gone? It felt like it had disappeared from beneath me. And with it, all my nice, reassuring sense of order.

But she wasn't asleep. She was still lying just as we'd left her, under the bedspread. But her eyes were wide open, and staring at the ceiling. She turned her head as I entered and, in what felt like the first time in ages, her expression was perfectly normal. No glassy-eyed stare, no contorted mask of anger, just an acknowledgement that I'd come into the room.

'I'm sick, aren't I, Casey?' she said quietly.

I nodded slightly. 'Yes, you are, love, I think.' I couldn't lie to her. I shouldn't lie to her. 'But the doctor's going to help you, okay? That's what he's there for. We've got an appointment arranged for you. Well, almost. For next week. And in the meantime, well, one day at a time, eh?'

She nodded.

'So, can I get you anything? I'm just about to make a start on tea. But do you want a drink and a nice salty snack to keep you going?'

'A drink would be nice. Orange juice?'

I nodded and smiled. 'Orange juice. Coming right up.'

I turned to leave the room, but just as I was through the door, she called me back.

'Casey, is Bob okay?'

'He's fine,' I reassured her. 'He's absolutely *fine*.'

'I had no idea I'd hurt him. Honestly, I didn't, Casey. I'll apologise to Kieron. I'm so, so sorry. I feel so terrible. I just don't know why I did it … it wasn't me … *honest*, Casey. It was like I was someone else … Oh, God, I'm so, so sorry.'

I hovered a moment, unsure whether to cross the room and give her a cuddle. But something stopped me. I just couldn't bring myself to. Not yet. My own son's anguish was still too raw for me. Instead, I smiled. 'Love, he's fine. And it's all done and finished with. Forgotten. We both know you didn't mean it. Okay?'

She nodded meekly. 'Okay,' she said quietly.

That was the thing, I decided, as I walked back downstairs. There was no point in berating or disciplining this child. It was as if, when she behaved as she did, she was absent. As if her life had become gradually more and more torn – more full of holes. She'd fall into one, act out, do and say terrible things, before, somehow, managing to find her way back to reality, unaware, in any useful sense, of what had happened.

I wished I knew more about psychology, could understand more. I didn't have a clue what was happening, but one thing seemed clear: that the holes, bit by bit, were getting bigger. How long before she fell down one so vast and deep that she couldn't find the means to climb out again?

And I was obviously in something of a hole myself. Or at least I must have appeared to be. Kieron and Bob returned a few days later, and, just as she'd promised, Sophia apologised, and the Easter weekend passed without incident. But I'd become aware of a new enthusiasm in the family for checking up on me, with Riley calling and popping round at an unprecedented rate, Mike calling from work on the flimsiest of pretexts, and even Riley's David taking to ringing me at odd times because he was either picking up Riley or dropping off Riley, and wondering, 'Is there anything you need, Case?'

Most odd, I decided. Very out of character. My family were fantastic, and had always been supportive, but this was something new. And though I suspected this was all designed to make me feel better, it actually had the opposite effect. Much as I loved them, I couldn't bear to think that what *they* thought was that I was actually drowning in all the mayhem. Or was I? If that was the vibe I was giving off, then I needed to get a grip and stop it happening.

But we were all, to a certain extent, holding our breath. John had called back – another long chat without progress, bar another update – as had the police, following up on the incident when she'd threatened suicide. I was actually shocked to hear from them, as it seemed completely out of the blue. I only put two and two together when I remembered that Bev (or perhaps Phil – it was all a blur now) had told me they'd be informed as a matter of course. I reassured them all was well now, and that some medical help was being sorted, and hung up with nothing more than a sense of bemusement and a new 'log' number to add to my files.

And, somehow, we reached the Sunday before the summer term – a week later – with nothing in the way of new developments, good *or* bad. Well, apart from the ironing pile, which had become a bit unruly, so I'd earmarked the early evening for a session in the conservatory. I might not finish it, but I did need to crack on with some of it. Sophia needed her school uniform, Mike needed shirts and Kieron needed his motley assortment of band T-shirts at least corralled into some sort of order.

I wasn't surprised to see Sophia appear in the doorway. She seemed to like the conservatory almost as much as I did. She was already dressed for bed, though it was only eight in the evening, and clutching the book of style tips by some celebrity fashionista that my mum and dad had bought for her for Easter. I'd been touched – I'd remembered to tell them that sweet treats were a no-no, because of the way the steroids affected her, and the book was a particularly thoughtful present.

Sophia threw herself into her favourite armchair and curled her legs underneath her, then grinned up at me.

'Tell you what, you must love ironing, Casey, judging by the size of the pile you've saved up there!'

'Pah!' I said, even though I couldn't help but smile at her witticism. 'I wish I did! But it's my least favourite thing in the whole world.'

She laughed. 'I know. I'm only teasing. Do you want me to do some?'

I was stunned by this offer but I was careful not to show it. And I certainly didn't need to be asked twice. 'Take it away, love!' I enthused, putting down the iron and beckoning her towards it. 'You'll be my best friend for life if you make a dent in that wretched pile.' I moved out from behind the board and grabbed my cigarettes. 'So be my guest!'

I didn't leave her sweating over a hot ironing board alone, however. I took the opportunity to stand in the doorway to the garden and enjoy the treat of an unexpected cigarette. And watching her, doing everything so carefully and conscientiously, gave me a real pang inside. Seeing her doing this simple thing for me, it was so hard to accept that there were these two completely different sides to this girl. I wished again that I had some proper understanding of the workings of the human mind – I really wanted to be able to make sense of it all. If you didn't know her, right now, you would think her absolutely normal – a sweet girl doing a typically girlie thing. She was just at that age – a touch before the rants of the later teen years – when girls typically like to do all those mumsy kinds of things, like helping with the ironing and learning how to cook. What a tragedy her mum couldn't see this.

But inside her – and as a result of what had happened to her mother, the things she'd seen – this other personality was lurking. Not typical of anything – not anything that I'd encountered, anyway – it was, I supposed, an amalgam of all the horrors she had been through in her short life.

But what was I doing? I wondered, as I stubbed my cigarette out. Stupid to give myself a headache trying to play psychiatrist. I should just be sure to capitalise on the pleasing here and now.

'So,' I said, getting comfy in my own favourite chair. 'What does your book recommend is the best look for a five foot nothing forty-something with black curly hair?'

That night in bed with Mike I felt strangely optimistic. It had been close on a week now since she'd had her last outburst. I didn't know if it was the knowledge that help was forthcoming, or just the effect of the school holidays, or just a coincidental period of relative calm. But I had this powerful sense that the doctors *would* be able to help her. That things *could* be looking up. That we could find a way through.

'She certainly seems happier,' Mike agreed. 'And more positive, too. As if she's come to accept that people really do want to help her.'

'Let's just hope it lasts,' I said. 'Because I think that'll be key to the whole process. Keeping her stable enough to accept whatever help she's offered.' I snuggled up to him. 'You know,' I said, 'something occurred to me earlier. It's mad, I know, but it really feels like fostering's our whole life now.'

'It would do. It is. It is *yours*, at any rate ...'

'No, I don't mean in terms of the hours we spend doing it. I mean I can't remember *not* fostering. Can't remember what it was like. Our old lives just seem a million miles away now. I feel we're different people now, you know?'

He laughed. 'Definitely. Kids! I think we just forgot how radically they change your life!'

'You can say that again,' I replied. 'And for the better, don't you think? I mean, I know this has been a nightmare so far, in lots of ways. But that's what it's about, isn't it? Lots of peaks and lots of troughs. But when we come out the other side ... well, it'll be just like Justin again, won't it? And there's no doubt about it – that was the best feeling in the *world* ...'

His answer was a mumbled 'mmm'. He was drifting off now.

And it was late. I switched my bedside light off and did likewise, my last thoughts all positive and optimistic ones. I couldn't know that between now and that 'other side' I'd mentioned lay the biggest – and scariest – trough yet.

Chapter 23

'Casey, it's Alan Barker. I'm so sorry to have to do this, really I am, but I'm afraid I'm going to have to spoil your day again.'

Monday. The first week of the school summer term, and I'd been having such a nice day.

My positive mood of the previous weekend had stayed with me. I'd woken up with it, taken it through making breakfast and getting showered, had it sit on my shoulder as I'd seen Sophia and Kieron off to school and college, and had it accompany me on the best and most protracted bout of spring cleaning I'd found time to do in many, many weeks. My house gleamed from top to bottom and I was pleasantly tired.

But now this. I looked at my watch. It was 3 p.m. Almost home time from school. And Sophia's head of year was on the phone. *Again*. I let a sigh escape. What now?

'Go on then, Alan,' I said. 'Go on, but break it to me gently.'

'Well, it's a little awkward …' he started.

'Awkward? In what way awkward?'

'Well, I can only report what I've been told.' He paused. 'And I have purposefully waited till the end of lessons.' Which was kind of him. 'But Sophia's been an absolute nightmare today, basically.'

I felt the sigh deepen. 'Go on.'

'Well, all the kids were out on the field after lunch, as is usual. And Mrs Cronin, the PE teacher, was out supervising a game of rounders, when she happened to notice a circle of boys standing in a circle further up the field, on the grass. And she was alerted straight away that something untoward might be happening, because she could tell one of the boys there was keeping a lookout.'

I remained silent as he paused, dreading what might be to come.

'Anyway,' he went on, 'Mrs Cronin naturally went to investigate, and that was when she saw Sophia. She was the only girl, apparently, in the middle of a circle of six boys, and I'm afraid she was … well, not fully dressed, shall we say, and, well, doing some sort of … well … erotic dance.'

'Oh, for God's sake!' I couldn't help but blurt out.

'I know. And I'm sorry to be the bearer of such unedifying news, believe me. Anyway, Mrs Cronin stepped in, of course, and sent Sophia immediately to my office, and then she corralled the boys together. And from what I can gather, they all told the same story: that Sophia had invited them to see her do some, ahem, "gymnastics" for them … And, well, they're teenage boys, Casey. Doubt they were slow in coming forward.'

'I don't know what to say to you, Alan, I really don't. What on earth am I meant to do with her? I have no idea why she does these things.' Which wasn't quite true. I had all sorts of theories on that, backed up by some pretty unpalatable evidence.

'Look,' he said. 'I'm not suggesting you "do" anything, to be honest. We're not suspending her for this. We're not even going to discipline her. These are a bunch of 12- and 13-year-old children, after all. I just wanted you to know. And maybe, if you have an opportunity, you could speak to her about the vulnerable situation she could put herself in if she continues to encourage such silly games.'

I felt relieved. At least that was one less stress to worry about. 'Of course I will,' I reassured him. 'And thanks for being so understanding.'

'That's okay,' he said. 'We all realise you have your hands full with this one.'

Never a truer word had been spoken.

I was canny, though. Much as I intended to deal with it, I made the decision to wait until later in the evening, when she'd already had her final meds for the day. That way, I figured, if there were any repercussions, at least an Addison's-related trauma wouldn't be one of them. In the meantime, preparing dinner, eating dinner, clearing away dinner, I kept my counsel. Though I'd put it in my log and mentioned her 'playing up' a bit at school to Mike, I decided I'd only go into details with him if I had to. No sense in the both of us getting stressed. Instead, I spent the time racking my brains trying to fathom the unfathomable, getting nowhere bar the same realisation as always: Sophia had multiple issues in her psyche *and* with her condition, so to try and tease logic out of her actions was futile. She was on such a balancing act with her meds, her illness had warped her personality, she'd almost certainly been the victim of some very erratic parenting, she had attachment issues and – my instinct – she had almost certainly been abused. How the hell did you make sense out of that lot?

I broached the incident on the field when we were in the kitchen together, making coffee. She was already in her night clothes, and we were all in that winding-down stage, Mike and I to go and watch something mindless on the telly, Sophia to head off up to bed.

But the winding down changed instantly into the opposite – a winding *up*.

'*Whaaat?*' she squawked indignantly. 'That is just *such a lie!*'

Mike had wandered back in from the living room at that point.

'Sophia,' I'd begun. 'I know what you did. One of your teachers *saw* you. You …'

'I did nothing!' she railed. 'Fucking nothing, okay?!'

'Sophia,' Mike snapped. 'That's enough!'

She swung around. 'And you can shut the fuck up as well!' she said, her face reddening and contorting. '*You!*' she spat. 'You are just shit on my shoe! You *pathetic* excuse for a man, you!'

It was such a shock, both the words and the way she'd suddenly unleashed them, that the pair of us were temporarily rendered speechless.

I wasn't having this again. 'Sophia!' I barked, hoping to stun her into silence. 'We are not going down this avenue, you hear me? We are not going to listen to that vicious tongue of yours tonight! Now get to your room and go to bed!'

I glanced at Mike then, whose expression was still one of incredulity. He'd been at the end of some barbs by her by this time, of course, but this one had completely caught him off-guard. I half-expected him to stand there and say, 'But what have *I* done?' He didn't, though. He couldn't. He'd been struck dumb.

But I hadn't. 'Move it!' I yelled at her again. And move it, to my gratitude, she did. She still stomped up the stairs screeching every profanity she could think of, but at least I'd got through to her this time. At least she'd gone.

'You okay, love?' I asked Mike.

'What the *fuck* was that about?'

I almost pulled him up on his language, but then I realised there was no one there to hear it, so who cared? I shrugged. 'What's it *ever* about, love?'

'But why me? Why all the vitriol? What had I done? Why *me*?'

We didn't hear another peep that night. Hurricane passed. Tornado over. But he kept shaking his head and saying it all evening.

My positive mood didn't extend to Tuesday morning. Even though it had been less of an outburst than he'd had to deal with previously, Sophia's vitriolic attack on him the night before had left Mike concerned for my welfare. Which in turn made me jittery. And he had a point.

'Look, love,' he said, as he brought me a coffee in bed. 'D'you want me to get her up for you, before I leave for work? Kieron's already gone' – we'd not said a word to Kieron, by agreement – 'and, well, you know, check out the lie of the land for you?'

I checked the time. It was still only seven. 'No, don't worry, love,' I said, shaking my head. 'You get off. I'll give her an extra ten minutes, so that if she is in a bad mood I'll only have twenty minutes of it to cope with till she leaves.'

It was incredible, I thought to myself as I kissed him goodbye, how we were beginning to normalise such outlandish and unpredictable behaviour. That was what happened, though; that was human nature. We'd taken to calling the sort of aggression and language that I would have pilloried my own two for – things like 'bad moods', 'acting up', 'going off on one'. And when she went into those fugues – that trance-like state, and all that talking to herself she did – that was 'funny' or a 'bit odd' or just 'spooky'.

But help was coming, I kept reminding myself. We'd have her hospital appointment through soon. And in the meantime – well, what else was there but to live with it?

I gave her the promised extra minutes, and went downstairs to the kitchen to get a second coffee. Bob, who'd shown no lasting effects of his own ordeal, thankfully, was already desperate to get out into the garden, so I unlocked the door for him, and by the time I'd done that it was time to call her down for her breakfast.

'Sophia?' I shouted up the stairs. 'Time to get up!'

No answer. I called again. Again, silence. I trudged back up the stairs to the landing. 'Sophia!'

Now I did get an answer. '*Fuck off!*'

Oh, God, I thought. Not all this again. I opened the door and put my head around it. 'Come on. I'm in no mood for your games *or* your foul language. So get up now, please. Come on. I mean it!'

And that morning it seemed she meant it too.

In an instant the duvet was hurled from on top of her and she'd sprung up, in bed, onto her knees. She then began making snarling sounds – horrible, scary noises – then picked up a teddy bear and hurled it at my face. As weapons went, it probably wasn't the most dangerous, but it took me by surprise and had been thrown with some force. And as such it couldn't have been a more provocative thing to do. But something told me a different tack might work here. So instead of yelling at her some more, I threw my head back and laughed. Perhaps that would confuse her into changing her own tack.

'Oh, dear,' I said brightly, picking up the unfortunate bear. 'Now poor teddy's going to need the doctor! Anyway,' I finished, 'spit spot. Time to get ready. Five minutes! Don't make me come back up here ...'

I walked to the door then, very calmly, and went downstairs.

I was shaken, though. Very badly shaken. She'd looked like a cornered animal, poised to attack me. She'd been practically foaming at the mouth. Once again the word 'normalise' floated through my mind. There was nothing

normal here. I felt we were on the edge now, a real preci-
pice. Her behaviour was becoming more and more erratic.
I went outside and had a cigarette, then came back in and
poured some cereal into a bowl, then went back into the
hall and called her downstairs again.

'*Fuck you, bitch!*' came the answer. Oh, *God*.

I raced back up the stairs again. I *had* to take control of
this situation. 'Get out of that bed!' I yelled, even as I
marched into the room. 'Get up and get dressed or I will
dress you myself!'

She laughed manically. 'You stupid fucking little fucking
whore! I thought I'd already taught you a lesson last time!'

She's 13, I kept saying to myself. She's only 13. She's a
child. I marched over to the bed and stood over her. But
before I could speak, before I could even think what to say,
she had punched me, hard, in the side of my head. I tried
to grab her arm, but, still kneeling, she launched herself at
me and began a full-on attack – punching me, pulling my
hair, biting me and head-butting, and I soon realised that
simply trying to defend myself was going to prove no
defence at all. I couldn't think coherently; all I knew was
that I had to restrain her. But how?

We'd been taught all sorts of things about how to handle
violent situations with children, but it was something my
dad had told me when I was a child that sprung to mind
now. He'd been a boxer when he was younger, and one of
the things he'd taught his children was that in self-defence
you needed to remember it was all in the eyes. 'Watch your
opponent's eyes,' he'd said, 'and then you'll know where
the next punch is coming from.' What bollocks, I thought

now. I couldn't even *see* her eyes. The slaps were coming thick and fast and she was just a blur of hair and limbs, but something else my dad said kicked in instead. Grab her arms and cross them. I must grab her arms and cross them. Being so much smaller it was vital that I use my whole body, if I had a hope in hell of overpowering her.

And I did it. I grabbed her wrists and quickly yanked them across each other, launching myself, at the same time, on top of her. We fell in a heap on the bed, her below and me on top, in as ungainly a position as it was perhaps possible to be in, being jerked up and down by her bucking, furious body.

'Get off me, you fucking whore!' she screamed.

And all I could do was scream right back at her. 'Is that right? I'm not some silly little girl you can knock about, you hear me? What exactly do you think you can do to me, eh?'

'Bastard, whore, motherfucker!' she spat in my face, writhing.

'I'll let you up when you shut the hell up!' I screamed back.

I was then startled by hearing a commotion downstairs, which had the effect of stunning us both into silence. 'Mrs Watson?!' The man was shouting so loud through the letter box that I could hear my name clearly. 'It's the police! Is everything okay?'

'Oh, thank God!' I thought. My neighbour must have heard the noise and called them! I sprung from Sophia. Now I'd be safe, even if she chased me. And she did manage to kick me, hard, as I bolted for the staircase, almost falling down them in my haste to open the front door.

'Oh, thank God you came!' I said, yanking it open to reveal two big policemen. 'Thank God someone called you!'

The younger of the two, stepping inside, shook his head. 'No one called us. We're here to follow up an incident report. But it sounds like you're having one right now!'

I nodded and explained, marvelling at this piece of good fortune, trying to flatten down my hair as I did so, feeling the sting of a cut as I smoothed my hand over my face. They were PCs Turner and Jamieson, PC Turner explained, upon which I promptly burst into tears.

The taller one, PC Jamieson, ushered me into the living room, while PC Turner set off up the stairs. 'Mrs Watson,' he said calmly, pulling out a small black notebook, 'you've clearly been assaulted. You're quite within your rights to press charges. Would you like to?'

I shook my head and sniffed. 'No, I wouldn't. She's sick, you see. She's got a health condition. She has psychological problems ... But it's all being sorted ... She's ...'

But I was stopped mid-sentence by the sound now coming from the hallway.

'Morning, boys!' It was Sophia, who'd come halfway down the stairs in her pyjamas. 'Oh, I see the witch has got to you first.' She pulled a face at me. 'Oh, boo-hoo! Is poor Casey crying?' Only she pronounced it 'cwy-ing', along with contorting her face into an exaggerated frown.

She then turned to the two policemen. PC Jamieson had stood up now. 'Jesus fucking Christ,' she observed. 'Aren't coppers young these days!'

PC Turner boomed so loud that I nearly exploded up from the sofa. 'Shut your filthy mouth, young lady, and get down here!'

'It's not *me*,' she said. 'It's *her*!' She jabbed a finger in my direction. 'She came up and attacked me in my fucking bed!'

PC Turner ran up the stairs then, closely followed by his colleague, and when he reached her he skilfully twisted her arm behind her back, before frogmarching her back towards her bedroom. First, though, holding her at the top of the stairs, he turned to me.

'Mrs Watson, Sophia is going to go and get dressed for school now, but if she doesn't I take it I have your full authority to take her to school in her pyjamas? And don't think I won't do it!' he growled at her. 'I'll march you right across the playground in them, if I have to. You get me?'

Numb with shock at this bizarre turn of events, I could only nod at him. But then something else occurred to me. 'But we mustn't forget to make sure she takes her pills first.'

Ten minutes later, fully dressed, and with her meds inside her, Sophia went to school in their police car.

Chapter 24

Alone in the house, finally, I burst into tears again. I was so tired of all this and it was made doubly worse because I didn't know what to do to make things better. I looked at the livid scratch that ran down my left cheek, and fresh tears spilled from my eyes. It would be joined tomorrow by some equally livid bruises, I knew. I felt useless – utterly useless. Unworthy of my position. How could a 13-year-old girl have driven me to this?

I paced the floor, then, trying to calm myself down. The policemen would be back soon, to take the statement they'd come to take from me in the first place. I couldn't bear the thought of them seeing me in this state. I didn't trust myself to phone John Fulshaw yet, either. Not without breaking down and wailing at him. I wasn't even sure I had it in me right now to write an accurate, unemotional record in my log.

Instead, I went out into the garden with my cigarettes, but lighting one, rather than calming me, just made me feel angry at myself. I was even too weak to give up smoking! I'd promised Mike I'd cut down, and had been doing so well lately, chomping away on horrible nicotine chewing gum and really making a sustained effort. But at the first hint of stress, what did I reach for? My fags. Hopeless, that was what I was. Hopeless.

But the minutes passed and, as I sat in the sunshine, I began to feel calmer, forensically replaying the morning's events in my mind. Rationally, I knew I couldn't have played things any other way. When Sophia wanted a fight, she wanted a fight, and that was that. Even John Lennon and Yoko Ono couldn't have pacified her. But the look as she'd left for school had made me shudder. If looks could kill … I knew what that saying meant now. She had lost it, really lost it, and I was the subject of her loathing. There was no getting away from that fact.

'Are you sure you're okay, Casey? Really sure?'

It was an hour later, the police constables having come and now gone, and I'd finally felt able to ring John with an update.

'I am now,' I said. 'Still a bit shaken, but I'll live. It's not the first time I've been in a scuffle with a teenager.' In fact it *was* the first time alone in my own home, without the support network of a whole school behind me. But there was no point in saying that. It just made me feel even less up to the job than I did already.

John sighed. 'Look, Casey,' he said. 'I know more bad news is the last thing you need to hear right now, but I'm afraid I have some none the less.'

'Go on,' I said. 'I don't think anything else could upset me today. Not after this morning.'

'Okay … They withdrew Grace's life support at 9 a.m. this morning. She died at 9.20.'

'Bloody hell! Since when was that sanctioned? I thought they'd planned on waiting till Sophia could say goodbye to her.'

'So did I. But apparently the grandmother told them to do it. Just her and Sophia's granddad were present. The uncle's apparently furious.'

'Oh, God, John. How am I going to break all this to Sophia?'

'You're not. Not today, anyway. Let me check on the funeral arrangements first. Given what's happened this morning, I think we should leave it for a couple of days. And look, are you sure you don't want me to come over or something?'

'No, John,' I said. 'There's only one thing I want right now, and that's to hear that you've made progress in finding help for Sophia. I just don't feel we're up to the task any more.'

'We have done, I promise. We have a provisional slot with Panel, just as soon as she's been assessed by the psychiatrist. They know how urgent this is, Casey. I've made that abundantly clear.'

This was a relief to hear. 'Panel', as they're called, are a team of senior professionals within social services, whose primary role is to decide what kind of fostering a child needs and, crucially, how much funding will be made available for it. Having a slot with Panel, in which Sophia's markedly more complex needs could be reassessed, meant there would finally be some action – and an end to what felt like this constant fobbing off. It was all very well, all this 'we're doing this', 'we're sorting that', 'we'll have progress on this shortly', but – and I gingerly touched the scab on my cheek – urgent, in the real world, meant *now*.

As soon as I'd said goodbye to John, I called Riley. Not to give her chapter and verse on my morning – I was determined not to burden her with it – but to see if she fancied bringing Levi into town, so we could do lunch and a bit of girlie shopping. Levi was over the worst of his chickenpox now; happy in himself, even if still a little scabby. It would be good to see him, and have a much-needed hug.

Thinking about Grace, cold and dead now, was weighing heavily on my mind. Would this be the straw that broke the camel's back for Sophia? Much as I knew it needed to happen to enable her to grieve and move on, I tried to put myself in her shoes, and it felt horrible. She was already so unstable, so full of rage, so full of heartache and, selfishly, perhaps, given what she'd already told me, I was gritting my teeth mentally at the prospect of having a suicidal teenager in my house. Yes, I'd sworn to help her, but it was so *hard*. It was one thing to rationalise her extreme violence as not her fault, quite another to accept that when it was squarely aimed at you.

But I knew Riley and Levi would prove to be the antidote, and I'd been right. After a lovely lunch, and the purchase of yet another bag, I began to feel my mental strength returning. And the bag was a beach bag, because the other thing I'd vowed to do while out with Riley was to plan a holiday – to jet away, somewhere hot and sunny and away from it all, just as soon as our circumstances allowed. In the meantime, however, it was very nearly end-of-school time, and I needed to get home and start on tea.

It was Kieron, however, who was home first. 'Guess what?' he said, almost the very second he arrived back. 'I've been invited to go on holiday with Lauren and her parents! To Cornwall! Which'll be great, don't you think?'

Bless him, I thought, knowing that what my 20-year-old son was really doing was asking my permission – seeking my approval. He hated making decisions, and was also stressed about change, so he needed me to tell him it was a really good idea before he'd have the confidence to actually go.

'How fantastic!' I enthused. 'You will *love* it! And it'll be good for you to get away from this madhouse for a bit.'

'Actually,' he said, 'about that … I've been thinking. I'm going to ask Riley if she'll look after Bob. Is that okay? I know you'll miss him, Mum, but I just couldn't bear it if … well, you know. I'd just feel happier knowing he's at Riley's.'

I nodded. 'Of course, love, I completely understand. And I'm sure Riley would love to have him.'

'And you've got enough on your plate, haven't you?' he added ruefully.

'Tell me about it,' I agreed, giving him the same edited version about the morning as I'd given his sister.

'Humph,' he said decidedly. 'I know I shouldn't say this, but you know, Mum, I am going to be *so* glad when she goes.'

Casey Watson

Which I knew Sophia couldn't have heard, as it was a full five minutes later when she got home. But when she came in it was almost as if she *had* heard – straight away I could see she had a face like thunder. 'There you go!' she spat at me as she came into the kitchen, plucking her lunch box from her bag and flinging it across the worktop. 'I didn't eat any of your shit!'

Nothing surprised me these days, so I didn't even gape. Not even when she glared towards the chips I was cutting and said, 'And I won't be eating any of *that* shit, either!'

'Sophia, just knock it off,' I said instead, more in sorrow than in anger. 'You know, I am really getting tired of all this.'

'Get used to it,' she snapped. 'Because from today I'm on hunger strike.'

I felt my heart sink. Was there no end to her manipulation? 'Don't be silly,' I said, pulling off the lid from her lunchbox, to see that she had indeed failed to eat a single thing. I removed the contents methodically, and placed them in the bin. Hunger strike. Brilliant. That was *all* I needed. And what was I supposed to do about it exactly? Tie her up and force-feed her?

'Sophia,' I said again. 'Don't be ridiculous. You know you have to eat, or you'll mess up your medication …'

But she had already stomped out of the kitchen.

I took a long, slow, deep breath then, and finished doing the chips. At least Mike would be happy, I thought wryly, as I rinsed them. Pie, chips and mushy peas with lots of gravy, his favourite dinner. Just the small matter of a

280

13-year-old hunger striker to deal with, and we could all enjoy a jolly family evening.

I would have to ring the GP again, I decided. Get some advice on what best to do. And though it was hardly rocket science – leave some tempting salty snacks in her bedroom, trust to hunger kicking in and taking over – I felt better for having spoken to Dr Shackleton. He'd also reassured me that he'd be happy to come out if needed, so at least I felt I had some professional support.

'But what about her pills?' Kieron wanted to know, after I'd hung up. 'How are you going to make her take them if she refuses?'

'I have no idea,' I told him truthfully. 'Just have to cross that bridge when we come to it.'

'Or,' he said, 'you could just ring the fostering agency. Just tell them you've had enough. Make them come and get her.'

I smiled wanly at Kieron's oh-so-simple solution. He had a point. It really could be as simple as that, couldn't it? And, heaven knew, not a soul could berate me. Fostering was supposed to be a job of work, wasn't it? Not a penance.

But every fibre of my being railed against giving up. Giving up on Sophia went against everything I'd signed up for. No matter how hateful, how hurtful, how horrible she was to me, I *had* to keep on keeping on with her. *She couldn't help it.* I had to keep that in mind at all times. *She was sick. She was crying for help. She couldn't help it.* And I also knew that I – along with Mike, and my own poor beleaguered kids – was all that stood between her and a secure adolescent unit. There'd be no putting her in a children's home, not with her history, and her illness. No, it would be straight to a place of incarceration. Which I knew would be the beginning of the end for her. You only had to take a quick look at the statistics to know how terrible the likely long-term outcome would be if *that* happened. Kids in those places almost never made it back to a normal life.

Since Sophia had taken herself off to the living room after her pronouncement – and I'd left her there – when I dished up I decided to take her plate in to her. It went against all my rules about sitting at the table, but perhaps the smell of the gravy would sway her just a little, and with the rest of us out of sight and out of mind in the dining room, maybe she'd be unable to resist. I'd already briefed Mike, who had sighed and rolled his eyes, as if, like Kieron, pleading, 'Why are we still *doing* this?'

Sophia looked up as I entered. Once again her expression was brutally hostile and I had to say it again, in my head: *She can't help this. She needs you.*

'You don't get it, do you?' she snapped. 'I'm not eating. End of.'

I had a bit of a brainwave, then, standing there, clutching her steaming dinner. 'Okay,' I said, placing it on the coffee table, along with cutlery. 'Don't eat, then. I'll leave the plate, but it's up to you. You should know, though, that I've already told the GP, and he's said that if you don't eat, and then refuse to take your steroids, you will definitely go into a full-blown crisis. And when that happens I have to follow the emergency procedure, so I will immediately call an ambulance, which will take you to hospital, where you will be fed and medicated, via drips, for as long as it takes. So this is pointless, all this. Just so you know.'

But she wasn't interested. 'Fine,' she said calmly. 'Do whatever you like. Makes no difference. I'll just do it again. A body without stress hormones can only take so much, you know. Eventually it'll work and eventually I'll die.' She turned back to the television. 'End of.'

For a second or two I just stood there and stared. How did you respond to that? What did you say? Nothing in the handbook seemed appropriate for the occasion. Did I rush to her, fling my arms around her and plead with her? Don't talk like this! Don't think like this! What are you *saying*? You are loved! You are cared for! It will all be all right!

How could I? When none of that was true? I wished I could say that my heart had gone out to her then. That in that instant I did feel her pain. But it was impossible. Her manner was so ice-cool, so measured. Don't think for a minute, she was saying, that you can stop me. Don't think that *I* think, for one minute, that you *do* care.

I went back to the dining room and ate my own dinner – well, a bit of it. My appetite, unsurprisingly, had disappeared. And when I finished, at Mike's urging, I did call the doctor, who promised to get to us within the next two hours. Which reassured me. Even if I couldn't get any food into her, at least I knew he'd see to it that she took her medication – administering it by force, if that was necessary. She sauntered into the kitchen just as I was finishing the call, and went straight across to scrape her untouched plate into the bin. 'You really think anyone can stop me?'

was her only comment, before she sashayed out and went up to her bedroom.

The three of us – plus Bob – then regrouped in the living room. It felt like we were in the middle of a siege. And Kieron was growing more adamant about things by the moment. 'Dad,' he said, 'I told Mum: you *have* to give this up. Not fostering, but *this* one.' He nodded towards the stairs. 'It's crazy. *She's* crazy.'

Mike nodded. 'I know, son. And you know what I honestly think, Case? I think the longer she's with us, the worse she's getting. Don't you? That can't be right, can it, love?'

I shook my head. 'No. Maybe we need to sit down and talk to Dr Shackleton. You're both right. We can't go on like this, can we?'

'No,' Mike said firmly. 'We can't.'

But it seemed that we weren't going to have to. Because five minutes later Sophia returned to the living room, and in doing so took all decisions about her out of our hands. Perhaps she *had* listened to my little homily earlier, after all. Perhaps the futility of refusing to eat anything *had* sunk in. Or perhaps she'd just realised she was as fed up with things as I was, and had decided to speed the whole process up a bit.

In any event, there she was, standing in the living-room doorway, ashen faced, her arms hanging limply by her side. And I was so mesmerised by the expression on her face that for some moments I completely failed to register what was happening. Indeed, it was Mike who alerted me, by leaping from the sofa, yelling, 'Jesus Christ, Case! Jesus! Oh, *God*!

Call an ambulance! Kieron, find some bandages! Anything! Just find *something*!'

It was then that I noticed all the blood. There was just *so* much blood. Pouring from both her wrists, dripping from her fingers, forming two dark spreading pools on the carpet.

She caught my eye then, as I leapt up myself, stunned. 'I'm sorry, Mummy,' she whispered. 'I'm so sorry.'

Chapter 25

Mike was incredible. While I stood there horrified, stunned into inactivity, he'd already scooped a drooping Sophia up into his arms and laid her down gently on the sofa.

'Ambulance, Case,' he said again. 'Go and call an ambulance.' The words sunk in and I finally juddered into action as, with incredible calm and instinct, he gently raised her arms to stem the bleeding. She was deathly pale, grey, and seemed to be losing consciousness. God only knew how much blood she'd already lost.

I snatched the phone from its rest in the hall and dialled 999, conscious of Kieron dashing past me, back into the living room, his own face looking green. I really thought that at any moment he might throw up. I thought I might.

Though it felt like it was happening in super-slow motion, it was probably only a couple of minutes before I'd given the emergency services our address and gone back into the living room, gaping anew at the grisly pools of blood darkening on the floor.

Sophia, droopy lidded, looked in my direction as I entered, and, seeing me, her body started jerking, racked by sobs. 'I'm so sorry, Mummy,' she said again. 'I'm sorry. I'm really sorry.'

Mike was now kneeling at the head end of the sofa, trying to carefully wrap strips of bandage round her flayed wrists – it was a pathetically thin roll of the stuff that Kieron had found from somewhere, and the blood was just seeping straight through it.

I sank to my own knees by Sophia's head and started stroking her hair, saying, 'Shhh, Sophia, shhh, sweetie. You'll be all right, don't worry.'

'I'm sorry, Mummy,' she said again. 'I'm so sorry.'

I looked to Mike, who shrugged helplessly. She was clearly delirious.

'It's all right, Sophia,' I kept saying. 'Shhh, it's all right.'

'Call me Sophie,' she said. 'Why don't you call me Sophie any more, Mummy? Like when I was little. Please call me Sophie. I'm so tired. I'm *so* tired ...'

The tears were pouring down my cheeks now. My heart was breaking for her. How had she done this to herself? What the hell had she used? I felt the weight of Kieron's arm around my shoulder. He squeezed it.

'Don't cry, Mum,' he said. 'Please don't. Don't be upset. This isn't your fault.'

Kieron's words just made me cry harder.

When the ambulance came, sirens blaring, a scant ten minutes later, it seemed everything – in contrast to the slow-motion reel earlier – sped up to an incredible rate.

Before I'd even really got my wits together Sophia was examined, attached to a drip, stretchered out and into the ambulance, and Mike was herding me to the door, pressing my handbag into my shaking hands.

'Go on,' he was saying. 'She wants you in the ambulance with her. Go on, they're waiting. Kieron and I will follow in the car.'

I did as instructed, half-blindly, stumbling up the steps to the back of the ambulance, and perched on a little pull-down seat while they made Sophia comfortable, attaching straps to her, checking and re-checking her vital signs, a blur of efficiency that made me shrink into my little chair, feeling useless.

She was growing less lucid and sleepier by the moment.

'Still with us, love?' asked the paramedic. She was a young woman who had a real air of reassuring calm about her. 'Still with us, Sophia?'

'It's Sophie.' Sophia mumbled. 'I'm Sophie ... where's my mummy?'

Where had this come from? I wondered. I remembered back to when Sophia first arrived and gave Riley a ticking off for calling her Sophie – God, it felt like a lifetime ago now – and wondered if her anger about people calling her Sophie was some sort of defence mechanism related to her mum. We all had our own versions of our kids' names – our private pet names. This had obviously been hers. I bit my lip to stop myself crying again.

'Can you come up here, love?' the paramedic was beckoning to me, I realised. 'Just sit by her. Important that we keep her awake.'

'Of course.' I stood, lurching as the ambulance began moving, and finding another space in which to crouch, close to Sophia's head. I took her hand. It felt so cold. 'It's okay, love, I'm here.'

Her eyelids fluttered and I felt a reassuring pressure around my fingers.

'She'll be okay, won't she?' I whispered to the paramedic. And at that instant the sirens once again started blaring. 'She'll be fine,' the paramedic said firmly, above the racket. 'You'll be fine, Sophie, love. Hey – you still with us?'

I felt Sophia's response as another reassuring squeeze. But when I looked up it was to see that, despite her brisk words, the paramedic's expression didn't quite match her voice.

As promised, Mike and Kieron had been right behind us all the way, and once we were disgorged from the ambulance and Sophia whisked away for treatment, the three of us were shown into a small waiting room. I felt completely drained, as if every single muscle in my body had been tensed up, and that, now I'd released them, I'd lost the power to stand up. I leaned against Mike, while Kieron went in search of a vending machine, unable to even raise the energy to talk to him. I had seen some things in my time, obviously, but the sight of all that blood was something I knew would stay with me for a long time. Mike was splattered in it – it had even crusted, brown and sticky, under his fingernails, and after a few minutes of just sitting with me, propping me up and holding me, when Kieron came back, he went off to find a sink in which to scrub them.

Kieron's expression was still grim, but his colour at least had returned now. 'You okay, Mum?' he asked, handing me a little white plastic cup of coffee. Black, the way I liked it. It was scalding.

I nodded as I took it from him, taking care to hold it by the rim. 'I'll be fine, love,' I said. 'Just a bit shaken up. I think we all are.'

'Do you think she'll die?' he said, in his usual, straight-to-the-point manner. No messing with euphemisms for Kieron.

I shook my head automatically even though I didn't know. She'd still been conscious, albeit barely, when we'd arrived at the hospital. I didn't know much about medical matters, but wasn't that a good sign? I felt sure remaining conscious was key.

As was the fact that she had come downstairs once she'd cut herself. She might not have been in full possession of her senses, but she *had* come down to find us. Had she wanted to die – *really* wanted to die – she'd never have done that. She'd have stayed where she was. An image filled my head then: the most distressing kind of image. Of my going up to her bedroom, ready to rail at her again about not eating, and about taking her hydrocortisone pill, only to find her dead on the floor. I shivered. How far away from that scenario had we been? Half an hour? It wouldn't take much longer than that, would it? Not if the bleeding went unchecked.

So she *hadn't* wanted to die. She had wanted to be helped to *live*. It was as clear as the glass on the door of the little waiting room. She'd wanted *help*. She had wanted to *live*.

I fought back a fresh wave of tears as the realisation hit me that she didn't even know yet that her mother was dead. That blow was still to come. Or would it be a release from her pain? I didn't know. I didn't know how I was supposed to feel about *any* of it, only that it filled me with so much emotion, it was all I could do not to shout it out loud.

But then distraction was there, in the form of a young doctor, who came and told us Sophia would indeed be okay. That they had transfused her and been pumping intravenous steroids into her, and that, thankfully, we'd got to her in time. She'd be poorly but there was no reason why she shouldn't make a full recovery.

At least, physically. In terms of her psychological condition, there was obviously much work to be done. *I know!* I wanted to scream. *I have been saying that for ages!*

But I kept silent. 'So if I can take some sort of history,' he told us. 'That would be enormously helpful. I understand from your husband –' he looked to Mike, whom he'd obviously already spoken to, perhaps when he'd gone to clean himself up a bit – 'that there's a psychiatric evaluation already pending?'

We spent a further half hour with the on-call doctor, explaining all the circumstances, the details of her background, and updating him about how things stood with Dr Shackelton. I also pulled out the emergency injection kit I'd had the foresight to grab as we'd left. 'Do you need this?' I asked. 'I thought I'd better bring it, just in case …' But even as I started speaking, my voice cracked and I welled up again.

The doctor looked at me sympathetically. 'All under control,' he said calmly.

It was impossible to sleep that night, even though all of us were exhausted, and when I woke the next morning I felt like a zombie. Somehow, however, normal life just resumed around me. Kieron went to college, Mike went off to work, and before it had turned eight the house, suddenly so empty, felt oppressive enough to make me want to leave it.

So when John Fulshaw called, just moments after nine, I was ridiculously grateful to hear the sound of his voice. I had planned on calling him as soon as the office was open, of course, and in the meantime had been manically cleaning – trying to get my home back into some sort of order. Right now it felt more like a crime scene. I'd actually been scrubbing the living-room carpet – a grisly business – when the phone rang, so I had to strip off a rubber glove before I could answer.

'Ah, you are there!' he said brightly. So brightly, in fact, that I felt guilt for having to quash his good mood.

It took me fifteen minutes to run through everything that had happened, and at the end of it he was indeed subdued.

'Come down,' he said. 'Casey, drive down to the office. If you're going to the hospital anyway, it's not going to be too much of an extra journey. Come on, come down and let's talk. This is not a good day for you to be soldiering on alone.'

'I don't know, John …'

'Or shall I come to your house? I can jump in the car now, if you'd like that better.'

'No, no. That's crazy. As you say, I'm going to the hospital anyway. But I'll come to you first. That makes more sense, with visiting … Okay, then. I'll see you in about an hour or so.'

I don't know why I felt so reluctant to go down and meet with John at the fostering agency offices. He was so much more than just our contact there and mentor. He'd become a good friend. But I wasn't sure I could face him. Any of them. I just felt so wired, as if my body was functioning purely on adrenaline. I felt permanently on the edge of the shakes, and just wanted to hide away and sleep.

Of course, as soon as I got there it was clear why I'd been so reluctant to go and see him. As soon as he jumped up and said, 'Right! Time to brew up some coffee!' I just lost it completely. Fell apart. Burst immediately into hot, frustrated tears.

But John was great. He just pulled out a chair and plonked me on it. 'You get it all out, Case. I'll go deal with the kettle. Go on,' he urged. 'Just allow yourself to weep.'

And I did. I sat and cried for a full fifteen minutes, my shoulders both heaving, gulping air, inconsolable, as the events of the last few hours – not to mention weeks and months – seemed to mass within me, clamouring for escape.

'I'm so sorry, John,' I sniffed, once the spasms had died down. 'I knew there was a reason why I didn't want to come here this morning. And now I know what it was.' I smiled wanly as he pushed my mug of coffee across the desk at me. It had grown cold, but I didn't mind. My throat felt raw.

'God,' I said, putting the mug down and plucking a tissue from the box on his desk. 'I feel such an idiot! You must think I'm such a bloody wuss! Coming all this way just to sit here and blubber.'

But he was having none of it. 'Don't be daft,' he said. 'You've just had a terrible shock, Casey! A terrible time altogether, let's be honest. And I'm amazed, now I'm finally getting the full picture, that you've held it together for as long as you have. And I feel responsible. You should have had much more support.'

'You did all you could, John,' I said. 'It's not like you haven't tried. And this is hardly your fault, all this, is it?' I gulped down more coffee. 'It's just the bloody system, that's all. And I don't know about you, but I for one haven't the energy to even *think* about what can be done about that.'

'But there's a bright side,' he said.

'There is?'

'Well, in a way. If it's not too macabre to voice it. At least the word "choice" has been removed from the equation. At least there's no more waiting for Panel and CAMHS, is there? She's where she needs to be, by default.'

'For the moment –'

He raised a hand. 'No, Casey. Until further notice. And whatever happens, she won't be coming back to you.'

'She won't?'

He shook his head. 'Now she's in the system, she's going to stay in the system. With all that's happened – well, it would be entirely the wrong course of action to even think about fostering as an option for her now. For the foreseeable future, at any rate, so you can rest a bit easier. You don't have to worry. Not your responsibility any more.'

Which should have made me feel as if the biggest weight had been lifted from my shoulders. But it didn't. I just burst out crying all over again.

John was nothing if not calm in a crisis, though. As a fresh wave of tears made it impossible for me to speak again, he simply went and made me another mug of coffee. And when I'd calmed myself sufficiently to tell him why I was crying, he sat, nodding sagely, understanding completely.

'It's just I hate this,' I said. 'I'm not in this to fail. And I feel I've failed *her*. And abandoned her too, John. I can't *bear* for her to think I've abandoned her. What'll that do to her? It just feels all *wrong*.'

'You're not abandoning her, Casey. You're supporting her. And before you ask, I've already spoken to the people I need to speak to. She's staying in hospital for a few days, while she recovers from her injuries, and then the likelihood is, subject to the psychiatrist's assessment, that she'll be transferred to a specialist adolescent mental health unit, where she can get the treatment she so badly needs.'

I'd had little experience of such places, though I did remember from my time running the unit in school about a girl – a tragic case; a chronically sick anorexic – and she'd come through it. Got better. Made it back to us. I pulled out another tissue and blew my nose, which felt as if it must be scarlet. 'And they think she'll recover?'

'Probably too early to say. But from the conversations I've had, that doesn't seem an unreasonable prognosis, not with the right support ...'

'But what *is* wrong with her? Does it have a name? *Is* it to do with her Addison's? I wish I knew more about all this stuff.'

'Casey, you can't know everything.'

'But *is* it? Or is it something else? Is she schizophrenic? Psychotic?' I was just grabbing words and I knew it. It was probably so much more complex than that.

'Who d'you think I am?' John said. 'Doctor bloody Kildare?!' His features softened then. 'Look,' he said, as I finished my coffee and told him I'd better think about heading off. 'Don't agonise, okay? Whatever it turns out to be – and my hunch is that it'll be a mixture of all sorts of pressures – you can still support Sophia. Go and visit her every day if you want to. Just do me one favour, okay?'

'What?'

'Don't beat yourself up. Don't feel you failed her. Don't feel *any* of this is your fault. You're my stars, you and Mike, and I can't have you wallowing in self-doubt, okay? And one day – and, honest, I'd stake money on this – Sophia herself will know that and be grateful to you. Okay?' he finished.

'Okay,' I said. I suddenly felt so much better. 'I tell you what, though, John. You might not be Dr bloody Kildare, as you put it. But you're a brilliant mind reader. Derren Brown, eat your heart out.'

I left smiling, but John had been absolutely right. Little by little, over the last few months, I had lost all confidence in my ability to do what I did. I climbed into the car feeling drained. And though I accepted what he'd said to me, I still wasn't sure what good I'd really done. I pulled my phone out to call Mike, thinking I'd just touch base with him, but in that instant I decided I needed to speak to someone else. Someone else who, happily, these days, didn't live too far away.

I checked the time. Just past twelve thirty. That would be perfect.

It was Justin I called, and he answered immediately. 'Hey, Casey!' he said. 'How are you?'

'All the better for speaking to you,' I told him. 'Fancy a McDonald's for lunch?'

Silly question, I thought. Was the Pope Catholic?

It took less than ten minutes for me to drive from John's office to where Justin now lived with his new foster family, and I arrived just as he turned the corner of the street. He always came home for lunch, and after catching up with, and getting the okay from, his foster mum, Glynis, I drove us both to the closest McEatery.

It had been a while since he'd left us, and though we kept in touch by phone regularly I'd purposely avoided being in touch too much, as it was important he settle with his new family.

But it was so good to see him, it felt like medicine.

He'd slimmed down, and also grown a fair bit since I'd last seen him – at 13 now, he was a good head taller than I was, and looked both well and, most importantly, happy. I felt so proud when he told me he was in the school football team now – one of the things that we'd really tried to engage him in was football; as in playing it, as opposed to sitting at a PlayStation operating the finger controls. I also glowed when he told me how lovely it was to see me. 'An' you look just the same, Casey! No older, I swear it.'

'Oh, you flatterer,' I teased him. 'Practising for chatting up the girls?'

I was most thrilled, however, to hear about his little sister – the baby his mother had had when he'd been with us, and whose existence, given how cruelly his mother had abandoned him, caused a lot of the heartache in his already desperate young life. He'd seen her recently, and it seemed regular contact was in place now, and I prayed for that state of affairs to continue.

And when I dropped him back at school it was with a real sense of hope for the future, as a boy waved and jogged across to walk back in with him.

'So why you up here, anyway?' Justin wanted to know, as he opened the car door.

I smiled. 'Honest truth? I just needed one of your big hugs.'

He looked at me for a moment, as he processed the simple statement. Then he leaned across and threw both of his now strong teenage arms around me, completely unselfconsciously, even though his mate was looking on.

'Sounds like a deal,' he said, releasing me, and grinning from ear to ear. 'You get hugs and I get a Big Mac meal. Come again soon!'

And with that, he was gone. And I thought I might cry again, but, instead, a sudden strength flooded through me, which chased all the threatened tears away. Justin was positive proof that I *could* do something useful. It was with a heart so much lighter than it had been in months that I headed back south, to visit Sophia.

Chapter 26

She looked beautiful, lying in her hospital bed, asleep. Really beautiful, just like her mother had. And so peaceful. How bloody wretched, I couldn't help thinking, to find peace of mind only when you were sleeping.

She was still hazy, I'd been told, about what she'd done to herself. She'd had it explained that she'd need to stay in hospital for a couple of weeks, and had apparently accepted this quite meekly. The sister who had greeted me seemed clear on one thing, however: that Sophia knew she was sick and in need of their help.

I didn't want to wake her, so I just sat nearby, in case she did stir, and contented myself with remembering John's assurances. I hadn't failed her. And even if it felt like I had, I was still here for her, and could support her for as long as she needed. If she wanted me to, I could be there.

'Poor love,' said a young nurse now, in hushed tones, as she passed. 'So young and so lovely. Why can't they see, eh? Everything to live for, yet they can't seem to see it, can they?' She looked from Sophia to me, then. 'Sorry, are you her mum?'

I shook my head. 'Foster mum.'

The nurse's expression changed then, as the complicated nature of Sophia's probable situation became clearer. It wasn't hard to make the leap, after all. You had a foster mum, you had problems at home. If you had a home at all. Whatever the reason, you weren't with your real family. But she didn't enquire further, just sighed a knowing sigh. She'd probably seen all sorts, as well.

I didn't expect Sophia to wake up because they'd already told me they'd given her a sedative. Time enough, I thought, to face the grim reality of her future when the emotional turmoil of the night's events – not to mention the implications for her Addison's management – had been properly addressed.

But just as I stood up, after half an hour or so with her, her eyelids flickered open and once she saw who it was she smiled a funny little smile. It really hit me then, stripped of all the make-up, all the artifice, just how young and how vulnerable she really was.

I placed a hand over hers. 'Hey,' I said. 'How you doing, sweetie?'

She blinked. 'Um, I'm not quite sure,' she said sleepily. 'Okay, I think.' She seemed to ponder. 'And hungry.'

This was something I could do for her, definitely. 'I'll get someone to see about some food for you then, shall I?'

She nodded slightly. 'That would definitely be good.'

I walked across to the nurse who'd spoken to me earlier, who was now at the nursing station, close by, writing some

notes. 'I know its way past lunchtime,' I said, 'but do you think there's any chance of getting Sophia something to eat? If it's allowed, that is. Some toast or something, maybe? With Marmite, if you have it. She loves salty things,' I added. 'It's part of her condition.'

The nurse nodded. 'Oh, yes. I'm sure that's fine.' She checked a note. 'She's not nil by mouth or anything. And we can always do toast,' she said, smiling at Sophia brightly. She raised her voice a little. 'Toast, love? We're famed for our toast on Ward 8, we are.'

I didn't doubt it. It was a young persons' unit, full of teenagers. Voracious appetites were probably the order of the day. At least for those recovering, at any rate.

'There,' I said, going back to Sophia's bedside. 'All sorted. But I'm going to have to leave you to it, now, I'm afraid. Got to get home and start on Mike and Kieron's tea. Shall I come back tomorrow?'

'Will you?' she seemed genuinely keen to hear that.

'Of course,' I said. 'Right here. Same time, same channel.' I hovered a moment, unsure whether to do what felt suddenly instinctive. And did it anyway. I leaned over and placed a kiss on her forehead.

'See you tomorrow, then, Sophia, love,' I said.

'See you tomorrow, then,' she answered. But then, as I turned to go, she clasped my hand in hers. 'Sophie,' she said. 'Remember?' Her eyes shone. 'You said you'd call me Sophie.'

She was one hundred per cent lucid. I knew it. I could *see* it. I felt my throat catch. 'Absolutely,' I replied.

* * *

In the end, Sophia didn't make her mother's funeral. It took place just three days later, and it was decided, in view of everything that had happened, not to tell her. With her still being so weak and emotionally unstable, the professionals felt that to make the trip from the hospital and attend the service, especially with the highly likely family tensions, was too risky – it might cause a marked deterioration in her mental state.

It was then that I think it sunk in just how seriously ill she'd been, and what a long road she had ahead of her to recover.

'A whole potpourri of stuff,' was how Dr Shackleton described it to me. She was clinically depressed, had been having acute psychotic episodes, and it had all been symptomatic of what had originally been flagged up as mild sociopathy, but which they now felt was indicative of an extreme stress reaction – not good for her condition, but also not unsurprising, considering the enormous traumas she had been through, together with her continuing guilt over her mother's 'death'.

In the end, for all my desire to understand what was happening in Sophia's head, all that mattered – and it *did* matter – was the general feeling of optimism among the medical professionals that with the right support – psychotropic drugs, cognitive, therapeutic, whatever – Sophia *could* be rehabilitated.

But in the meantime, after ten days in hospital, during which I did visit daily, as promised, she was to spend the coming months in an adolescent mental health unit, about an hour or so's drive from where we lived.

'So what about these paintings?' Mike wanted to know, as we got her things together. He'd taken a few days off work to support me, and I couldn't have been more grateful to have him around. I'd taken up spontaneous random crying as a kind of new hobby, it almost felt like, and it was so unlike me that I even mentioned it to Dr Shackleton when I went down to the surgery to give him Sophia's now redundant hydrocortisone injection kit to dispose of. His response had been clear. What else did I expect? He reminded me how it was when you're at home with a new baby: just the emotional whirlwind, the lack of sleep, the anxiety about the future ... you'd need a hard heart, he reassured me, not to feel tearful – not after what I'd been through.

I looked at the two canvases Mike was holding up for inspection, the two from Jean that she had chosen to go on her bedroom wall. She also sent a card, bless her, which I knew would please Sophia.

'The blue one,' I decided. 'Put the other one in the box.'

We'd been involved in the whole process, and since almost all Sophia's worldly goods were with us we had to make the decision for her – which she was happy to leave with us – about which of her things we should bring to the unit, and which were destined, in the short term, for our loft.

'Funny you should say that,' Mike said. 'I would have guessed the exact opposite. But then, that's what I love most about you, my darling. Always contrary ...'

'You mean mysterious and unpredictable, don't you?'

'Nope,' he said, grinning. 'Just contrary.'

The whole family had rallied round for the day of Sophia's move, and I was grateful. Not just because it reminded me just how precious my family were to me, but also because it sent a clear message to Sophia that, even though she was almost alone in the world, in terms of her blood relatives, she would at least know the Watson clan were there for her.

Kieron's Lauren had made a picture – a montage of snapshots from her *Wicked* party – and Riley had made a lovely hand-painted card, from her and David, including poster-print handprints and footprints from little Levi. And, inspired by this, even Kieron, perhaps the most relieved she no longer lived with us, did something similar with Bob's paws. It was saying something that the blue paw prints all over the kitchen floor didn't even make me snappy. They made me smile.

And the adolescent unit, when we saw it, filled me with hope and happy thoughts. It was small, set in lovely gardens, and had a palpable air of optimism. It was nothing like my mind's eye imaginings of such an establishment: all locked gates and shadowy figures, looking lost and forlorn.

No, I thought, as we unloaded the car of the possessions we'd brought with us, I knew I could rest easy at least on that score.

Sophia had now been told about her mother. But if I was tense about seeing her in the aftermath of that – and I was – I needn't have worried; so locked in her own troubles, she'd apparently barely registered it. According to John, she had been told the news by her uncle, who'd visited her in hospital, and, apart from commenting to the ward sister that she was 'glad Mummy was properly asleep now', she'd displayed nothing in the way of emotion. It's not sunk in yet, I thought. But then, with her sedated and sick, how could it?

Ironically, as we'd left home, I'd seen marked on our kitchen calendar the next scheduled date she'd been due to go and visit Grace. How much water had passed under all our bridges since I'd written that? An awful lot, most of it turbulent. But now all was peace and calm – even if chemically achieved, as it was in Sophia's case – and as Mike and I helped her sort out and put away her belongings it felt almost as if she was doing nothing more unusual than arriving at a boarding school for the first day of term. Only with a better room. It was on the first floor, with a view over the surrounding countryside. It would definitely have passed muster for a rural B&B.

'It is scary,' she confided in me, again looking and sounding so much more her proper age. 'All these strangers and all these people asking questions.'

'You'll soon settle,' I told her. 'And Mike and I will come and visit you again next weekend. By which time I don't doubt you'll have made some new friends.'

She lowered her voice. 'Except they're all mad here,' she answered. Then she completely surprised me by nudging me in the ribs and bursting out in great peals of laughter.

'How do you think she seems?' I said to Mike when we left her half an hour later, having promised to be back the coming Saturday. 'She certainly seems to have developed a sense of humour about it all.'

'Impossible to say,' he mused. 'A little odd, a little not-quite-really-with-it. But I suppose that's to be expected, if she's on so much medication.'

'I think she'll be *fine*,' I said, looping an arm though his as we walked back downstairs. 'And I'm not just saying that, love. I really think it.'

And I was doing just that when our progress was arrested by a voice.

'Mr and Mrs Watson?' It was a male voice. We turned around. 'Casey, isn't it?' the tall man before us now asked. 'I'm James Johnson, Sophia's uncle. I recognised you straight away,' he went on, gesturing to his head. He half-smiled then, at my obvious confusion. 'Sophia's been telling me all about you,' he explained. 'And showing me pictures from her memory box. Photos …' Now he pointed towards my head. 'I would have recognised you anywhere,' he said. 'By the black hair.'

And the lack of inches, I thought, but didn't say. I looked more carefully at him. You could definitely see the likeness. He looked quite well-to-do. A professional. His suit looked expensive. And I remembered what I'd been told about the family finances.

He looked a little tense, a little embarrassed, though. 'I just wanted to say thanks. I know we've not spoken, but, well, we really are very grateful.'

I wondered about the 'we'. Which 'we' would that be?

'We've just been doing our job,' Mike said gruffly. I don't think either of us knew the lie of the land here. But the man shook his head.

'No, you've done *way* more than that.' He spread his

hands. 'Look, it's been a mess. It's still a God-awful mess. But I just wanted to let you know that we're – *I'm* – extremely grateful. You know the score about what's happened. Chapter and verse – probably more than I do. But I just wanted to let you know that, well, we all know Sophie owes you her life. As will she, of course, eventually, God willing … but, well, I just wanted to thank you. Whatever else is true about what's happened in my family, it really matters to me that my sister's – her mother's – legacy isn't another needless death.'

Neither of us had an answer ready to roll when he finished speaking, so some seconds passed while we both tried to work out what to say. In the end it was me who spoke.

'Thank you,' I said to him. 'As Mike says, we were only doing our job, caring for Sophia. But, well, as I say, thanks. I hope it works out for you all.'

'Me too,' he said. He actually seemed like a nice, normal man. Perhaps he'd come good after all. Step up, as they say, to the plate. Perhaps he already was. He was *here*. That was the main thing. He had accepted some responsibility. Which was all good. Now the future looked just that bit brighter.

'Chapter and verse,' I whispered to Mike as we said goodbye and walked to the car. 'That's what we have to say to John Fulshaw next time. That we ain't not doin' nuffin' till we get chapter and verse.'

'Good luck with that,' he grinned, getting into the car.

* * *

'That says butter chicken!' I repeated. 'Look that's a double "t", not an "n"!'

'It's definitely my bhuna, mum. Come on, give it here and let me open it.'

'Be my guest,' I said to Kieron, 'but a pound says I'm right!'

It was the following Saturday evening and we were having the best day ever. Mike and I had been up to see Sophia, and spent a perfectly pleasant hour with her in the sunshine, after which we'd gone back to her room – which was now looking more lived in, and I'd been moved to see three things on her little bedside table. A photo of all of us, a get-well card from her granddad and, best of all, a lovely photo of her mother, in a silver frame.

I didn't know why, but there was something about that collection of items that gave me all the hope I needed to know that, ultimately, all would be well. Or at least she'd have a shot at it – I wasn't that naïve; nothing in life was certain – but at least the confidence that she was in with a fighting chance.

And I'd returned home to a surprise Mike been keeping from me for days now, when he mysteriously fired up his laptop and then Kieron's printer and, after a couple of mouse clicks, out had spewed two tickets. He'd secretly booked us a week in Corfu, leaving in less than forty-eight hours.

And now we were all assembled, and it was a Watson family take-away. The three of us, plus Lauren – she and Kieron were off to Cornwall in the morning – plus Riley and David and little baby Levi, who didn't much care for curry but had grown extremely fond of poppadoms – he was sitting in his high chair sucking on one right now.

'Well, I don't care whose curry is whose,' Riley said now. 'I've got my lamb pasanda, so I'm all sorted down my end.'

'Hang on, love,' David said. 'Didn't you order an extra naan?'

They exchanged looks. 'This the perfect moment?' Riley mouthed at him, grinning.

He nodded. 'Oh, I think so.'

We all stopped squabbling over foil trays and looked. 'Perfect moment for what?' I said. 'Go on.'

'No, *you* go on, Mum.' Riley was grinning too. 'You're supposed to ask, "Why d'you need to order an extra naan?"'

'You're not!' This was Mike, slightly more on the ball than I was. Though in fairness, I had had a lot on my plate.

'I am,' she said brightly.

'Blimey,' Kieron echoed. 'I think she is, too!' It clicked. 'Eating for two?' I asked, still not quite believing it.

'See!' Kieron said, as my eyes began misting. 'A pound, please. I *knew* it was my bhuna!'

Epilogue

Four years on, Sophia has made astonishingly good progress. After an extended spell in hospital, and then in a specialist adolescent unit, where she underwent cognitive behavioural therapy, came the good news that her uncle and aunt wanted to welcome her back into the family. As a consequence, after a period during which she made a gradual transition, she went to live with them full time when she was 15. She was then able to resume her education and is now studying for GCSEs, and hoping to go to college and study beauty therapy.

The management of Sophia's Addison's disease continues to be challenging, but with the support of her aunt and uncle she is taking responsibility for her health, motivated in part, or so her uncle tells me, by her relationship with her little nephew, who adores her. And though she never re-established a relationship with her grandmother, sadly now deceased, her granddad visits her regularly and never forgets her birthday.

As for me and my family, well, there's obviously no deny-ing that taking care of a complicated child like Sophia was, and remains, one of the most challenging things we've ever done, and I spent many hours, both while she was with us and for some time after, questioning my ability to do such a job, both from a personal point of view and in relation to my loved ones. Was I right to put the family through such stress? Ultimately, however, we're all agreed it *was* a good thing. We were there for her at a time when she had no one to help her, and we all learned so much, and also grew as people, along the way.

And, perhaps, it was coming through the experience of Sophia that gave both me and mine the tools we would need for our next challenge. Two siblings, needing urgent refuge from a damaging and dangerous home life. Within weeks that Corfu holiday would begin to feel like a distant memory …

For more information about Addison's disease, go to www. addisons.org.uk